Connected

ALSO BY DANIEL ALTMAN

NEOCONOMY: GEORGE BUSH'S REVOLUTIONARY
GAMBLE WITH AMERICA'S FUTURE

Daniel Altman

Connected

24 Hours In The Global Economy

MACMILLAN

First published 2007 by Farrar, Straus and Giroux, New York

First published in Great Britain 2007 by Macmillan
an imprint of Pan Macmillan Ltd
Pan Macmillan, 20 New Wharf Road, London N1 9RR
Basingstoke and Oxford
Associated companies throughout the world
www.panmacmillan.com

ISBN 978-0-230-01629-3

1 3 5 7 9 8 6 4 2

A CIP catalogue record for this book is available from
the British Library.

Designed by Gretchen Achilles
Printed and bound in Great Britain by
Mackays of Chatham plc, Chatham, Kent

TO THE WELCOMING PEOPLE OF

HONG KONG AND BUENOS AIRES

CONTENTS

CONTENTS

Every day, newspapers and television broadcasts are full of numbers that supposedly tell the public how the global economy is doing. Like the markings on a thousand thermometers, the numbers go up and down: stock market indexes, payroll data, interest rates, quarterly earnings, trade deficits, you name it. The problem is, none of these numbers tells you how the global economy actually works.

But what if you could go behind the scenes, pulling back the curtain like Dorothy in *The Wizard of Oz*? What if you could freeze the global economy for a sliver of time, just long enough to get a really good look at it? Then you'd have a pretty good idea of what was connected to what and who relied on whom. You'd see how the global economy is like an enormous machine crammed with six billion interlocking cogs and wheels—one for every person inside. Unfreeze the action, and the cogs and wheels will whir away as the world's workers spring back into action.

Not everyone's wheel is the same size, but everyone's wheel matters. To use another metaphor: think of the proverbial butterfly that beats its wings in the air over Australia and helps to cause a hurricane thousands of miles away in the Gulf of Mexico. Like the earth's own atmosphere, the economy is a closed system—everything's connected, and every action by an individual instantly affects everyone else.

Sometimes this fact is lost in the countless hours of commentary on television and radio, to say nothing of the endless articles and books, about a topic vaguely called globalization. Touting opinions conceived from afar, they tell you what to think. Yet much of the resulting debate amounts to "globalization good" or "globalization bad." And that kind of name-calling doesn't do much to help you cope with the changing world.

The only empirically obvious truth is that the forces often labeled "globalization"—the integration of markets, the spread of ideas, the formalization of the world trading system, and whatever else you care to place under the umbrella—are here to stay. Moreover, there's not much subtlety in the jingoistic pronouncements of a laissez-faire true believer, nor is there much nuance in the screams of a black-clad protester outside a major trade summit. Pundits are often guilty of the same crime; their big ideas and generalizations can't possibly encompass the reality of such a diverse world. It's also a little arrogant to assume that everyone should think about today's sweeping changes in the same way. Mightn't it be better—and more interesting—to take a broad sampling of the facts and judge for yourself?

This book will give you the tools to get started. From one day—June 15, 2005—you'll see fourteen snapshots from around the world. Then you'll find out why each of them illustrates something bigger, a trend or truth that's affecting the entirety of the global economy. Plus, you'll hear from the people who make the cogs and wheels turn, everywhere from Damascus to Dili, Brussels to Bangkok. They'll describe, in their own words, how their own actions fit into the big picture. You'll get perspectives from all walks of life, ranging from the head of a central bank on the white-tablecloth circuit to a migrant worker in a city of smokestacks. You'll not only see what decisions they make; you'll see why they make them. Along the way, you'll find quick guides to the fundamental markets that link the global economy together: stocks, credit, currencies, and oil.

Each chapter also strives to ask questions in a new way. By taking a counterintuitive approach, it encourages you to develop original insights outside the hubbub of the existing debate. For example, can a poor country become rich too quickly? Do companies need crises in order to stay competitive? Can corruption ever be a good thing? Does economic growth really raise living standards?

This book won't tell you what to think, but it might just help you to develop a way of thinking. It doesn't claim to resolve the big questions, but it can help you to find some answers. All you need is curiosity, an open mind, and a willingness to cast your thoughts back to June 15, 2005. As that day began, at midnight in New York, most of the residents of the world's financial capital were asleep. But elsewhere in the world, news of the global economy was streaming in. Billions of connections would send reverberations back to New York before long . . .

Connected 24 Hours In The Global Economy

CHAPTER 1

NEW YORK
12:03 A.M.
JUNE 15

STOCKHOLM
6:03 A.M.
JUNE 15

"ERICSSON AND NAPSTER TO UNVEIL ONLINE MUSIC SERVICE" WHEN DOES WORKING TOGETHER REALLY WORK?

A scratched-up old train pulls in to the small station at Helenelund, just a few stops from the center of Stockholm. Outside the station, a road leads through a leafy working-class suburb. It passes under a low-slung highway, and there, across a two-way street, is a six-story cement building with the word "Ericsson" on the side. Next to it is another one, this one faced in brick. Behind them are two more. And there, off in the distance, the name of one of the world's biggest builders of telephone networks is visible again.

Six thousand miles away, at the wrong end of Los Angeles's trendy Melrose Avenue, a plain office block lies unmarked except for a white sign that bears an abstract image of a cat wearing headphones. A couple of blocks down the street, a heavy metal band is scorching its way through a set in a studio that used to be

3

someone's house. These two buildings are the headquarters of Napster, a former file-sharing service that is now an online music store listed on the stock market.

On the face of it, the two businesses make one of the oddest couples in the corporate world. One company is a pillar of its nation's corporate identity, a leader in design and manufacturing for over a century. The other is an upstart that began life as an illegal network of tech junkies and only recently became a respectable brand. Ericsson has more than fifty thousand employees in 140 countries. Napster has a couple hundred, most of them located in those two largely anonymous buildings on the edge of Beverly Hills. Yet in the global economy, the age-old telecommunications giant and the cutting-edge music retailer had no trouble finding each other.

For some time, Ericsson has been helping the operators of mobile phone networks to sell music to their customers, says Svante Holm, Ericsson's sales manager for applications and content. Some of them want to slap their own name on the services, but others think that there's a better way.

"A lot of them say, we are not a music store, that's not our core competence," Holm says, speaking—how else?—from his mobile phone on a train somewhere in Europe. Instead, these operators want to piggyback on an established brand in the music world. Though it's less than ten years old, Napster may hold the answer.

"We looked at the different brands in the industry, and we saw that their brand was recognized more than anybody else for legal and illegal downloads," Holm recounts. "We actually called them up," he says. "We flew over to L.A. and met their president and their business development team. That was the first meeting, really, and then it all went from there."

4

In this case, Muhammad was not expecting a visit from the mountain.

"We were like, 'Wow, that's a very interesting opportunity. I didn't even think about partnering with you in this way,' " says Larry Linietsky, Napster's senior vice president for worldwide business development. "And then over time, we began to understand what they were doing." Where Ericsson had a technical platform looking for a brand, he explains, Napster had a brand looking for as many platforms as possible.

It took six months of negotiation, but Ericsson and Napster came up with an online music service that would deliver songs to mobile phones and personal computers interchangeably. "The timing was perfect," Linietsky says. "There's nothing else like it out there today."

This time, working together really worked; Ericsson's corporate customers wanted online music for their mobile phone networks, and Napster was glad to supply it—along with its hot brand name. But that's not always how it goes. The road to corporate hell can be paved with extremely good intentions.

Companies link up for reasons ranging from the idealistic to the downright venal, and they do it in several different ways. The most minor can be sharing technologies, as American and Japanese car manufacturers have done for decades. After that, there are several steps up the ladder to a complete merger, which can take the form of anything from two companies joining together under an all-new banner to a hostile takeover followed by layoffs and liquidation.

The most successful linkups are usually built on a combination of comforting similarities and useful differences. Though that notion seems fairly obvious now, it wasn't always so.

In the 1960s, ambitious executives like James Ling of LTV and Harold Geneen of ITT constructed gargantuan conglomerates made up of dozens or even hundreds of often unrelated businesses. The rationale was to insulate investors against the ups and downs in any one industry by diversifying across several sectors. The reality was disappointing; with little in common, the component businesses were often hampered rather than helped by coming under unified management. In addition, executives sometimes used profitable businesses to subsidize those that were failing instead of simply letting them die. Their priority, it seemed, was not to make a profit for investors but to keep their own empires intact. Still, within a few decades, almost all of the conglomerates had crumbled or dissolved.

These days you can usually find a strategic reason for a merger announcement, even if it's not immediately obvious. An apt case study comes from eBay's acquisitions. In July 2002, the leading Internet auction site bought PayPal, a Web-based system for buying and selling products, for $1.5 billion. At that time, eBay had its own payment system, called Billpoint, but PayPal's was more popular. PayPal's technology, like Billpoint's, could be combined with eBay's existing auction platform. By bringing on PayPal—with its well-developed payment infrastructure and its valuable brand name—the company would provide a streamlined, immediately familiar tool for buyers and sellers alike.

Then, in September 2005, eBay offered $2.6 billion—with up to $1.5 billion more in performance-based bonuses—for Skype, one of the pioneers in voice-over-Internet telephony. Why did an Internet auction site need a telephone service? The reason wasn't obvious right away, but there certainly was one. Several companies with big online platforms, like Yahoo!, Google, and Microsoft, were getting into the voice-over-Internet business. If, one day, they decided to offer auction services, then they'd also have an added feature—voice—that eBay lacked. Nobody knew whether customers would want to talk along with their auctions . . . but they might. With a voice partner in place, eBay wouldn't have to worry about getting caught in an unfair fight later on.

Even mergers that make sense on paper can run into trouble because of personal and cultural factors. In 1997, when Morgan Stanley, one of Wall Street's top investment banks, merged with Dean Witter, a similarly big name from the world of financial brokerages, it was the latest in a string of mergers bringing these two seemingly complementary types of businesses together. Yet the corporate cultures were jarringly different—a hierarchical, bread-and-butter retail brokerage firm versus a sparkling hot-house for financial wizards—and their respective leaders were intent on hanging on to power. They were so intent, in fact, that they touched off an eight-year battle over the future of the company. The infighting didn't end until Philip J. Purcell, the Dean Witter man who had been leading the merged company, resigned in June 2005. His replacement, installed by rebels on the board of directors, was John Mack, the former Morgan Stanley president who was passed over for the top job eight years earlier.

And those two companies were both based in the United States. When Daimler-Benz and Chrysler got together in 1998, the results were even messier. Daimler-Benz was a classic German conglomerate, backed by big banks and with its fingers in a variety of transport industries ranging from heavy trucks to airplane engines. Its name meant solidity and permanence, if not the cutting edge of technology. Chrysler was a down-the-line car company that had set a new standard for efficiency in the costly design process during the early 1990s but was shackled by a history of financial problems. In the past, its emphasis had been more on innovation than on long-lasting quality.

At first it seemed as though the merged companies had little interest in cooperating, even in the tried-and-true format of basing their vehicles on similar chassis. The new company's problems were amplified by several lawsuits related to the merger. But the main problem was figuring out which corporate model to adopt: that of Chrysler, striving to retain a lean-and-mean focus on building cars, or Daimler-Benz, a giant that relied on its workers' loyalty and its reputation for quality.

In 2000, amid calls for the resignation of the company's chief executive, a well-known investors' rights advocate said, "It may be better to have a miserable end rather than endless misery." As the economy slumped in 2001, a downturn in the global car market made the company appear even more bulky and uncompetitive, a product of empire building by power-hungry managers. It took five years for the chief executive, Jürgen Schrempp, to resign, a decision that raised the company's share price by 9 percent in a day, and other senior management from the German side soon followed. In the meantime, the economy had picked up, and the merger looked like it could finally work.

For both Morgan Stanley Dean Witter and DaimlerChrysler, part of the problem was the idea that the marriages would be those of corporate equals. When two businesses of similar size get together, it's not always obvious who should take control or whose culture should dominate. It may seem, in hindsight, that both merged companies made the wrong choice. The real failure, however, may have been to make the hard choices: which staff to cut, which operations to close, even which directors to force out, in order to stay true to a single vision of the new company. As they learned, there is little point in pursuing such a big merger anything less than wholeheartedly.

Culture clash isn't the only thing that can sink a corporate marriage, though. Sometimes, one spouse quickly finds out that the other is basically a gold digger. When the high-tech boom of the late 1990s sent the share prices of Internet companies skyward, some of them decided to turn their newfound paper wealth, which was based mainly on investors' eager expectations, into real assets. The shining example was America Online, the Internet service provider that arranged to buy Time Warner, one of the world's biggest media companies, in 2001. Initially, there was talk of synergies: how AOL's platform could carry Time Warner's content to larger audiences. But nowadays the deal is seen more as AOL's clever way of trading its Internet-bubble-inflated shares for Time Warner's real, tangible assets—in other words, as a steal. Indeed, the new-media-plus-old-media equation doesn't even fit anymore. It is AOL's Internet hand-holding service, not Time Warner's mature media empire, that is now seen as teetering on the brink of obsolescence.

For each of the evils described above, however, there can be a contrasting benefit. The most obvious is economies of scale. When two companies that do the same thing get together, they usually find that they don't need quite so many managers and back-office staff; duplicate departments for human resources, accounting, and similar functions tend to disappear. More controversially, the motivation for a partnership is often simply a lower cost of production for goods or services. That's the driving force behind so much of the outsourcing now used by companies in rich countries.

But on a more subtle level, buyouts can also enliven the buyers. Adding a hungry, up-and-coming division to a big firm can be just the thing to shake up a mature business and bring in new ideas—something Andrew Ertel, the chief executive of Evolution Markets, was taking advantage of on June 15.

Evolution Markets, which is based in New York, provides a setting for companies and countries to trade pollution permits handed out, respectively, by governments and treaties. All over the world, countries have found that emissions of carbon dioxide and other pollutants can be controlled by issuing these permits. They provide the lowest-cost way for society to reduce pollution.

The permits to pollute exist because it's not easy for governments, on their own, to know which companies can cut emissions most cheaply. All the governments have to do is issue permits covering the target amount of emissions, either by assigning them to companies—mostly in the energy and manufacturing sectors, which generate more pollution than service-sector businesses—or by putting them up for auction. In either case, companies can buy and sell the permits until they're left in the hands of the ones for whom cutting emissions is the most costly; those companies, clearly, are the ones to whom the permits to pollute are most valuable. The other companies are better off selling the permits and cutting their emissions to obey the law; for them, it's the cheaper option.

Evolution Markets is in the business of making this trading happen. Ertel was in Slovakia to check on Evolution Markets' joint venture there.

7:30 A.M. BRATISLAVA (1:30 A.M. NEW YORK)

I arrived late last night from London, where I was working to shore up our emissions brokerage desk in London (which is on top of the market, and we want to keep it that way) and meet with long-standing clients.

So I roll out of bed in Bratislava after a deep slumber—thank God for Ambien—and meet up with the senior management of Evolution Markets' Slovak joint venture, Evolution Menert. Our breakfast is at the hotel café's outdoor balcony, which overlooks a refurbished plaza in the Old City and the heavily secured American embassy. Greeting me are Ivan Mojík, a former official with the Slovak Ministry of the Environment and now director of Evolution Menert, and Miroslav Wöllner, Jr., the young, ambitious business director for the joint venture.

Our one-hour breakfast turns into a four-hour affair as we have an extensive, and at times animated, discussion of the state of the business and our plans for expansion.

Although we have the industry's most experienced emissions trading team working for us in the U.S., staffing is a huge issue for us in Europe—especially central Europe. Expanding in a region whose economy is in transition to cover an emerging commodity market, such as emissions, is a big challenge. Ivan, Miro, and I review a stack of résumés from prospects in Hungary, Poland, and the Czech Republic to support our regional expansion.

I'm also looking for the full 360, so we delve deep into the Slovak market: the business situation in the region; an update on arcane Slovak politics; efforts to improve the energy infrastructure and bring more renewable energy to the country; and, perhaps most important, our emerging competitors. The good news is that although there are lots of competitors in the region, our market share is strong.

The guys at Evolution Menert have ten new deals in the pipeline that will bring central European companies into the European emissions market to sell carbon allowances. The European emissions trading market is dominated by major western European energy companies. Bringing the central European players to the market has been a core part of our overall global emissions brokerage strategy for winning market share from the big guys.

Evolution Menert plays a key role in the success of Evolution Markets' global carbon market brokerage business for precisely this reason. Our joint venture gives us access to a supply of credits and carbon allowances that differentiates us from our more than two dozen competitors in the global carbon market.

This is a classic example of a joint venture that works, and it works because we have a partner we trust and that is able to deliver what is expected. The joint venture is also an example of how a Wall Streeter like myself and a small-business man from Slovakia can come together to create a thriving business.

Our meeting breaks at 1:00 p.m. Slovak time. Ivan heads off to meet with clients. Miro checks back in at the office.

I take thirty minutes to see the Old City. The plaza where my hotel is located is a beautiful renovation at the center of Bratislava's Old City. It oozes Old World charm, but venture ten blocks in any direction and you get a taste of the more recent Communist past. The two conflicting Bratislavas—one being renovated for a storied past with streets jammed with Porsches and BMWs, the other staid and depressing remnants of the past they are trying to leave behind—show the success of the nation's new economy and the work yet to be done.

12

I always try to break away for a few minutes during my overseas trips, time to decompress and experience a little of the local culture. Today, as with most of my overseas "breaks," I am looking for a present for my wife—my number-one fan, and I'd like to keep it that way. I hit a few antiques stores with little success.

Around 1:30 p.m. I meet back up with Miro for a business lunch. This time we talk in detail about the prospects for creating so-called greened assigned amount unit (AAU) transactions. These deals permit central European countries to sell the greenhouse gas emissions allowances they get under the Kyoto Protocol and reinvest the proceeds in projects that further reduce emissions. Miro tells me both the Slovak and the Czech governments are interested, and I know from my contacts that we have some intense interest from a Japanese buyer.

Evolution Markets worked with Miro when he was at the Slovak engineering firm Menert and Ivan when he was at the Ministry of the Environment to structure the first such "greened AAU" deal in 2001. The deal is the nexus that now bonds the joint venture.

An hour later, I hop in the car with Miro. He drives me the two-plus hours to the Vienna airport for the flight back home. I doze while Miro pounds diet Red Bull. He has been up late working on a proposal for a client and studying for a law exam. Energy and drive like Miro's is everywhere in central Europe.

We cross the border at 3:45 p.m. I make a mental note to get a new passport. No pages left in this one. I count seventy-three countries visited and am reminded of my business partner's famously sarcastic line, "Business travel is glamorous."

We arrive at the Vienna airport around 4:30 p.m. I have about an hour until my flight. I hole up in the airport lounge and try to take care of U.S. business matters until my flight departs. My BlackBerry gets a true workout—this is clearly the best productivity tool I've ever had.

I board the 5:20 p.m. Austrian Airlines flight to JFK. A couple of movies, a nap, a few chapters of the Dan Brown novel on the National Security Agency, and lots of e-mails later, I arrive in New York. Good to be home.

Ten-thirty p.m. Eastern Daylight Time: I arrive back home and peek in on the kids first thing. I take a breath—already preparing for another day—and head off to bed.

The moment when a new international joint venture begins is always filled with hope and expectation. Sometimes, however, the reality fails to measure up. In times when almost any chief executive, anywhere in the world, can be asked, "What's your China strategy?" quite a few companies rushed into Beijing, Shanghai, and Guangzhou just a little too quickly. One of the most notorious disappointments was a joint investment by companies including Germany's Siemens, France Telecom, and Japan's NTT in Unicom, one of China's biggest telecommunications firms.

In 2000, after just a few years, the government forced the foreign investors to take their money back, along with a small profit that was probably just a fraction of what their stakes were really worth. The foreigners had little choice but to comply; the government maintained the controlling interest in the company, and they probably wanted to stay on good terms for future opportunities. By mid-2005, despite the continuing reform of China's markets, some big banks and investors were losing interest in Chinese share offerings and other deals. The government's short-term greed—or at least its unwillingness to share even a modicum of control with foreigners in an important market—may have cut into China's long-term economic growth, if only slightly.

So what did all these potential pros and cons mean for Ericsson and Napster? Investors seemed to view the partnership as a big deal for the small company and a small deal for the big one. On June 15, Napster's stock on the Nasdaq market, a completely electronic stock exchange, opened 7 percent higher and closed with a gain of 2 percent. In other words, investors finished the day believing that the pile of money one could someday earn from holding a share of Napster—discounted a bit for the time it would take to collect it—had increased by 2 percent.

Ericsson's shares also rose, but by less than 1 percent. That's still a better response than the one that greets many mergers and buyouts, where the market picks a winner and a loser—or worse, two losers. Even considering all the benefits that can come from working together, investors often see acquisitions as a zero-sum game. In cases of empire building, they're probably right.

In this case, investors seemed to agree with Larry Linietsky; the fit for Ericsson and Napster looked pretty good, at least on paper. And despite their extraordinarily different histories, the two companies' employees seem to have a youthful, informal attitude in common. Over in Stockholm, young people stroll through the gleamingly clean hallways wearing T-shirts and shorts, with their mobile phone microphones looped over their ears and sometimes even under their noses. Back in Los Angeles, where the preferred footwear ranges from running shoes to combat boots, the Napster crew is always ready for an impromptu basketball game behind their studio building.

Nevertheless, it's easy to get the impression that Napster

moves at a somewhat faster pace than businesses in most other industries. On the sidewalk outside the studio, Becky Farina, Napster's communications manager, notes that her company structured the leases on both its buildings to end at the same time, in case it needed to move to bigger digs. But she also says, "To the extent we can make this ours, we want to. We'll be here a long time." So exactly how much time is left on those leases? Two years, she says.

Working with a partner five thousand miles away can also be difficult, and it has required a lot of costly travel. "We're doing a lot of meetings both in Europe and in the U.S., in New York and L.A., where they have their main offices," Holm says. "They're actually coming out to Stockholm quite a bit."

The two companies' workers can't always be in the same place, though, and keeping in contact by telephone has been essential—even though the companies are separated by nine time zones. Indeed, Holm says, "The one thing that can be a little annoying is the time difference. Either we stay up really late at night talking to them, or they get up really early in the morning." In the global economy, however, even this obstacle can be turned into an opportunity. "When we stop working on it in Europe, they start working on it in the U.S.," Holm says of the project. "It seems like day or night there's always something being developed. It never stops."

CHAPTER 2

NEW YORK
3:02 A.M.
JUNE 15

TOKYO
4:02 P.M.
JUNE 15

"JAPAN CHARGES MITSUBISHI HEAVY, 17 OTHERS FOR RIGGING CONTRACTS" CAN GOVERNMENTS MAKE GLOBAL MARKETS MORE COMPETITIVE?

High in a monolithic gray office building in the center of Tokyo, a clean-shaven, bespectacled man of middle age is about to jump out of his seat. Or at least that's the way Toshiyuki Nanbu looks, with his hands poised eagerly on the arms of his chair. With a palpable excitement, this twenty-three-year veteran of Japan's Fair Trade Commission is describing the moment when his agency finally secured indictments for price-fixing against a bevy of Japan's industrial powerhouses.

"Ten years ago, twenty years ago, we could never think of such a thing, with a big-name company," he says. The reason this can happen now, he explains, is a cultural shift in the way Japanese people regard competition. While Americans may take for granted that competitive markets offer the most benefits to consumers—lots of choices, lower prices—the experience of economic development in Japan did not always teach that lesson.

The postwar administration of General Douglas MacArthur, Japan's American steward, attempted to give Japan the same tools for regulating markets as the United States: an Antimonopoly Act based on the U.S. Antitrust Act, and the FTC, designed to be like the Federal Trade Commission in Washington. But Japan's economic development was not a story of a thousand flowers blooming in a free-market garden. Rather, it was one of careful coordination between industrial conglomerates, abetted by the central government and intertwined with the nation's biggest banks.

For decades, Japan's FTC languished in a powerless limbo, despite being a nominally independent agency within the government. The old Ministry of International Trade and Industry (MITI) deliberately hampered the FTC's activities, Nanbu says. It introduced policies that substituted collusion for normal market forces, in order to protect big Japanese companies from imports and downturns in business activity.

"The ministries had big power to affect the activities of businesses by using the so-called administrative guidance," he says. "Businesses tended to accept it, because it was beneficial for them. It restricted competition. It was very easy for them to follow, because it was easier than true competition."

Though a "leniency clause" in the regulations prevented the FTC from taking action against companies that colluded to control markets, the agency did start trying to educate people about the benefits of competition. The point was that in markets where buyers or sellers colluded, they would use their power in the market to fix prices at artificially low (as buyers) or high (as sellers) levels. As a result, fewer transactions would take place than if the market were left to its own devices, and society would lose out on some of the gains from trade. Those gains occur whenever a transaction makes both the buyer and the seller better off— which, by definition, applies to virtually every transaction in a market where buyers and sellers are free to do what they want.

The FTC faced one particularly imposing obstacle in this quiet crusade, however. Its officials could argue that Japan would have flourished even more quickly in a more competitive environment, but no one could know for sure. What the Japanese did know was that their system had worked—at least it had until the 1980s.

The Japanese government was influencing trade at home and abroad by, on the one hand, helping its own companies to collude and consolidate while, on the other hand, hampering foreign companies by making imports and the establishment of Japanese subsidiaries more difficult. By this time, however, even MITI was starting to worry about the flood of Japanese imports coursing into the world's markets. If a backlash kicked up among foreign consumers, the damage could be far-reaching. And then there was a watershed.

Almost simultaneously, two crises rocked the Japanese economy. In 1989, the bubble of inflated prices for real estate and financial assets suddenly burst. Both had shot up in the previous decade along with Japan's rapid economic growth, but in the end the profits didn't match up with buyers' heady expectations. In the same year, the United States classified Japan, along with India and Brazil, as a country whose trading practices were unfair to American businesses. The trade deficit in the United States had recently peaked, and a search for scapegoats had ended—to some degree justifiably—with Japan.

Within a year, the United States had negotiated an end to some of Japan's restrictions on imports, like strict licensing rules imposed by the government or domestic companies' control of sales networks, especially in high-technology areas. But even bigger changes were taking place in the domestic economy.

"This phenomenon stimulated the discussion that restructuring of society and business activities is required in order to recover from the depression or bubble burst," Nanbu says. The change in mood was striking. The government, apparently after a bout of post-bubble introspection, began to move away from its central role in promoting economic growth and allowed the private sector to function more on its own. Major industries were deregulated. The enormous corporations that wove together banks and manufacturers, often with very little shareholder control, were dismantled. It would be easier for investors to figure out what companies were really worth. And for once, people started listening to the FTC.

Laws ensuring competition were bolstered, and the leniency program was cut out of the Antimonopoly Act. Fines for violations were increased, and mandatory punishments were introduced for criminal violations of business statutes. The FTC started to offer lectures to junior high school students to teach them about the benefits of competition. The Japanese economy could, in theory, reach greater heights if it abandoned its collusive tactics. More university students started studying competition law. Most remarkable of all, the impetus behind enforcement shifted from the government to the private sector as companies started asking for investigations of their competitors' practices.

"In general, the level of knowledge of the market mechanism has increased," Nanbu says. He tells with pride how, in the midst of Prime Minister Junichiro Koizumi's budget cuts, the FTC has attracted small increases in funding and staff. Starting in 2006, he adds, the agency will even have a program to promote whistle-blowing by employees who witness uncompetitive behavior—an unheard-of notion just a decade ago.

Nanbu cites all these forces as improving the FTC's deterrent power. The most visible yardstick, however, is the number of prosecutions the FTC helps to bring. The June 15 indictments charged some of Japan's biggest builders—divisions of giant corporations like Kawasaki, Sumitomo, and Mitsui—with secretly rigging bids for government contracts to build steel road bridges from 2003 to 2005. In truth, the scheme may have been around for decades.

It's all in a year's work for the revitalized FTC, Nanbu says. "Some journalists said it is a symbolic case, but we don't think so. The reason why we bring this case is we can get enough evidence to start investigations." But he also sees taking down high-profile companies as part of his job: "We put a high priority on serious cases that make a great effect on the general public in Japan."

The same questions about headline grabbing have been asked of Eliot Spitzer, the former attorney general of New York State, who brought one of several bid-rigging cases against leading lights of the insurance industry in September 2005. The charge was that former bosses at Marsh & McLennan's insurance arm got their competitors to submit exaggerated bids so that their own bids would look better. By that time, Spitzer had already extracted guilty pleas from executives at five big insurers. Spitzer has also crusaded against malfeasance at mutual funds and investment banks, and the mere rumor that he is taking aim at an industry has been enough to send share prices plunging. His initial sally against Marsh & McLennan, accompanied by guilty pleas from executives of American International Group and implications for two other insurance giants, destroyed $26 billion worth of share value in a single day. Costly lawsuits can put a dent into a company's reputation and profits, whether or not it's found guilty.

Yet there is something troubling about the apparent ease with which he and Japan's FTC have found their targets. Even in mature democracies with strong laws and relatively little corruption, the largest and most scrutinized companies still try to cheat consumers and other businesses through collusion, just like the insurance executives did. Poorer countries may witness embezzlement and monopolistic behavior routinely. Dictatorial rulers dole out entire industries to their friends and skim money off the top for their offshore bank accounts. But most of the culprits could never hope to engineer scams on the billion-dollar scale that their American and Japanese counterparts have managed. The Japanese bridge bid-rigging alone may have affected over $3 billion worth of contracts every year.

Of course, undermining competition doesn't always mean crime. Sometimes it's hard to know where to draw the line. For instance, does a local cable company have a monopoly on television services, or is it still in competition with broadcast and satellite carriers? Other times, the government itself raises barriers that prevent new companies from joining the fray.

The most basic barrier is a government franchise, a legal monopoly that permits one and only one company to offer a certain product—something Adam Smith, the father of modern economics, railed against in his landmark tome, *An Inquiry into the Nature and Causes of the Wealth of Nations.*

The reasons for a franchise vary. In Sweden, spirits are only sold by a government-run alcohol monopoly, on the theory that limited access will cut down on the harmful side effects of drinking. In Russia, the government is re-creating a franchise from its oil and gas companies, which were sold off at cut-rate prices after the Soviet Union disintegrated. The rationale there is less clear, but it smacks of a consolidation of the government's domestic power and its ability to sway world markets. In the United States after September 11, 2001, airport security became a government-run franchise, because Congress concluded that private agencies were doing a lousy job.

In these cases, the lost benefits of competition have been traded off with supposed gains in other areas. The same is true for less restrictive barriers against competitive markets, like those that exist in the European Union's markets for services. When, for example, a Czech travel agency wants to set up an office in Munich, it has to jump through a whole new set of bureaucratic hoops; its licenses from the Czech Republic are no good in Germany, despite the integration of the EU's economies. By allowing these barriers to remain in place, the EU has allowed national interests—in many cases, national protectionism—to trump the sort of competition that benefits consumers.

Protectionism, even by wealthy countries, still stands in the way of competition around the world. On January 1, 2005, an international agreement on trade in textiles expired. The end of the Multifibre Arrangement, as the original pact was called, was the culmination of a ten-year phaseout of tariffs and quotas and three decades of negotiations. Not surprisingly, big exporters like China had signed contracts with companies all over the world to supply clothing after the agreement passed into history. Yet the market had barely been free for days when the United States and the EU, taking note of a huge increase in imports, sought new restrictions on Chinese textiles, claiming that they were being dumped onto the market in contravention of the World Trade Organization's rules.

Sure, free trade might be better for everyone in the long term. But politicians usually work on a shorter schedule—an election schedule. Even though cheaper textiles might be good for consumers all across the United States and the EU, politicians will usually do whatever they can to prevent factories closing and jobs being lost in their districts. Throw in a little horse-trading, and their colleagues will often help out.

It took more than ten months, but China eventually consented to new quotas in both the United States and the EU. In the meantime, tens of millions of sweaters, trousers, brassieres, and the like were held up in transit, to the undoubted consternation of importers and exporters alike. The only beneficiaries were other, less competitive textile exporters. For example, on June 15, the chairman of Mauritius's Export Processing Zone Association, an industry group, greeted China's deal with the EU enthusiastically. "We are obviously very happy," said Ahmed Parkar in an interview with the Reuters news service. "This will allow our industry some more time to adapt to the new trading environment." A decade, evidently, was not enough.

The United States and the EU, with their sharp elbows, are not the only culprits. While Japan may be learning to accept and even encourage competition at home, the country's attitude toward international markets is not so embracing. When the World Trade Organization reviewed Japan's trade policies in 2005, it reported that a complicated set of technical standards and health regulations needlessly hampered imports of several kinds of manufactured and agricultural goods. Japan had average tariffs of 70 percent on imported dairy products, and levies of up to 1,124 percent on grains like rice—who knew it could be so expensive for rice to cross a border? With imports pushed out, the price of rice in Japan was fixed at $1.99 per kilogram in 2003, compared with world prices of about $0.30 to $0.35 per kilogram for Thai and American rice, respectively. The WTO also calculated that the government's subsidies to farming actually exceeded that sector's contribution to gross domestic product.

Manufacturing tariffs were low in most industries, but barriers to foreign entrants in the service sector were varied and complex. For example, foreigners were not allowed to buy more than a third of the voting shares in NTT, the national telephone company. Companies wanting to provide harbor services at Japan's many ports would have to guarantee a 50 percent increase in employment over the current providers. In 2003, a change in the law allowed foreign securities dealers to work with Japanese exchanges directly, without opening local branches, for the first time. In theory, it would be much easier for the rest of the world's financial firms to compete with Japanese banks—for example, by selling shares in Japanese companies—but only with the explicit permission of . . . the prime minister.

Japan is not alone in this. Even among countries where the government takes a firm line on maintaining competition in its markets—in the United Kingdom, authorities can investigate businesses that earn "excess profits" without much other proof of anticompetitive behavior—those same markets are sometimes closed to competitors from abroad. Equally frustrating for businesses is the sheer variety of legal regimes and customs rules that they must satisfy to import or export in different countries. While many types of products, from disk drives to eye exams, have been standardized internationally in the past few decades, traders still have to jump through seemingly endless hoops just to buy and sell.

In terms of hoop jumping, a manager for a multinational chemical company's business in China might as well be a champion show pony. In the afternoon of June 15, one such manager (who must remain anonymous by corporate policy) was in the middle of planning marketing, service, sales, and production for a new plant set to come online in January 2006.

12:00 P.M. SHANGHAI (12:00 A.M. NEW YORK)

Even though lunch started at 12:00, I am still doing e-mails and eating lunch at my desk. Some of the business discussions are regarding the various legal entities we have in China. Each legal entity has certain specific rights—for example, import and export of raw materials. We are setting up a manufacturing plant which will import raw materials (globally sourced), utilize Chinese raw materials, and produce finished goods for either domestic sales or possibly for export.

In order to have the optimal structure to satisfy the Chinese legal requirements, various discussions (e-mails and phone) were being talked about with our legal team. I also went through the reports of visits to current and potential customers written by our salespeople. The potential customers number in the thousands. How do we manage this huge number with limited sources and also try to determine how many will exist over the course of the next two to four years? Managing the large numbers of potential customers and ensuring the follow-up is carried out is quite complex.

For each stage in his company's plan—importing raw materials, combining them with Chinese raw materials in production, selling locally, and exporting—the manager and the company's lawyers need to make sure the operation is aboveboard. Instead of having one subsidiary that can accomplish all of the company's objectives, the company has to deal with several subsidiaries holding individual licenses. All of this costs time and money.

When rich countries erect barriers to trade, both formal and informal, they hurt businesses from rich and poor countries alike. That means they hurt people—not just shareholders, but employees as well. Businesses that want to sell their goods and services in certain countries can't. Businesses that want to import raw materials, parts, or finished products from other countries can't. The barriers also hurt consumers. They're left with fewer choices and higher prices for goods and services. In addition, they're often charged higher taxes to finance subsidies to domestic companies or to pay for expensive regulatory regimes.

The problem is partly political. Specific industries can mount focused, well-financed lobbying efforts to defend their interests. Consumers are a diffuse bunch; though the overall benefits of open markets might be massive for them—lower prices, more selection, better quality through competition—very few have enough of an incentive to push for change all by themselves.

Occasionally, political leaders can break this impasse. In recent times, governments in rich countries have started to accept the notion that poor countries may need to protect their own markets while freely accessing foreign markets in order to see their economies grow. It's not a particularly shocking revelation, since that situation is exactly what helped Japan and South Korea go from rags to riches. It's also a potentially farsighted view on the part of the rich countries, since it's in their interests to cultivate nations of middle-class consumers as future markets for their own exports. The key is that the protection should be allowed for a limited time only, perhaps less time than in the case of those two Asian success stories.

This view had been championed by some economists—notably those from Japan and South Korea—for several years before being accepted by the United States, the European Union, and other major traders. Part of the reason for the delay was that its proponents applied the view to developing countries in general. Naturally, the first country to hop into the queue for special treatment was China, especially as it prepared to join the WTO. Yet giving free access to Chinese exporters while receiving none in return was not a prospect that the United States and the EU relished. As a result, the treatment is now applied only to a few dozen of the world's poorest countries, whose exporting capacity is far too small to scare the more powerful business interests in the world's big economies. Undoubtedly, some other deserving candidates have been left out.

Even when companies from one country do gain access to markets in another, problems with internal competition can still arise. Around the world, regulatory regimes can be as different for competition as they are for trade. These differences tend to affect big companies the most, since they are the ones most likely to gain a dominant position in a market.

Microsoft is a case in point. The U.S. Federal Trade Commission, the Justice Department, and state attorneys general pursued the company, through investigations and court cases, on and off from 1990 through 2002. The accusations surrounded big issues in the computer world: that Microsoft colluded with International Business Machines in the software market, that Microsoft forced its Internet browser on customers, and that Microsoft modified licensed software so that it couldn't be used along with competitors' programs.

Microsoft eventually settled these lawsuits, plus most of the others brought by companies and groups of consumers, for a total amount that could reach $9 billion—roughly what the company earns in a good year—in money and software vouchers. Yet that was far from the end of the story. In 1998, Japan's FTC had raided Microsoft's Tokyo headquarters, in a show of force usually reserved for drug gangs and tax cheats. The accusation then was that the company was compelling Japanese computer makers to offer bundles of Microsoft software rather than individual programs, and making it difficult for competing brands to be installed. The company later agreed to stop its illegal practices. But another raid came in February 2004, when the FTC accused Microsoft of forcing Japanese computer companies to give up rights to patented technologies in exchange for deals to sell their machines with Microsoft software. Again, Microsoft desisted.

In the meantime, the European Union had begun probing Microsoft's operations for evidence that the company was using its dominance in the market for personal computer software to kill competition in the market for server software. That investigation began in 2000, and in 2004 the EU fined Microsoft 497 million euros (about $600 million), a ruling the company appealed.

Clearly, many of Microsoft's problems were of its own making. Dozens of lawsuits, with their resulting rulings and settlements, don't magically appear without a company pushing the bounds of what's legal. Yet the burden of compliance—what Microsoft could have done to stay within the law, and what it must do to abide by the authorities' decisions—might have been lessened if different countries coordinated their enforcement. That is, if the American, European, and Japanese lawsuits had been rolled into one, under a common set of standards, then the company, courts, and regulators could have saved a lot of time and money.

But it's not for this reason that people like Ajit Singh, a professor at Cambridge University, have proposed an international competition authority. Singh's motivation is the recognition that many poor countries simply don't have the means or expertise to prosecute a company like Microsoft by themselves—just as they don't necessarily have the wherewithal to negotiate favorable trade agreements with the United States or the EU. Such an authority might create an extra incentive for multinational businesses to stick to the straight and narrow, by adding a fourth major arbiter of competition (after the United States, the EU, and Japan). It could also make compliance that much more difficult, though, by setting up a fourth set of rules.

And there's one more factor in the balance, too: sovereignty. In recent times, the United States has shown little interest in supporting international agreements, such as the Kyoto Protocol on controlling pollution, the International Criminal Court, and even the Anti-Ballistic Missile Treaty. It's unlikely that the United States would embrace an international competition authority if it meant allowing anyone else a say in its own domestic enforcement. So the question becomes, how can the economic benefits of shared regulations be balanced with strong incentives for good behavior and the preservation of sovereignty?

The WTO has already supplied an answer, if an imperfect one.

It provides a forum for setting trade rules using a shared set of standards. In addition to the shared rules, the WTO creates incentives for good behavior through its dispute settlement system, where countries can bring grievances and receive permission to punish wrongdoers. And sovereignty is completely preserved, since each member has veto power over every change in trading rules. There are problems, of course. The veto power means setting trade rules can take years; the most recent round of negotiations, involving 150 countries, had been going on for five years at the time of this writing. Also, the rules can be extremely complex, with all sorts of escape clauses built in; though countries may agree to freer trade, they always reserve the right to raise tariffs if imports flood their markets too quickly. The dispute settlement system can be toothless, with several rounds of appeals taking years. But still, the template exists.

The introduction of new competition rules usually meets with the same sort of opposition as open markets for trade. Again, there are entrenched minorities with lucrative interests to protect. Again, the potential beneficiaries are a diffuse group of consumers, and some businesses. The differences were clear, for example, when the *South China Morning Post* interviewed dozens of Hong Kong's business leaders and economic experts about bringing a competition law to the Chinese territory.

This was the statement from Wellcome, one of two supermarket chains that dominate the territory: "We believe that Hong Kong's enviable international reputation for free trade has been assisted in great part by laws that have kept intervention to a minimum and allowed the free market to work naturally." And this is what Lee Kwong-Lam, the vice president of the Hong Kong Food Trades Association, a suppliers' group, said was his personal opinion: "The supermarket sector is now monopolized by two operators. We are at a disadvantage when negotiating with them and they always impose additional requirements."

Likewise, consider these two responses. From Shih Wing-Ching, chairman of Centaline Holdings, a major real estate firm: "A law will mean restrictions in fair competition and will be in favour of certain people. The government should ideally do as little as possible in business competition." And from David Webb, a local advocate for shareholders' rights: "Hong Kong consumers, entrepreneurs and SMEs [small- and medium-sized enterprises] deserve a level playing field free of price-fixing, restraints of trade, market carve-ups, bid rigging, retail price controls and other anti-competitive behaviour. But to be effective, the watchdog established by a competition law must have teeth."

Beyond the obvious and conflicting vested interests, culture can still pose a problem for the embrace of competition. Despite the progress in Japan, Nanbu says he thinks competition will always be a second-class value there.

"The difference between Japan and the U.S. and Europe is that Japanese business society, it's very deeply rooted in their mind to tend to violations," he says. "Japanese society cannot get rid of that method."

Perhaps, though, a modicum of cooperation can sometimes help to *preserve* competition. In November 2005, Toyota and General Motors met in Tokyo to discuss various forms of co-operation in making cars. Secret talks between these ardent competitors would normally be enough to send chills down any regulator's spine. But the meeting was one of the first steps in an attempt to help General Motors become more competitive. Toyota's executives were worried that their company's strong position in the global market could lead to ill feelings from consumers, especially if General Motors crumbled in the face of Toyota's strength.

The mere fact that Toyota saw this possibility as a public relations problem suggests that some consumers, at least in the markets where Toyota and General Motors are major players, understand the benefits of competition. If Nanbu gets his way, Japanese consumers will be sensitized as well, and more likely to welcome competition in Japan's own markets.

CHAPTER 3

NEW YORK
3:09 A.M.
JUNE 15

HO CHI MINH CITY
2:09 P.M.
JUNE 15

"INTEL SIGNS AGREEMENT TO HELP DEVELOP 'DIGITAL VIETNAM'" DO MULTINATIONAL COMPANIES BRING PROGRESS OR PROBLEMS ABROAD?

A nighttime drive along Nguyen Van Troi Street—Ho Chi Minh City's version of the Las Vegas strip—is a study in outrageous contrasts. The graceful colonial villas that house official offices behind forbidding metal fences have been swamped by trendy cafés, bars, restaurants, and shops open until the wee hours. The patriotic banners hanging nearby, all in gold letters on a red background, are barely legible in the blinding light of thousands of tubes of neon.

Is this really a Communist country? Not on your life. The entrepreneurial tradition is just too deeply rooted. Dozens of private businesses dot the sidewalks. At first you don't notice them under the dim streetlights, but then you see the plastic stools sitting around a little outdoor stove, or a small case filled with waffle cookies and candies. There aren't as many of these mini-enterprises as there used to be, though. New storefronts selling everything from silk bathrobes to spa treatments are popping up all over Ho Chi Minh City. Likewise, the old Honda Dream mopeds are quickly giving way to racy new Yamaha scooters. Entire families still pile on just like they used to, but they're not wearing plain white shirts and dark trousers anymore—now it's tight jeans, designer tops, and plenty of makeup.

Vietnam didn't get this way all by itself. Foreign companies have had a hand in the country's growing prosperity. Naturally, they didn't get involved out of charity. They're trying to find cheaper places to make their products, or new people who might buy them.

It's a mission that has often led to controversy, with accusations ranging from substandard treatment of workers to wrecked indigenous cultures. But arguments against companies reaching around the world to produce or sell are being washed away, if not always answered, by the twin tides of trade and investment. The more relevant question today is whether these multinational relationships can be managed in a way that benefits both guests and hosts.

Intel, the microchip maker, would respond with an emphatic yes. The company has been operating in Vietnam since 1997, the year when several countries in the region experienced financial crises that deterred many other businesses from investing. In 2000, the United States opened trade relations with Vietnam for the first time since the two countries went to war. And it was then that Intel sent Than Trong Phuc home.

Phuc left Ho Chi Minh City on the last night it was called Saigon, in one of the last helicopters to take off from the roof of the American embassy. Soon afterward, he was adjusting to life as a newly minted California teenager. Today, three decades after he fled Vietnam, he is the living embodiment of Intel's shrewd strategy for expansion into developing countries.

It's a sweltering summer day outside, but Phuc and Le Quoc Anh, a Vietnamese-American born in Virginia, are sitting at a conference table in the cool comfort of Intel's air-conditioned offices. Phuc, a trim man with a gray-flecked mustache who runs the operation, is flipping through a slide presentation on his laptop while Anh, his jovial public relations manager, takes notes. As each slide pops up on the projection screen, Phuc's steady gaze checks with his audience to make sure his explanation has sunk in. One slide elicits a special mention, though.

"This is the Communist Party of Vietnam Web site," Phuc says brightly as the projector shows an image taken from a Web browser. "We made the headline!" And indeed, there on the screen is Intel's name, in an announcement of the deal that is supposed to bring Vietnam to the cutting edge of the digital era. "I thought the day would never come," Anh adds.

Phuc and Anh agree that if they brought this slide to their immigrant friends in the United States, they would not believe it. But cooperation with the government is the name of Intel's game in Vietnam.

In a way, it has to be. Foreign companies' access to Vietnam is still tightly controlled by the government, and the government has a profound involvement in the lives of Vietnamese. "The government's role in Vietnamese society is pervasive," Phuc says. "Their influence and their mindshare is everywhere." Rather than seeing this unusual situation as a handicap, however, Intel has tried to exploit it.

From the moment Phuc arrived in Ho Chi Minh City, he set

about cultivating government officials. His initial step was to understand their goals. The first, he says, is to increase the use of personal computers and the Internet. The second is to make Vietnam an exporter of high-tech items, and preferably those that don't require a lot of equipment to produce. "In manufacturing on the hardware side, the capital cost is big," Phuc explains, adding that Taiwan already has the upper hand in that market. Instead, he says, "the government wants Vietnam to be an exporter of information technology. All you need is a brain." With a million graduates entering the workforce every year, the need for these jobs couldn't be plainer.

Intel's goal is clear, too, and Phuc makes no bones about it: sell more chips. But rather than simply hanging out a shingle and waiting for customers to arrive, Phuc spends most of his time actively working to develop the market. That means coming up with an endless stream of ideas for putting people together with computers, since more demand for computers implies more chips.

And so it came to pass that Intel, with just a handful of people working out of an office in Ho Chi Minh City, became the driving force for Vietnam's entire computer industry.

Phuc divided the market into three segments, separated by income. The high end presented no challenges; they'd buy whatever computers they wanted. The low end probably couldn't afford to buy any computers, so the question was how to give them access to software and the Internet in a community setting. That's when Phuc got to know Vu Duc Dam.

Vu was vice chairman of the people's committee in Bac Ninh, an inland farming province in the north. He had studied abroad and was interested in promoting Vietnam's digital future. But what would Bac Ninh's poor farmers do with computers?

The answer, in part a product of Intel's constant brainstorming, is now on show at two hundred community centers across Bac Ninh. Each one houses five personal computers and one printer. A local Web site created by the agriculture ministry offers daily crop prices. In addition, online maps clearly show the boundaries of land allotments, previously a frequent topic of disagreements. The system can also be used to set up distribution routes.

For farmers, it's a valuable resource. For Intel, it's one thousand chips sold. For Vu, it's prestige. Like all politicians, says Phuc, he has his agenda. "They want to be seen as doing something good for their constituents, just like in the U.S." And now, just a year after Bac Ninh signed the "e-province" agreement with Intel that got the ball rolling, Vu is one of the country's three vice ministers of post and telematics. "I'm not saying it was our program, but it helped," says Phuc, who will shortly be on his way to negotiate a bigger deal for community computing . . . in Hanoi, with Vu.

Though farmers sharing computers is all well and good, Intel's prime target was always the middle segment of the population, a group Phuc now estimates at about three million households with income of $2,000 to $6,000 annually. How could Intel encourage these people to stretch their budgets and become new customers?

Working with the government's Communist youth group, Intel developed a program under the brand Thanh Giong, the name of a legendary Vietnamese hero who magically overcame disability to beat back the enemy of his people. To beat back the enemy of illiteracy (and thus unemployment), the program would sell computers costing $265, $320, and $420. Intel acted as matchmaker between Taiwanese suppliers and Vietnamese assemblers, whom it also helped with testing, debugging, and quality control.

Then the marketing began. The government's communication organs ensured that people soon knew the Thanh Giong brand name. "The press is government-owned—free advertising!" Phuc says with a chuckle. With a caravan of buses carrying its employees, the assemblers, and the press, Intel began a chain of road shows in almost half the country's provinces. They rented space in community centers and schools, where they demonstrated and sold the computers. Each event cost about $2,000 to arrange—a puny sum by Western standards—and at each event the Intel brand appeared next to Thanh Giong. In addition, Intel hosted free conferences for the software industry.

So far, the Thanh Giong systems have been selling at a rate of three thousand a month. "Intel doesn't do this for free," Phuc says. "We don't even take a loss." Though the program began in just a few provinces, now all sixty-four have followed the Thanh Giong lead. "And of course," Phuc adds, "we helped everyone."

Phuc's approach, which he credits in part to the ideas of Intel's chairman, Craig Barrett, has become a model for Intel divisions throughout Southeast Asia and eastern Europe. The government is planning another Thanh Giong program to reach small businesses, which it hopes will triple in number in the next five years. The "digital Vietnam" agreement that Intel's chief executive, Paul Otellini, signed on June 15 includes a stunning plan for the future: computer labs in all schools, e-government programs in all provinces, personal computers in all nine hundred hospitals and 260 universities, rural Internet rollouts, and even wireless Internet covering entire cities.

But Phuc is not satisfied. Unlike some of the European initiatives, the Thanh Giong program doesn't include any direct subsidies to encourage people to buy computers. "That's our next target," he says, rubbing his thumb and fingers together with a look of utter seriousness. "What is missing is for the government to move from a cheerleader to putting money in this program."

Intel has succeeded in Vietnam because its goal and the government's are roughly the same: more Vietnamese using more computers. Essentially, Intel gave the government a menu of options—all of which were good for Intel—and followed up on the ones the government liked. The company has taken advantage of cheap marketing and played up to local traditions. At worst, it can be accused of encouraging people to spend their money on computers instead of other things, perhaps including necessities. The situation could hardly be better.

Intel hasn't always been able to avoid controversy, however. Like other companies, it has been blamed for being a badly behaved guest. For instance, by building a large plant in Kiryat Gat, an Israeli town that belonged to Palestinians before 1948, Intel became a target for boycotts from pro-Palestinian groups. They accused the company of helping Israel to limit Palestinian families' ability to regain their ancestral homes.

There is no shortage of other stories, especially involving American businesses. Coca-Cola has been suspected of fouling the water supply near one of its plants in India. Several clothing and footwear manufacturers, including Nike and the Gap, were long accused of supporting unfair labor practices in the factories they used in Southeast Asia. In Nigeria, citizens' groups charged

Chevron with failing to share any of its profits from exploiting the country's oil—for example, by building infrastructure or hiring local workers. That dispute actually led to a major change in the company's policies, according to its chairman, Dick Filgate. "We now have a different philosophy, and that is do more with communities," he told the Associated Press at the time.

The Chevron case was also something of an exception, because local people led the fight against the company. More often, it is activists in the wealthy nations who protest the behavior of their own multinational companies—at least, those folks are the ones who make the headlines. In part, it's because they have more freedom, information, and resources than people in poorer countries. Yet because of their distance from the people they claim to represent, their actions often raise questions about whose interests are really being served. It's a dynamic that people pushing for better living standards in developing economies often lament. "If they'd only listen to what I was saying," said James Wolfensohn, then the president of the World Bank, in an interview with *The Prague Post* before the bank's annual meetings, held in the Czech capital in September 2000. "A lot of protesters don't have a clue what we're doing or what we're trying to do."

Still, history is filled with examples of companies from rich countries taking advantage of looser regulatory regimes in poor countries in order to do business at lower cost. These days, sometimes it's the companies that are buckling under to ethical compromises insisted upon by their hosts, like Google's agreement to censor its Internet searches in China. Yet the social costs of these practices—whether environmental, cultural, or economic—can sometimes be balanced against visible social benefits.

One of these occurs when a business with investor- or worker-friendly practices enters a country with lower standards, either by opening a subsidiary or by buying a local company. In many cases, these companies are required to make their favorable practices universal, wherever they do business. Sometimes this happens as a result of laws in their home countries. For example, when an American company buys a subsidiary abroad, it has to report on its new operations in much the same way it accounts for its domestic activities. Other times, it is the result of agreements with employees. When Skoda, the Czech carmaker, became part of Volkswagen, its workers began to benefit from a coalition of workers' councils covering Volkswagen's production facilities all over Europe, and later all over the world (with the exception of China).

A few countries have recognized the power of these effects, and they have actively sought out foreign participation in their economies. In November 2005, the Chinese government decided to allow foreigners to buy into thirteen hundred state-controlled companies. The intent, according to officials quoted at the time, was to make the companies more competitive and responsive to investors. By bringing foreign owners into the Chinese market, the government could hope for a gradual improvement in practices without actually changing any laws—a sort of laboratory experiment. A month later, the official in charge of supervising China's state-owned businesses, Li Rongrong, recommended that they sell shares on foreign markets before listing in China. The rationale was the same, with the added bonus that the businesses would have to adopt more transparent accounting methods.

For the most part, however, it is still up to individual companies to find their own way. Intel had to sell its sales ideas to the

Vietnamese government because, as in many emerging economies, the government controlled access to the market on a case-by-case basis. In countries that are further along in economic development, the process of persuasion usually works directly from seller to buyer.

One of the people at the heart of this process is Andreas Naumann, head of European business development for Moody's Investors Service. His company sells an invisible product that has become part of the fabric of financial markets: credit ratings. Whether you're a company or a government, you can hire Moody's to assess your ability to manage and repay debts.

Now, you might ask, why would a company want to pay for this service—why not let the lenders do it? Surely, the information is most valuable to them. That's true, but think what would happen if credit ratings didn't exist. Then every investor who considered lending money to a company, for example, would have to do his or her own investigation of the company's finances. All that work would be duplicated countless times. If a company could get a universally acknowledged stamp of approval, however, then it would instantly become more attractive to investors—no extra work needed. For that reason, companies are willing to pay for an appraisal; for many, it's the price of admission to the financial markets.

At least that's one of the main selling points that Moody's and its competitors—predominantly Standard & Poor's and Fitch Ratings—can use with potential borrowers. On June 15, Naumann was in Berlin, planning his next big pitch in Israel, seventeen hundred miles away. Like any modern salesman, he was trying to figure out a way to avoid going door-to-door in his campaign to win new customers.

44

4:00 P.M. BERLIN (10:00 A.M. NEW YORK)

I had just finished a meeting with representatives of a major bank group and was deep in thought about our conversation when my cell phone rang. It didn't take me long to recognize the very familiar voice at the other end, that of Gil, the chief executive of our affiliated rating agency in Tel Aviv. I eventually found a quieter place to take the call, and we got straight down to the subject at hand: a mutual event we had originally planned for July.

The idea, born during a recent business trip to Israel, was to invite the treasurers of the major Israeli cities to a special event jointly hosted by our local partner and ourselves. We would then explain the concept and value of credit ratings, the typical assessment process, and of course the rating methodologies of the two rating agencies. We would use a case study of an already rated city to add some useful flavor. The key point here is to go for one very concentrated gathering rather than individual meetings with each of the cities, which would be both time-consuming and, at least for me, logistically challenging. Also, if it went well, we could hopefully create a working-group atmosphere, which could be a first step toward actually starting a relationship, plus it was also a chance to further strengthen the relationship between Moody's and our partner in Israel.

The risk, however, is a low response rate, so the critical question has clearly been finding a way to turn the odds in our favor. Gil was calling to tell me about his bright idea: he had just spoken to the local association of Israeli municipalities and gave me a brief summary of their conversation. They seem to be keen to team up with us and would even help us secure the attendance of not only the treasurers but also some of the key decision makers, the mayors. The only flaw is that we would now need to postpone the whole event to September because of the organizational changes we'd have to make. However, we both ended our conversation feeling quite upbeat about our plans and looking forward to a successful cooperation.

Because Israel is a market economy, Moody's has to win its customers one by one. The central government's involvement is minimal, except in setting the legal framework that allows foreign companies to offer their services. As a result, no business or municipality will be forced to buy Moody's ratings; each one's leaders will make a decision on their own, after considering the company's sales pitch. Likewise, if Moody's is confronted by local corruption, it cannot go crying to the central government; it must access Israel's legal system like any other business.

In this way, the burden of responsibility for the effects of foreign companies on Israel's development is mostly transferred to the customers themselves. To be sure, Moody's still has to behave itself according to the law of the land. But if its activities in Israel have any harmful side effects, then Israelis themselves will share the blame.

That's not so much the case in Vietnam. Because the central government holds so much power, local authorities and state-controlled businesses would have a hard time trying to curtail Intel's activities, were they to harm any particular communities. And if Intel were to encounter corruption from petty officials, the central government would sweep it away.

"The government here has looked at Intel and wants Intel's investment in the country," Phuc says. "We get almost everything we ask for." If low-level officials try to extract bribes, he says, "we push back."

So far, Intel's involvement in Vietnam has steered clear of major controversies, and that's not surprising. When the goal is higher living standards, it's hard to argue that money spent on computers and digital literacy is wasted. One could make a case for diverting the cash to more basic matters of public health or primary education, but there would be room to disagree. And it's unlikely that such a case would ever be heard, because of Vietnam's closed political system. Israelis who believed their local governments were throwing away money on Moody's credit ratings could demonstrate, show up at meetings to protest, or kick out their mayors. Vietnamese can only rely on the government's sense of obligation to the citizens who helped to install it a generation ago.

It's a meaningful difference of accountability that underpins an enduring truth: the multinational ventures that bring the worst stories of worker abuse, corruption, and mistreatment of the environment tend to be in countries where power is concentrated and backed by force, rather than by an egalitarian legal system.

There are several ways to deal with the risks of working in countries of this sort. One is to impose rules on the multinationals in their home countries, perhaps even limiting the countries where they could do business. That solution comes with two big caveats, though: (1) rules governing conduct are hard to enforce, because evidence of wrongdoing must be collected overseas, often in an atmosphere where foreign legal authorities have little standing, and (2) companies can avoid the rules altogether by moving to new homes where the regulatory regimes are less onerous. Even manufacturers with big factories can do this; they just move their administrative headquarters and turn their factories into an overseas subsidiary.

Another solution is to let the market take care of the problem, with the help of some independent monitors. The monitors—like newspapers and nongovernmental organizations—provide information about multinational companies' behavior, and investors or consumers can judge for themselves whether they want to buy shares or products. Good behavior often costs money, of course, as shown by the "fair trade" goods now on sale in many wealthy countries. To achieve fair-trade certification, buyers of commodities must pay suppliers a premium that they can reinvest in developing their business—a premium that consumers must ultimately help to pay. And like the fair-trade goods, the shares and products of companies that distinguish themselves as "ethical corporations," even passing up profitable opportunities in order to stick to preset standards of behavior, are often luxury goods. They're for people who can afford to accept lower profits or higher prices that may come with the companies' ethical codes. People with less money are left to support the supposed evildoers—a somewhat distasteful state of affairs.

Finally, there is the option of a tribunal, where citizens of any member country can sue companies from other member countries for bad behavior. With this device, strong legal accountability can be exported to places where it does not already exist. Doing so, however, implies some usurping of local sovereignty. Moreover, companies might try to avoid doing business in the signatory countries. Both of these factors could discourage countries from signing up—rich countries to protect their companies from prosecution, and poor countries to raise their chances of attracting investment.

The tribunal system is currently being used in the European Union, where member governments have already agreed to give up some of their control over local affairs. The EU has an advantage, of course; most of its markets are too lucrative for companies to avoid on legal grounds.

There are also international treaties that seek to regulate corporate conduct, such as the International Labor Organization's eight conventions on fundamental human rights. These conventions rely on local enforcement, though, and they haven't been ratified by all the ILO's members. Vietnam hasn't agreed to the two items guaranteeing freedom of association (the right to meet and develop relationships with anyone you want) and collective bargaining (the ability to unionize), but neither has the United States.

Things are changing, though. Ironically, the same corporations that activists once castigated for using sweatshops in poor countries may now be the entities most responsible for spreading progressive labor practices. For example, Gap Inc., which was once criticized for using exploitative clothing suppliers on three continents, has more recently been praised for coming clean about its violations of labor laws, pledging to reverse them, and even solving a dispute between workers and local bosses in Cambodia.

The company only changed its ways after years of sustained pressure from activists and consumers. But the case proved that under their watchful eye, multinational companies can bring progress as well as problems. When the activists' voices and consumers' pocketbooks make visible examples out of offenders, it's much less likely that others will test the limits of acceptable behavior.

NEW YORK
4:00 A.M.
JUNE 15

HONG KONG
4:00 P.M.
JUNE 15

CREDIT MARKETS AND CURRENCIES

Money may make the world go round, but credit makes it go round faster. If you don't want to spend your money right now, someone else will be happy to do it for you—and they'll pay you interest for the privilege. Alternatively, you may want to spend money that you don't have. In that case, naturally, you'll be the one paying interest.

Credit serves a crucial function in the global economy. It allows individuals, companies, and governments to buy things they need now based on their ability to pay in the future. The implications of this simple idea are powerful indeed. Individuals can use credit to smooth out the rough spots in their careers, borrowing when times are tough and repaying when things look up again. They can also use it to invest for the future, by buying a house or a college education. Companies can use credit to get new ideas off the ground, or to open branches in new markets, before the cash from sales starts rolling in. Governments can use credit to invest and to smooth out rough spots, too, but they can also use credit markets to fine-tune the economy . . . at least they can try.

The world has many financial centers, but it has only one credit market. That market is open twenty-four hours a day, and it encompasses every single type of credit: government notes, corporate bonds, short-term loans like commercial paper, mortgages, car loans, plastic cards, and all the other IOUs you can imagine. The market is like the world's oceans; add a drop to the Atlantic, and the water level everywhere else will rise. Add a dollar to the credit markets, by being willing to lend it, and obtaining credit becomes that little bit easier for every single borrower in the world. Different countries have different rules for lending and borrowing, but those rules are like filters—the water still flows through them.

This integration is a result of countless connections between borrowers and lenders. For example, when a government or a big company needs to raise money, it usually uses a handful of the world's biggest financial firms to find lenders—that is, to sell its bonds. On June 15, CIMB Group, an investment bank based in Kuala Lumpur, Malaysia, announced that it would draw up plans for a set of bonds that would help poorer Islamic countries to raise money for economic development. But CIMB Group wasn't going to sell the bonds alone. HSBC Holdings of London, Deutsche Bank of Frankfurt, and Dubai Islamic Bank would all be part of the offering.

To sell the bonds, the financial firms would tap their respective pools of clients all over the world. Those clients—private individuals, pension systems, investment funds, other banks—would weigh the new bonds against all their other options before buying. They would consider how risky the bonds were, how long the underlying loans would last, and how easy the bonds would be to resell before that time ran out. The would-be creditors would compare them with other bonds, but also with other investments: short-term credit, stocks, derivatives, real estate, you name it. By choosing one option but not the others, they'd affect the supply of credit for every type of borrower.

That's the key, because the credit market—like every other reasonably free market—works on the principle of supply and demand. Borrowers demand credit, and lenders supply it. The prices in this market are interest rates.

Because of all the interconnections, a change in interest rates for one type of credit can affect every other interest rate. To understand why, it helps to start with some of the shortest loans in the world. Every night, banks in the United States lend each other cash to ensure that they hold the reserves required by law. The Federal Reserve—the nation's central bank—manages the market by determining the overall supply of cash. It injects cash into the supply by buying government bonds on the open market, and sucks out cash by selling the bonds into the open market and then sitting on the proceeds.

When the supply of money shrinks, it's that much harder for banks to borrow the cash they need in these overnight loans. As a result, they end up paying higher interest rates. But where does the money come from to pay the higher rates? The banks end up charging their own customers higher rates, too. Pretty soon, short-term credit—which includes loans made over days, weeks, or months—is getting more expensive throughout the economy, and throughout the world. And when credit becomes more expensive, it's tougher to do business. That's why the Federal

Reserve often shrinks the supply of cash when it's worried about inflation; by pushing up interest rates for short-term loans, it's hoping to put the brakes on an economy in danger of over-heating. A report of high inflation can therefore send markets tumbling, as investors anticipate higher interest rates, lower employment, and lower demand for goods and services.

Equally important to the growth of the global economy, if not more so, are long-term interest rates. Mortgages, government notes, corporate bonds—all of these are loans that last for years, not days, and they form the bedrock of investments in housing, infrastructure, and innovation. Investors from around the world can bundle and trade these loans after they're issued, which is why their rates of return can change even while the loan is still active. You might make the same interest payment on your mortgage every month, but the rate of return for the owner of that mortgage—your bank may have long since sold it on the open market—will depend on how much he paid for it. Furthermore, if your neighbor wants to take out a new mortgage, the interest rate she has to pay will depend on the rates of return of all the other comparable mortgages in the world. Who would back a bank, after all, that lent money at a less-than-competitive rate?

Long-term loans' interest rates don't always react to changes in short-term rates, because their chances of repayment may depend more on long-running trends in the economy: the kinds of things that could affect a person's lifetime income, a government's tax revenues, or a company's sales. In fact, sometimes the credit market finds itself in a situation where long-term loans are paying lower interest rates than short-term loans, even when they're all for the same borrower. (The U.S. government, for example, borrows money for time periods ranging from one month to thirty years.)

This may seem perplexing, since over a longer time period more stuff could go wrong. But investors may think, for instance, that the economy is heading for a tumble, and that in the future, consumers and businesses won't want to spend as much money as they're spending now. With less demand for credit in the future, interest rates will slip. There may still be strong demand for short-term loans now, but eventually it could disappear—and that's what investors are betting on.

The credit market, therefore, provides not only a means of financing the future but also a means of predicting it. That trait, together with the market's universality, is why people all over the world follow its movements so carefully.

It's that same integration of the credit market that makes understanding currency markets so important. Credit only flows easily from country to country because currencies do, too. An entrepreneur in Indonesia can raise money in the United States, the European Union, and Japan because she knows that she'll be able to convert lenders' dollars, euros, and yen into rupiah without too much trouble or cost.

Foreign exchange makes it possible. Whether it's a teenager holding a wad of bills on the street in Dakar or a pin-striped trader in one of London's shiny skyscrapers, you can usually find someone who'll take the money you have and turn it into the money you need—for a fee. Yet currencies are more than just ways to pay for things in different countries; they are assets and investments unto themselves. It's worth keeping that in mind if you want to understand what makes currency markets move.

At the most basic level, currency markets are like any markets;

they react to supply and demand. If the Bank of Japan decides to double the amount of yen in circulation, then anyone who wants to hold on to a given amount of yen will find it a lot easier to come by. But if the Bank of Japan decides to cash in some of its mammoth reserves of American dollars by selling them for yen, the rest of the world will feel yen getting scarcer. All other things being equal, the price of yen in terms of other currencies—that's the exchange rate—will react as you'd expect to either situation.

The biggest movers of currency markets are often large-scale economic trends. Let's say the United States suddenly hits another rich vein of productivity, like it did in the 1990s. Businesses are able to make stuff more quickly and more cheaply, new products are being invented, employment surges, and consumers' demand for goods and services goes through the roof. Corporate profits are on the rise, and stock prices are, too. Foreign investors will want to get a piece of the action. But first they have to get hold of some dollars.

Shares in most publicly traded American companies, as well as stakes in private companies, are usually sold in dollars. Fortunately, investors who need to buy dollars can usually find someone who wants to sell. Foreign exchange traders buy and sell about $2 trillion worth of currency every day, which makes theirs the richest market in the world. Moreover, the markets are open around the clock. After Hong Kong and Singapore, two of the world's major trading centers, close at 4:00 p.m. local time, you can go on trading in Frankfurt, London (the world's biggest foreign exchange market), and then in New York.

Even in such a big, liquid market, a flood of investors trying to buy up American shares can still affect the equilibrium, driving up the dollar's value. This kind of change can have massive implications. For one thing, Americans will find it cheaper to buy goods and services from abroad. When they go to purchase euros, yen, or other currencies, they'll discover that their dollars can buy more of them. Foreigners, similarly, will find American products more expensive.

At this point, it probably sounds like a country seeking to export more just needs to figure out a way to make its currency less expensive to foreigners. But alas, it's not that simple. In fact, if the currency loses value, it may even have the opposite effect, at least in the short term.

Say you own a restaurant in Moscow that specializes in fondue, and every week you receive an enormous shipment of Gruyère cheese, straight from Switzerland. In order to lock in a low price for all that cheese—you want some stability in your costs, after all—you've signed a three-year contract with a Swiss supplier.

Now, say the Swiss franc suddenly gains value. Looking at the Russian economy as a whole, you might think this was a good thing for the balance of trade. With a more powerful franc, the Swiss might import more Russian goods, and Russians might import less from Switzerland. At your restaurant, though, it's a calamity. You have to pay for all that Gruyère in Swiss francs, so at the new exchange rate you're going to have to stump up more rubles for the same amount of dairy goodness.

As far as the Russian economy is concerned, it looks like your imports are increasing, because you're spending more rubles. Any upturn in exports of caviar or downturn in imports of watches—both of which would help the Russian trade balance—will be offset by the behavior of businesses like yours. The situation will

stay that way, too, until you and your counterparts can renegotiate those long-term contracts or find cheaper suppliers.

The complexities don't end there. Every example so far has
assumed that the underlying prices of goods and services didn't
change. But sometimes changes in a country's prices can actually
explain changes in its exchange rates.

Let's say that the U.K. is experiencing rapid inflation without
any corresponding boom in the economy. Products from the U.K.
are now more expensive to foreigners—they need more pounds
to buy them. Rather than pay more, foreigners may decide to import from elsewhere instead. With less demand for the U.K.'s
products, there's also less demand for pounds. As a result, the
pound starts to lose value in the foreign exchange market.

Investors, too, may start to flee the pound. The inflation in
the U.K. means that returns on investments there won't be worth
as much in the future; that same dividend or interest payment
won't buy as many goods and services as before. Investors are
likely to sell off investments from the U.K. before the pound
drops further. Next they'll want to turn the pounds they receive
into other currencies. But when everyone wants to sell pounds,
the currency's value falls even faster.

This situation was a part of life for years in Turkey, until the
country began to control its runaway inflation. Prices were rising
so quickly by the late 1990s that supermarkets used liquid crystal
displays, rather than paper tags, to show how much their products were going for on a given day. As prices shot up, the Turkish
lira's value tumbled—sometimes by more than 10 percent in a
week.

All in all, the value of a given currency is subject to just as bewildering an array of influences as that of a stock, bond, or apartment on New York's Upper West Side. Currencies may well be the hardest to analyze, though, because so much of the action in the foreign exchange market is unseen. Central banks, financial firms, and even a few private investors trade billions of dollars without any fanfare, and often without the markets realizing what happened until well after the fact. Moreover, every factor that makes foreign exchange convenient—the speed and volume of the market, the dozens of trading centers, the countless ways to complete a transaction—also makes figuring out what's going on more difficult.

For example, by the time the Hong Kong market closed on June 15, the dollar was starting to gain ground against the euro while remaining practically unchanged against the yen. Did the economic relationship between the United States and the euro area change in a way that wasn't reflected in the U.S.-Japan relationship? Perhaps. Or maybe a bunch of American investors decided to sell stocks from the euro area and exchange the proceeds for dollars. Either way, there were far too many possible explanations, all of which could have been right for at least some investors, to be sure exactly what happened.

Nevertheless, anyone with an interest in the global economy ignores the currency markets at his own peril. Think you know the price of oil? You'd better know it in euros if you're running a fleet of trucks in Milan. Think you know why a Sri Lankan textile exporter's business is booming? It might just be because the rupee's cheaper, not because the company's doing anything right. Think you know how much that Japanese carmaker's takeover bid for a Canadian parts supplier is worth? It'll be worth something else next week, once you account for the exchange rate.

Fortunately, keeping track of currencies isn't too hard. Rates are published in most big newspapers and on several Web sites, some of which track almost two hundred widely traded currencies. It's certainly worth your while to know what's happening, even if it's often tough to figure out why.

CHAPTER 4

NEW YORK
5:15 A.M.
JUNE 15

QINGDAO
5:15 P.M.
JUNE 15

"CHINA'S HAIER CONSIDERS MAYTAG BID" WHAT DETERMINES THE GLOBAL ECONOMIC PECKING ORDER?

Qingdao, a hazy seaside city of 2.6 million people in China's northeast, has long been one of the country's exporting centers. For more than a century, people all over the world have enjoyed its Tsingtao Beer, a legacy of German settlers who also built the city's towering cathedral. But as of this writing, Anheuser-Busch of St. Louis, Missouri, owned almost as much of Tsingtao as the Chinese government did. The real powerhouse in Qingdao today is an appliance company called Haier that makes everything from pen-sized mobile phones to refrigerators so big you could stand inside. If you don't know about Haier, you will.

You only have to meet Wei Duan to know why. Even on Haier's immense Hollywood back lot of a campus in Qingdao's dusty outskirts, where legions of workers in identical blue short-sleeve, button-down shirts trundle from building to building by shuttle bus, Wei sticks out. She's got the blue shirt, too, but she's also sporting bleached hair pulled back in a ponytail, tight, boot-cut jeans, and pointy, low-heeled shoes.

For this brand manager in her twenties from Xi'an in central China, the style is an obvious holdover from her time studying business in Nottingham, England, and working in the financial hothouse of London's Canary Wharf. Wei returned to China, though, for a very definite reason.

It wasn't money. "In Haier, none of the salaries is very high," she says. But the workers are young—an average age of twenty-three here in Qingdao, all with university degrees—and they're enthusiastic about making Haier an export leader. "They want to realize this dream," Wei says, for themselves and for China.

For much of its two-thousand-year history as a unified nation, China has been the world's great economic power. Some Chinese see the twentieth century, with its legacy of American domi-nance, as a blip; they're looking forward to a return to economic leadership. That's part of why companies like Haier aren't lining up to be bought by wealthy foreign businesses, making a quick buck for their owners. Rather, they want to be the ones doing the buying.

Still, Haier isn't simply barging into the world's markets and expecting to dominate from the start. As Wei can tell you, in almost perfect English, there's a very shrewd strategy behind Haier's expansion.

Up a flight of steps in the boxy cement building housing Haier's overseas department, Wei and her boss, Han Feng, who is the company's marketing general manager, pull up chairs at a plain conference table. In fact, except for the fancy printing whiteboard from Panasonic, and the Motorola mobile phone and Sony VAIO laptop sitting on the table, everything here is plain—

white walls with no adornment, fluorescent lights, linoleum flooring.

Expense has been spared here, as with Haier's salaries. The skimping ends, however, with the products. Haier is a high-end brand in China, known for its post-purchase service, Wei says. But Wei and Han, a soft-spoken man not much older than she is, know that it will take time for Haier to achieve preeminence among the seasoned consumers of the United States and Europe.

"A lot of big names already existed in the mature markets," Han says. "We are not a big brand. We don't have a lot of money for advertising, public relations, and media." Choosing one's battles, therefore, becomes extremely important. "A lot of big brands are fighting for the big markets, so we want to avoid the crowds," Han explains.

As a substitute for marketing, Haier uses research. The company has a "culture center" where marketers study the preferences and psychology of consumers in other countries. They use what they discover to design niche products, like box freezers for the United States with a bottom drawer, so owners don't have to reach down into the icy interior; big washing machines for Pakistan, where families are large, and small ones for Japan, where people like to run a load every day; and mobile phones for the elderly, with oversized fonts, large buttons, and a louder speaker. Each product line, from Haier's washing machines to its wine cellars, includes up to fifteen varieties to suit different markets.

Among these are small refrigerators, a market Haier now controls in the United States, where the line includes a special model for college students with a built-in laptop stand. The company deliberately targets young consumers, Han said. "The university students will be the consumers in the future."

To sell its products around the world, Haier sets up joint ventures with local companies in big markets. A typical example is its partnership with Sanyo in Japan. In exchange for the use of Sanyo's entrenched distribution network in Japan, Haier offers its own sales infrastructure in China. "So for the two brands, this is a win-win situation," Han says. Once Haier's white goods such as refrigerators become popular overseas, Wei adds, the black and brown goods like flat-screen televisions and MP3 players will follow.

Tactics such as these have allowed Haier's sales to grow by an average of 68 percent a year—that's not a typo—for the past two decades. The company now has two thousand sales outlets in India. It sold a million major appliances in Japan over the past four years. It's making inroads in South Korea, where big names such as General Electric and Toshiba have faltered. And its products are in Costco and Home Depot warehouses across the United States.

But the company lacks prestige in the top markets. The "Made in China" label is still a liability rather than an asset. "How to change this kind of image is very hard for us," Wei says.

Hello, Maytag. Americans knew the always-on-call, never-needed Maytag repairman as a symbol of the brand's reliability. But by mid-2005, the company itself had seen better days. Its costs of production were high, and it had recently settled a class-action lawsuit pertaining to its clothes washers. It was ripe for a takeover and a fresh start.

Haier didn't want Maytag for what it built, though, or even for its brand. Haier wanted Maytag for what Maytag knew, and for what buying it would mean.

"We want to promote Haier," Han says, "but we want to acquire advanced management philosophy and technology." Moreover, Wei says, consumers would see the reflected glory on Haier of such a high-profile acquisition. It was for a similar reason, she adds, that Haier bought the former headquarters of Greenwich Bank, a stone-columned monolith on Broadway in New York City: "We want to hit the people and give the first impression 'Haier is such a strong company.' "

By this point, the story may be starting to sound familiar. Two decades earlier, another emerging economic superpower on the Pacific Rim was buying up trophy brands in America and Europe. For a brief moment, it looked like Japan might gain the double crown of the world's undisputed economic leader: the biggest economy in the world, and the highest living standards. But Japan's drive toward supremacy—one heralded by countless books and magazine covers—stalled and then crashed at the end of the 1980s.

As recounted in Chapter 2, Japan crashed rather than just slowing down to a regular pace, in large part because of overoptimism. Investors from around the world, but particularly from Japan, saw the country's economic future as one of unlimited prosperity. They bid up prices for Japan's scarcest resources—land and real estate—and also sent shares in Japanese companies through the roof.

Those companies chose to believe the illusion. Into the mid-1980s, their borrowing rose sharply as they hired more workers, bought more equipment, and built more factories and offices to house them. The Bank of Japan, controller of the country's money supply, did little to slow the by-now-careening bandwagon.

Inevitably, it ran off the road. Investors began to realize that their expectations were too great, that Japan was already pushing the bounds of its capacity to produce. But they also started to see how the bandwagon had picked up so much speed: the tortuous ownership structures of Japan's biggest businesses, in which banks were often tightly entangled, gave the businesses a level of access to money that didn't always correspond to their profitability; demand for Japan's products simply fell behind the country's capacity to produce. And collusion within major industries, often aided by the government, didn't help to make matters clearer. Investors had a hard time figuring out what companies were really worth, and that's part of why they believed the illusion of Japan's bubble for so long.

China shares these risks, if for slightly different reasons. Its leading companies can also have knotty ownership structures, thanks to the involvement of the government, the army—which happens to be one of the country's biggest business empires—and their many tentacles. Its banks also have a history of making decisions without careful regard for risks, and they have had balance sheets filled with junk loans as proof. China Construction Bank, the first of the country's major banks to sell shares to the public, shed a staggering $46 billion in loans with little chance of repayment in the six years leading up to its initial public offering in 2005.

Investors may be overestimating China's ability to keep growing, too. In the global economic pecking order, it's always easier to follow than to lead. Countries trying to catch up to the most advanced economies can save time by copying technologies and techniques that the leaders had to spend time developing. While their living standards are lower, their businesses can also get away with paying lower wages than their competitors in wealthy nations.

As the followers catch up to the leaders, however, two things happen. First, wages rise alongside the improving skills of the labor force. Second, as the followers move into higher-skilled occupations, they have to do more of the nitty-gritty work of research and development themselves. For that reason, economic growth—like most things in economics—tends to show diminishing returns over time. Just look at how Japan's economy grew, adjusting for changes in prices of goods and services:

DECADE	AVERAGE ANNUAL GROWTH RATE
1960s	10.2 percent
1970s	4.5 percent
1980s	4.1 percent
1990s	1.2 percent

Compare that with how the American economy developed over the same period:

DECADE	AVERAGE ANNUAL GROWTH RATE
1960s	4.2 percent
1970s	3.2 percent
1980s	3.3 percent
1990s	3.3 percent

Some analysts have predicted that China's economy will slow down much less rapidly than Japan's. In 2003, researchers at Goldman Sachs, an investment bank based in New York, published one such report that quickly became a sensation in the financial world. It predicted the next five decades of growth for four of the world's emerging powerhouses: Brazil, Russia, India, and China. The report said China was already decelerating, from its growth rate of about 10 percent annually in the 1990s to more like 7.5 percent in the first decade of the twenty-first century. But it also predicted that China's growth rate wouldn't drop to that of the United States until the 2040s.

If the predictions turn out to be right, China will easily pass the United States to become the world's biggest economy. Indeed, China might find itself permanently lagging the United States in this oft-cited measure of well-being.

To understand why, think about what happened in Japan. In 2005, material living standards in Japan, where the economy had finally regained a feeling of normalcy, were roughly equal to those of France, Germany, and the U.K. None of those countries was on its way to catching the United States, however. In the United States, the average person's buying power was about a third higher, and the figure was also growing faster than in Japan or the European countries.

That group has become a pack trailing the leader. Fundamental aspects of the Japanese and European economies—possibly their laws, regulations, cultural norms, levels of financial sophistication, even geographies—are holding them back. The United States, with its entrepreneurial spirit, strong legal system, diverse population, and freer markets, has achieved a higher capacity to innovate and grow. The four runners in the trailing pack can catch up to one another and hold one another's speed, but it would probably take a change in those deep factors for one of them to break away and challenge the United States.

There are several packs trailing further behind, too. At the back of the race—and often losing ground—are the least developed countries, such as Sierra Leone, Haiti, and Laos. In the middle are comers from eastern Europe and North Africa. The question is, which pack is China in?

Right now, it's hard to say. But in the Goldman Sachs report, China's economic growth rate drops to about the same level as that of the United States by 2050. It drops because China may not always be able to keep racing forward the way it has in the past decade or so. Much of China's growth has come from taking existing products and making them more cheaply in enormous volume. As its workers gain more skills, however, they will start running out of things to copy. They'll have to start inventing their own products, with higher and higher levels of technology. In other words, they'll be competing with workers in the United States, Europe, and Japan on equal terms. And at the moment, they don't seem like obvious winners.

For 2006, the World Bank ranked China 91st out of 155 countries for the ease of doing business. China offered a particularly difficult climate for the process of starting a business, getting credit, dealing with licenses, and paying taxes; it ranked no higher than 113th in any of those categories. According to the World Bank, an entrepreneur would have had an easier time in Yemen or Kyrgyzstan. For 2002, the International Monetary Fund used an "economic freedom index" to rate the ability of countries' institutions to lay the groundwork for growth. China scored 3 out of 7—the same as Niger, one of the world's poorest countries. By contrast, the United States ranked 3rd in the World Bank's survey and notched a full 7 out of 7 in the IMF's chart.

If these hindrances don't disappear, then China may find itself hitting a wall, as many long-distance runners like to say. It might have the biggest economy in the world by 2050, but with a population so large that China's average income would still be only about half of the average income in the United States. Growing at the same rate, and barring a major change in population, it would never catch the United States in that second measure of economic progress: material living standards. And there is a chance that, as in Japan's case, its growth would slow even more. Even as the world's economic behemoth, it would still be stuck among those middle packs in the race for higher living standards—going forward, yes, but not gaining on the leaders.

In the meantime, other countries seem to want to answer the question of packs on China's behalf. Researchers and politicians in Brazil, India, Iran, South Africa, Syria, and Vietnam have all suggested that their governments could follow the "China model" for economic growth. Taken literally, that would mean setting up the same institutional framework—a sort of quasi-capitalism moderated by an authoritarian government—and trying to compete in the same sorts of markets: textiles, plastics, machinery, and so on. Several of these countries already have higher living standards than China does, but they're envious of its rapid growth. Most of them will find China a hard act to follow, though, and not just because of its immense human and natural resources.

China is changing rapidly, and for that reason it could be in a "pack" by itself. Upon its acceptance to the World Trade Organization in 2001, China's government promised to loosen its grip on trade and commerce, and also to clear away some of the bureaucracy and corruption that have discouraged foreign companies from doing business there. But the country's institutions still have a long way to go before China's living standards will approach those of the world's wealthiest nations.

Another risk China has run, one that Japan did not face so starkly, comes from the side effects of its headlong dash for economic growth. As China prospered, its environment paid the price. Water shortages dog the central and southern parts of the country, and air pollution is a tremendous problem in the east. By the mid-1990s, China was second only to the United States as a source of emissions of carbon dioxide, carbon monoxide, nitrogen oxides, and other volatile compounds. For sulfur dioxide, it was number one—by a mile.

Meanwhile, the gap between China's rich and poor rapidly widened. China made enormous strides in reducing poverty between the early 1980s—after it took the first steps toward a market economy—and the mid-1990s. But since 1996, there has been little change in the share of the population living in poverty, by almost every measure, and inequality has been rising steadily.

Tens of millions of Chinese have gone from being poor in the countryside to being poor in cities. The number could rise into the hundreds of millions by 2020. When workers are poor in cities, however, their labor can go to work for manufacturers who export products to the rest of the world. The seemingly endless supply of low-wage laborers is what has allowed Chinese exporters to keep undercutting their competitors' costs on world markets.

In the United States in the early twentieth century, the poor in cities sent their children to school, and the children laid the groundwork for American economic dominance. But not all Chinese may be willing to wait for that process to reach its culmination, and unrest is building. Official figures reported seventy-four thousand protests over living conditions, working conditions, local corruption, forced relocations, and other issues across China

71

CONNECTED: 24 HOURS IN THE GLOBAL ECONOMY

in 2004; there were eighty-seven thousand in 2005. Tensions were often exacerbated by unpaid wages. China's National Economic Research Institute reported that migrant workers were owed about $12.5 billion in back wages, just from the previous few years. The protests sometimes became violent and were, at times, viciously suppressed by the government's forces or by hired thugs.

If these protests became organized and linked across regions, several threats to China's economic growth could emerge, from pro-Marxist backlash—as some eastern European states have witnessed—to open revolt. The government in Beijing was sufficiently worried about these possibilities to make dealing with the side effects of China's growth the central theme of its annual planning meeting in October 2005.

Regardless of these drags on its growth, China is still very likely to become the world's biggest economy—if not in 2041, as Goldman Sachs predicted, then sometime in the second half of this century. China's population of 1.3 billion virtually guarantees it. In the meantime, China may already feel like the world's most influential economy, at least in some arenas. By constantly ratcheting up its demand for commodities such as oil, gas, and steel—a process whose recent easing is sure to be temporary—and by continuing to lead the world as a target for investment by foreign companies, China will always be seen as the one pushing on prices and interest rates.

Generally speaking, China's impending dominance will not pose a danger to living standards in wealthy nations. There has been and will be a painful transition as manufacturing jobs, and even some jobs in the service sector, leave countries like the United States and Germany for cheaper homes in China. But trading with China has been a boon to consumers in these same countries, as their money goes further with relatively inexpensive Chinese products.

Living standards aside, however, there are areas where sheer size really counts. It's hard to underestimate the importance of the United States, the current leader, in the global economy. In total, the world produces about $40 to $45 trillion worth of income each year. More than $12 trillion of it comes from the United States. If you add up the value of all the buildings, equipment, cars, washing machines, and every other long-lasting item in the United States, the total comes to about $38 trillion. And that doesn't include a lot of the value of American companies. Their share prices are based not just on the value of their assets but also on the expected value of their future profits.

When the U.S. economy moves, the rest of the world pays attention. Sometimes they don't have a choice. Dozens of countries link their currencies to the dollar. Some keep a permanent and fixed exchange rate, like Ecuador; for years, its sucre has been worth one twenty-five-thousandth of a dollar. Others, like Barbados, Panama, and even China, allow their currencies to fluctuate, but only in a narrow range.

Most do it to prevent inflation. It works because fixing a currency to the dollar is usually a commitment to keep it in scarce supply. To start with, maintaining a stable exchange rate with the dollar requires that investors believe that a currency will hold its value. If they didn't, the currency would start trading informally at a discount; outside of the country, no one would be willing to buy it at the exchange rate set by the government. That's exactly what's likely to happen if the government starts printing lots of money—for example, to pay its own debts. With buckets more money chasing the same number of goods and services in an economy, prices are bound to rise—inflation. But when the currency is fixed to the dollar, the government can't print tons of new cash. If there's more and more of the currency around, investors will start to doubt whether they will always be able to exchange it for dollars. Then the currency's value will drop outside the country. Importers and the government will have a hard time buying products from abroad and paying off debts, and eventually the fixed exchange rate won't even hold up inside the country. After all, if a currency's value is dropping, why would anybody sell her dollars for it?

When prices rise in the United States, though, it affects everyone. Dollars suddenly buy less in the United States, but the same amount of stuff abroad. The same goes for currencies linked to the dollar. Every currency that's *not* linked to the dollar will buy less in the United States, too. It's no wonder, then, that a report on inflation from Washington attracts a lot of notice. The inflation report could also affect global markets for credit, albeit indirectly, as explained in the interlude titled "Credit Markets and Currencies." As investors from around the world came to grips with the report, Ashraf Laidi, a currency analyst in New York, was at the nexus.

7:00 A.M. NEW YORK

As I made my way to the office, I called our junior analyst to discuss the overnight move in the Canadian dollar and how the market was doing ahead of a flurry of economic releases that morning. I arrived at the office shortly after 8:00 a.m., checked the market, answered a few e-mails from clients asking questions about the incoming data releases, and called to order breakfast.

One of the day's most anticipated data reports was the May inflation report for the United States. Markets from New York to New Delhi awaited this report, as it showed the extent to which prices for goods and services were growing in the U.S. The dollar has had a tremendous run so far this year, appreciating 11 percent against the euro, 6 percent against the yen, and 5 percent against the British pound. The main reason for the strengthening was that U.S. (short-term) interest rates rose from 1 percent to 3 percent over the past year, which increased the yield on dollar-denominated bank accounts by about 200 percent.

The inflation report ended up showing inflation to have been negative in May, meaning that prices for goods and services went down instead of up. Initially that would have hurt the value of the dollar, because it meant that the U.S. central bank might not have to consider raising interest rates. But the market shrugged off the report, because traders argued that the main reason for the decline in prices was a temporary decrease in energy prices. And since everyone knew that energy prices went back up in June, people reasoned that inflation would be back up the following month.

Almost each and every business reporter and financial TV anchor was speaking about the inflation report. Many traders were seen on TV being interviewed about the same report. Nonetheless, we were alerting our clients just the preceding evening and earlier that morning that the key report to watch would be the one on foreign capital flows, due at 9:00 a.m. That report showed how much money foreign investors (non-U.S.) were pouring into U.S. stocks and bonds. Indeed, once the clock struck 9:00 a.m., my monitor flashed the data of what ended up to be the most influential report on the U.S. dollar and U.S. bonds for the week. The report showed that foreign investors' net purchases of U.S. assets (stocks and bonds) came in at

$47 billion in April, much less than the $57 billion trade deficit the U.S. incurred over the same month.

The $47 billion means that foreigners bought $47 billion worth of U.S. assets more than they sold, while the deficit means that the U.S. paid out more for its imports of goods and services than for its exports by a difference of $57 billion. This was the second month in a row that the U.S. trade deficit was greater than the surplus of how much assets foreigners bought from the U.S. The last time this had happened was in October 2004. The dollar began dropping instantly once the news hit the screen. Thirty minutes later, the dollar lost seven-tenths of a cent against the euro, falling from $1.204 to $1.211. Put in another way, that means that the value of one euro rose from $1.204 to $1.211. In a market where nearly $2 trillion changes hands daily, seven-tenths of a cent, or 70 pips, can mean hefty losses or profits for traders who transacted in amounts with $1 million face value. Once the report hit, I posted a quick note via Internet for our clients to read alerting them to the significance of the report and what it meant for the dollar and the major currencies. Since our clients trade currencies by speculating on the periodic changes in one currency versus another, the resulting drop in the dollar after the report presented ample opportunity for clients. It also meant great risk for those who were holding the dollar prior to the release of the data.

Once I finished alerting clients on the report, I began further dissecting the numbers, to see what part of that foreign money went into U.S. stocks and which went to bonds, as well as which countries showed the biggest gain (loss) in purchases of U.S. assets. As I started the number crunching, I received phone calls from the financial press asking, "What does the [Treasury] report show?" "What does the report mean for the dollar and the U.S. economy?" and "Why should we care?" I stated in my general response that if foreign purchases of U.S. stocks and bonds continued to be less than the trade deficit, then the U.S. central bank would have to continue raising interest rates to keep those foreign purchases and investments flowing into the U.S. The risk with that possibility is that further interest rate increases may hurt the U.S. economy at a time when energy prices are near their record highs, causing consumers to pay record rates for gasoline and companies to pay soaring prices for transportation fuel. Higher rates would also mean rising mortgage costs for home owners and new home buyers.

At 3:00 p.m. I was finally set to order lunch to eat at my desk.

By the time China is the world's biggest economy, the yuan's movements might attract as much attention as the dollar's. At the moment, the United States is able to finance its massive debts, incurred by both the private and the public sectors, because securities denominated in dollars—that is, the stocks and bonds that companies and governments sell to raise money—are in such heavy demand around the world. Many foreigners are happy to take these pieces of paper in exchange for the promise of future payments, because they still think the American economy offers an unbeatable combination of safety and high returns. But the euro is already threatening the overall demand for dollar-denominated securities by offering big buyers, such as East Asia's central banks, a chance to diversify their holdings. If the yuan becomes a stable, commonly traded currency, and the Chinese economy becomes a stable climate for investment, then the dollar will be even less prized. Either Americans will have to pay back their debts sooner rather than later, or they'll have to pay higher interest rates in order to attract the same amount of foreign lending and investment.

In addition to raising capital easily, the biggest economy in the world can do some things that other economies can't, and these tend to be the things that create fear in far-flung quarters: building a world-beating military, surging to the front of the space race, holding up international treaties, and the like. The United States has done all of these things, as did Germany and Britain before it (with the exception, of course, of the space race).

If China follows in their footsteps, it will risk falling into what Paul Kennedy, a historian, has noted as an almost inevitable decline. Countries in the dominant position are repeatedly tempted to overreach, spreading themselves too thin in the pursuit of a greater empire—be it military, political, or just economic. Britain couldn't keep its colonies; Germany let extreme ideology and wild ambition outrun its productive capacity; and even the United States is straining the limits of its military might. The historical parallels stretch back to ancient Rome. And China might be more tempted to overreach than its predecessors, because even as the world's biggest economy, its people still won't be the world's richest.

China's leaders have often said that they will not use their economic bulk to become an aggressive power. If they simply mean no more aggressive than the United States, the statement may not be so reassuring. Instead of Afghanistan and Iraq, China may choose to "liberate" Taiwan and the assortment of other islands and ocean waters it disputes with Russia and Japan. Yet because China lacks a democratic government, it's especially difficult to handicap its chances of becoming a warmongering bully rather than a benign merchant state.

For the moment, China's conquests are restricted to foreign companies. Even in this area, there is resistance. When China's Lenovo bought IBM's personal computer business, there was fairly little fuss; the business just wasn't cost-effective, and IBM wasn't doing much assembly or manufacturing in the United States anyway. The American government required a few concessions for security reasons, but then let the deal go through in March 2005.

The smooth sailing was over when the China National Offshore Oil Corporation (CNOOC) tried to buy Unocal, an American oil giant, in late June 2005. The bid came as crude oil prices were setting records almost daily in a race toward $60 a barrel. Fearing Chinese dominance of this vital market and a resulting erosion of American self-sufficiency, politicians in Washington immediately let fly with threatening rhetoric about regulatory investigations, congressional reviews, and the conditions domestic workers might expect inside a Chinese company. CNOOC dropped its bid of $18.5 billion, and homegrown Chevron stepped in to buy Unocal for about $700 million less.

China could run into more problems if it tries to buy any of Europe's big brands. There, officials do not hesitate to throw up roadblocks, even with little legal basis, when their countries' trophy properties attract foreign interest. In the summer of 2005, the governor of Italy's central bank, Antonio Fazio, stubbornly ensured that Banca Antonveneta would remain in Italian hands after interest was expressed by a bank not from China, nor even from the United States, but from the Netherlands. A few weeks later, the French prime minister, Dominique de Villepin, practically rallied his citizens to the barricades after rumors circulated that PepsiCo might buy Danone, the French titan of packaged foods and bottled water. The rumors later turned out to be unfounded.

Haier didn't succeed in bagging Maytag, either. After further consideration, the Chinese company stepped aside, leaving no obstacles to a takeover by Whirlpool, the American appliance maker. In the end, however, China's money is bound to win out. Its companies have shown that they're willing to pay top dollar, or top yuan, for foreign competitors. Its government has also demonstrated patience. Shortly after CNOOC failed to buy Unocal, another Chinese oil company with links to the government, called the China National Petroleum Corporation, outflanked Indian competition for PetroKazakhstan, a Canadian business with vast assets in central Asia. The price: $4.18 billion—almost one and a half times the value of the business's assets, according to the Kazakh government.

With these sums being kicked around, it's no surprise that foreign investors are taking notice. They feel China's influence in markets like the one for crude oil long before word gets out to the media and the public at large.

Donald Straszheim was the chief economist at Merrill Lynch, one of Wall Street's financial giants, before he started his own firm. Though Straszheim Global Advisors first set out to provide independent research on countries and markets around the world, its focus quickly narrowed to China. On June 15 it had an office in Beijing as well as its headquarters in Los Angeles, and China's energy needs had already been on Straszheim's agenda for some time.

We keep close track of economic events, activities, and data because that is our business—to be informed and to help our clients make better decisions with their investments and their businesses. So we regularly look at the data and the key stories that are being written, as well as some longer-term matters which we think are important and that the media does not follow as closely.

In particular, this time we are focused on China and the energy sector. China is an economy that used to be interesting, but now it is important. Any company that is not paying attention to China is totally asleep, and it is clear to any outside observers that China is changing the world.

So we are putting a series of reports together on China and energy in general, as well as more detailed reports on coal, oil, natural gas, hydroelectricity, and on alternatives like wind, solar, geothermal, biomass, etc. And we are looking at other issues—ethanol, energy, and the environment, China's appetite for foreign purchases of what we call secure sources of fuel for her economy (oil, gas, coal, etc.).

In the meantime, foreign companies are trying to engage with China. It will be the biggest consumer market in the world for pure sales, even though most of its consumers won't be among the world's wealthiest. It will also be the world's biggest exporter.

That's why, a few hours after Haier's interest in Maytag hit the newswires, Bill Zollars's mind was focused on China. As chief executive of Yellow Roadway Corporation (now YRC Worldwide), a commercial transportation company with roughly seventy thousand employees in more than one thousand locations worldwide, Zollars knows how to move products from factories to ports and into businesses and homes. His company has a strong interest in providing the logistical support for China's industrial future. Here's how his day started out:

6:30 A.M. KANSAS (7:30 A.M. NEW YORK)

Got up and worked out for thirty minutes, then got ready for work. Since it was garbage day in the neighborhood, took out the garbage cans before taking the ten-minute drive to the office. Once there I read *The Wall Street Journal*, *The Kansas City Star*, and *The New York Times* (as I do every morning), then checked e-mail that came in overnight.

First meeting of the day involved a pension reform legislation update from our vice president of government relations. This is a major issue for us, as for most companies, and seems to be moving along well in Congress. Then on to a meeting regarding our China strategy and my meeting there the last week of June, which includes a speech to Tsinghua University as well as a meeting with our employees, a joint venture partner, and a number of government officials. As part of the briefing I practiced my pronunciation of several Chinese phrases which will be used in the speech (in an effort to avoid an international incident).

We have been working on our China strategy for two years, and we met to talk about the final terms of our joint venture, which was announced this past Friday. We had members of our China team there, and following the deal discussions we talked about the trip I will be making next week to Beijing and Shanghai, which will allow us to highlight the deal and raise our profile in China.

Joint ventures such as YRC Worldwide's, which is with Shanghai Jin Jiang International Industrial Investment, provide China with some of the know-how that Han mentioned as a motivation for Haier's interest in Maytag. It's unlikely that China will always get the best out of these partnerships, though. As long as the government insists on Chinese control of these ventures in certain sectors, such as telecommunications and securities trading, foreign companies probably won't bring in their best staff or resources. And as long as other governments see China as a potential threat, both economically and militarily, they won't allow cutting-edge technologies to be shared in these ventures.

Now and in the future, China will have to rely on its own engines of innovation. Haier has already learned this lesson. Back in the 1980s and early 1990s, the company grew by buying competitors and related businesses, as well as by making its production lines leaner and more efficient. Then Haier began to expand its exports, with the key being the development of those unique, niche products. By analogy, China Inc. will be able to grow for a time simply by relying on low-cost manufacturing and acquisitions. But at some point, it will have to come up with its own special sauce—and not just the hoisin variety.

This vital focus on innovation could be difficult for China to maintain. Its political system doesn't prohibit people from becoming rich—it's hardly Communist anymore—but it doesn't encourage people to question authority, either. Along the same lines, there's not much encouragement for challenging the status quo through new ideas. A well-known Chinese professor of genetics publicly bemoaned this state of affairs in 2005. "What China has not realized, if it truly wants to go to the next level, is that numbers are not enough," said Tian Xu of Yale and Shanghai's Fudan University. "You must reward innovation, and reward scholarly work."

It's a worry that Wei shares, back in Qingdao. She complains about Haier's rigid hierarchy; she has to submit any new idea to her boss before she can share it with the relevant person or department. And Haier, Wei says, is more progressive than most Chinese companies. Nevertheless, she says attitudes are changing as more young people enter the workforce. The source of that change, she adds, is China's increasing engagement with the rest of the world.

CHAPTER 5

NEW YORK
6:06 A.M.
JUNE 15

BRUSSELS
12:06 P.M.
JUNE 15

"EURO GROUP MUST BE MORE FORCEFUL WITH ECB —JUNCKER" WHO REALLY CONTROLS THE WORLD'S MONEY SUPPLY?

It's hard not to be surprised by the grandeur of Brussels. For the capital of a democracy of ten million people, it boasts more than its share of bombastic architectural follies. Massive stone colonnades line cobblestoned plazas. Sunlight bounces off gilt-tipped domes. Larger-than-life statues of kings on horseback stand proudly in well-kept parks.

Several of these monuments are the products of Belgium's colonial exploits—and "exploit" is the right word, for the country's occupation of the ironically named Congo Free State was extraordinarily cruel. It was also extraordinarily profitable, as mining and the profits from rubber exports soon allowed Belgium's King Leopold II to control a small but non-negligible share of the global supply of gold, which was the world's common currency at the turn of the twentieth century.

A century later, Brussels is a center of power again, as the capital of the twenty-seven-member European Union. Berlaymont, the aircraft-carrier-like edifice that has been the nerve center of the union since 2004, easily dwarfs anything Leopold II ever built. It's nothing like the enormous palace he completed roughly a century earlier; the endless corridors of the oblong, four-winged building are covered with plain carpet, and the walls are just removable panels.

The European commissioners stationed here manage a realm far wealthier than any Leopold ever saw. But control of this empire's common currency, the euro, does not reside in Brussels. Instead, the viziers who set interest rates and the size of the money supply for twelve of the union's nations reside in Frankfurt, almost two hundred miles away.

The founders of the European Union chose Brussels as the seat of its most potent institutions, both to create a buffer between France and Germany and to separate those institutions from the sway of the local superpowers. Similarly, the creators of the euro deliberately separated its custodians from the rest of the EU's government, in law as well as in geography. On a day-to-day basis, the actions of the European Central Bank are completely independent of the politicians and commissioners in Brussels. Its governors are appointed by the euro area's twelve finance ministers, but they serve for a minimum of five years. The bank's budget is paid for by the euro area's subsidiary central banks, not by the government in Brussels.

While the European Commission, the European Parliament, and the member governments control the EU's taxes and spending, the ECB controls the money supply and some aspects of the financial system. In the past few decades, this kind of firewall between the bosses of fiscal affairs and monetary systems has been a basic tenet of mainstream economic policy. The reason for it comes down to differences between the political cycle and the economic cycle.

Say the economy of a country is growing at a moderate rate, with a steady level of unemployment. A politician with an election coming up might want to give the economy an extra spark by expanding the money supply and lowering interest rates. With lower rates, credit would be easier to come by; consumers and businesses might spend more money, leading to more new jobs. But doing so might also drive prices upward at a perilous rate, if markets for labor and goods started to tighten up during the resulting boom. Likewise, a politician might be hesitant to shrink the money supply—driving the process in reverse—to slow down an already-booming economy in danger of runaway inflation if there was a substantial risk that doing so would cause a recession.

Taking the decision out of politicians' hands and placing it in the lap of unelected officials whose main job is to fight inflation is supposed to solve these incentive problems. In many industrialized countries, it seems to have worked; average inflation rates have dropped steeply in places where the central banks have been made independent. But it has also made some politicians in the European Union very unhappy.

On June 15, their number included Jean-Claude Juncker, Luxembourg's prime minister and finance minister since 1995. On the eve of what promised to be an acrimonious summit meeting between the European Union's heads of state, with economic matters at the top of the agenda, Juncker took a rhetorical ax to the hallowed firewall.

"Many ministers want to persuade the central bank to change policy as regards interest rates," he said, implying their desire for a cut. "The bank has to remain independent," Juncker added, "but there is no reason why it should not take advice or listen to the views of other people, in this case the finance ministers." After that back handspring of logic, he said, not so cryptically, "The time has come to strengthen the initiative capacity of the euro group [of finance ministers] when expressing our views to the ECB."

For Juncker, these comments were something akin to a parent trying to regain the upper hand with a wayward teenager. For decades, he had been a tireless backer of economic integration in Europe. Like many other politicians, he saw it as a way to bind Europe's powerful nations together so tightly that war would be inconceivable. Juncker was born in 1954, but his father had been conscripted by the German army in World War II and forced to fight on the blood-soaked eastern front.

Juncker's involvement in the European project reached its apex in 1992, when members of the European Union signed a treaty in Maastricht that laid the groundwork for the close economic ties that exist today. Much of the chapter on monetary union, which would culminate in the euro's birth in 1999, was written by Juncker.

Yet by June 15, the euro had become a thorn in several governments' sides. That morning, the currency was worth about $1.20—12 percent less than its all-time record of $1.36 six months earlier, but still a rate that some finance ministers considered too high.

Though the euro had debuted on January 1, 1999, at $1.18, economic conditions had changed since then. The euro area's

trade surplus in goods and services had narrowed by over a quarter in the previous nine months, to 78 billion euros, compared
with 111 billion euros in the nine months before. In other words,
the balance between the region's imports and exports was starting to tilt more toward importers. The politicians wanted to see
their exporters in the driver's seat again. With a less valuable currency, they thought, euro area consumers would buy fewer imports, and foreigners would be able to afford relatively more
exports. They didn't control the exchange rate directly, of course,
but they weren't shy about saying which way they thought it
should go.

These concerns didn't hold much water with the ECB, however. Some of the countries in the euro area, like Ireland and
Greece, were growing so quickly already that fanning their economic flames could have done more harm than good—they
might have fallen victim to rapid inflation, as outlined in previous chapters. Moreover, sky-high oil prices and the simultane-
ous recovery of the American, Japanese, and possibly German
economies had the central bank's governors worried about gener-
alized inflation for the first time in several years. Higher oil prices
would eventually feed into higher prices for the euro area's goods
and services, as would enhanced demand from the world's big
importers. Cutting rates in hopes of devaluing the euro would
just enhance those risks.

Juncker had a seat at the table, though. As the first permanent
chairman of the euro area's group of finance ministers, he was
the only elected official allowed to attend the biweekly meetings
of the ECB's governing council. But under the European Union's
rules, he couldn't vote in any decisions. Those rules set up very
clear lines between the ECB, the ministers, and the European

Commission, the administrative body that essentially runs the union. The tables were turned once a month, however, when Juncker and the other finance ministers from the euro area met with the ECB's president, Jean-Claude Trichet, and the commissioner and director-general for economic and monetary affairs.

The director-general during Juncker's chairmanship was Klaus Regling. The discussions at those monthly meetings were unusually intimate and frank, Regling recounts, but there were still limits to what people such as Juncker could say. With only about thirty people in the room, Regling says with a chortle, these euro meetings represented "the smallest group in Brussels."

"People can talk freely, confidentiality is much more assured, but it's an informal body," he adds. "This is the closest one can have in the euro area to when the Federal Reserve chairman and the secretary of the Treasury meet over breakfast or lunch. Obviously we need a few more people in the room in Europe."

Since Juncker took over, Regling says, the informal dialogue has intensified—up to a point. "Advice in a strict sense is excluded under the treaty," he says. And when it comes to Juncker's restive remarks, Regling takes a milder interpretation. "What he probably wanted to say is one needs close dialogue, like the Fed chairman and the secretary of the Treasury—very open on a confidential basis, but it doesn't mean that you can tell the other side what to do." In the United States, the chairman of the Federal Reserve (who is in charge of monetary policy) and the secretary of the Treasury (who oversees fiscal policy once it's approved by the president and Congress) may speak often about the state of the economy, but they have no direct say over each other's decisions.

Maintaining the divisions between the monetary policy makers, the politicians, and the bureaucrats can be a bit of a tightrope act in other areas, too. Every two years, the ECB and the European Commission independently prepare reports on the EU members that have not yet joined the euro area. But they still do a bit of informal coordination. "To the extent possible, we try to avoid coming to different conclusions," Regling says.

Lately, though, that tightrope has been used for a tug-of-war. Politicians from some member states have argued for a weaker euro and even lower interest rates while the ECB has moved in the other direction. Regling says he doesn't expect it to change very soon. "We know that in any big monetary area, whether it's the U.S., China, or Europe, there have always been different cycles in different parts of the country," he explains. "Never expect a complete synchronization."

With this in mind, it shouldn't come as a shock that the same tug-of-war had been occurring in the United States less than a year earlier. In June 2004, the Federal Reserve began raising interest rates to fend off expectations of inflation. It was also giving itself some room to maneuver, since the target for short-term rates had been set for a year at just 1 percent; when rates are close to zero, there's little the Fed can do to give the economy a boost in a crisis. But politicians began to grumble. The most vocal of these was Jim Saxton, vice chairman of Congress's Joint Economic Committee, who repeatedly called on the Fed to stand pat rather than lift rates further.

Neither central bank took the politicians' advice. The Fed never looked back after its meeting on June 30, 2004, raising rates in every subsequent meeting through the next two years. The ECB never did cut interest rates; it kept its benchmark short-term rates at 2 percent until December 6, 2005, when it pushed them up to 2.25 percent. The concession to the euro area's weaker economies was, if anything, waiting that long. Had the ECB raised rates earlier, recession-stricken Italy and hobbling France might have felt the pain even more acutely.

While the independence of the world's two biggest central banks may be assured, the situation varies much more widely elsewhere. In the U.K., independence is a fairly new thing, instituted in 1997 as soon as Tony Blair became prime minister. For the most part, it has been respected. But in Japan, politicians exert almost constant pressure on the governor of the Bank of Japan to raise or lower interest rates. They can even, under some circumstances, delay the bank's decision-making votes. And though the bank's governor serves for five years and can be reappointed, none has been given a second full term since 1962.

Since 1991, Canada's central bank has agreed with the parliamentary government to try to keep inflation near a target level. That target is now 2 percent, or as close as possible within a range of 1 to 3 percent. The Bank of Canada is accountable to the country's parliament but still manages Canada's short-term interest rates and money supply with considerable autonomy, working toward the dual goals of achieving the inflation target and promoting steady growth in the Canadian economy.

On June 15, David Dodge, the bank's governor, was speaking to an audience in Winnipeg, where he credited that target with underpinning the nation's economic strength. Dodge also toasted the bank's commitment to transparency. "Monetary policy is more effective," he said, "when people understand what we are doing and why." Judging by his schedule of speeches, meetings, and media events, no one could call him secretive.

WINNIPEG, MANITOBA (ONE HOUR BEHIND NEW YORK)

I was chairing the first day of a two-day meeting of the Bank of Canada's board of directors. Once a year, we hold a board meeting away from our headquarters in Ottawa, Ontario. This one was in Winnipeg, Manitoba.

I had flown directly to Winnipeg from a weeklong trip to China and Japan, where I had attended meetings with other central bankers and delivered two public speeches. I was a bit jet-lagged, so I was up quite early for breakfast and briefing sessions on the regional economy, which lasted most of the morning.

I met with staff from the bank's communications department for a market briefing and a final read-through for a public speech, which I delivered to the Winnipeg Chamber of Commerce at lunch. I talked about some of the changes taking place in the global economy, and said that I was encouraged by the adjustments that Canadians are making to improve their competitiveness and seize new opportunities that arise from these global changes.

Immediately after the speech, we held a press conference, as we usually do after my public speeches in Canada. About a dozen reporters attended the press conference. More attended a media lockup at our Ottawa headquarters or listened to a live Webcast of the speech and press conference.

The afternoon was spent with the board, meeting with local business leaders to discuss business conditions in Manitoba. In the evening, I hosted a reception and dinner with the local business community, accompanied by my wife, senior bank staff, and board members. I delivered another short speech, about the Bank of Canada's seventy-year history and its role in the Canadian economy, and answered questions from the audience.

After the reception, I took a quick walk and went to bed—the jet lag was catching up to me, and our meetings started again at 8:30 a.m. the next day.

In other countries, links between the central bank and the rest of the government can be extremely intimate—and far from transparent. India's central bank has remained under political control, despite the country's other shifts toward economic modernization. The situation moved Anand Chandavarkar, a former adviser for the International Monetary Fund and author of a book on central banking in developing countries, to write the following in India's *Economic and Political Weekly* in August 2005: "Why and how the Reserve Bank of India (RBI) alone has remained immune to India's critically acclaimed economic reforms, and to the worldwide trend of radical reform and legal independence of central banks, is a baffling conundrum that has hardly attracted any attention. Nor has it figured on the agenda of any political party."

The latter observation may not be so surprising. It takes a far-sighted political party, or at least one burned by the experience of rampaging inflation, to propose granting a central bank its independence. The more natural desire for politicians is simply to keep their mitts on the bank's levers as long as possible.

Of course, this doesn't always hold true. In some of the world's smaller economies, having their own currency and the apparatus to support it would be a disproportionate burden. To solve the problem, they adopt existing currencies as their own; for example, Panama uses the dollar, and Monaco uses the euro. These countries can't control their own money supplies, as their needs are too small to affect the decisions made in Washington and Frankfurt. But it's a trade they're willing to make.

Even in medium-sized countries, a bad experience can sometimes lead a government to give up part of its control of the money supply. That's what happened in Argentina in 1991, when the government decided to link its peso to the U.S. dollar. Inflation in Argentina had reached 200 percent *per month* in July 1989, after years of fiscal deficits were financed by printing money. Fixing the value of the peso at $1 and pledging that pesos would always be convertible into dollars ensured a sort of discipline. The government would only be able to print more money if it could still buy back all the pesos in circulation, using its reserves of dollars and other strong currencies. With this commitment in place, inflation rapidly subsided.

Scores of countries around the world fix their currencies' value to the dollar, the euro, or even to so-called baskets of different moneys. Smaller countries usually look for a mix of safe currencies that reflects their trading relationships; for this reason, many East Asian economies that export to the United States have currencies linked to the dollar. But according to various calculations, independent central banks may still be in control of only about half of the world's money supply. The implication is that bouts of high inflation, and therefore precarious swings in the global economic cycle, may be occurring with unnecessary frequency. And even where a link to a strong currency is in place, problems can still arise—as Argentina soon found.

Argentina grew strongly for six of seven years after hitching the peso to the dollar, but the government didn't take full advantage. It failed to collect a substantial surplus in all but one of those years (in part for reasons discussed in Chapter 6) and later added heavily to its existing debts. The private sector borrowed more, too, since Argentina had finally become a place deemed safe for investment. But by 2001, the burden of those debts had become too great.

The government could no longer make its interest payments. Provincial governments started issuing their own currencies to cover their bills. After a series of attempted bailouts by the United States and the International Monetary Fund, Argentina decoupled the peso from the dollar in January 2002 and allowed its exchange rate to slip. This action cut the value of the government's debts, and the private sector's as well. It also led to an exodus of chastised foreign creditors, many of whom received only pennies on the dollar for their loans and bonds, and cast millions of Argentines into poverty. Some lost their jobs, but many more suffered as the value of their incomes and savings—at least in terms of foreign currencies—dropped by almost three-quarters in just five months.

This time, however, the government managed to convince the public that it could restrain inflation without hitching the peso to the dollar's wagon. It clamped down on public expenditure, so that it wouldn't be tempted to print money indiscriminately, and allowed the currency markets to determine the value of the peso. By the second half of 2005, prices were rising by about 10 percent annually—not exactly the target of about 2 percent used by many wealthy nations like Canada, but almost under control. Unemployment was down to 11 percent, identical to the level in several western European economies. The country was definitely poorer, having paid the price for its salad days in the 1990s, but it was on its way back.

By this time, however, a similar situation was causing a very different kind of friction across the Pacific in China. Like Argentina, China had fixed its currency to the dollar—though without completely guaranteeing its ability to buy back all the yuan in circulation, as Argentina had. The Chinese government still had to stack up its reserves of dollar-denominated securities, though, for two reasons.

First, because of China's big trade surpluses, there is more foreign currency coming into the country than going out. The excess always ends up with the central bank. Here's why: When an American wants to buy some goods from a Chinese seller, the American first has to buy some yuan. So the American goes to a bank or money changer and trades dollars for yuan. Then the American pays the yuan to the Chinese seller and receives the goods in return. But where did the yuan come from? Ultimately, all yuan originate with the central bank. The central bank doesn't give them away, though; intermediaries have to pay for them, with dollars or other strong currencies. When Chinese businesses want to buy American goods, the process works in reverse. Thus, when China's exports outweigh its imports, the central bank will end up with a lot of dollars.

Second, countries in China's position will often try to buy up even more dollars, in order to defend their fixed exchange rate. No one would ever pay more than that official rate to buy yuan, but they might pay less. For example, if people thought that the Chinese government might lower the fixed exchange rate tomorrow—something American politicians have been begging for, as detailed below—they might trade yuan among themselves today at a price below the official rate. To counter this undermining of the official rate, the Chinese government could use its reserves of dollars to buy back yuan from the public, thus creating extra demand to push the unofficial price back up to the official rate.

Dollars don't come in unlimited supply, though. China's demand for dollar-denominated securities in 2005 was pushing up the greenback's value relative to other currencies. The value of the dollar depends on both supply (thanks to the Fed) and demand (thanks to buyers), and control of that value was shifting ever so slightly toward China. Rather than being tossed along the waves of fluctuations in the dollar's value, like smaller economies with linked currencies, China was affecting that value directly.

In early 2005, China was having no trouble maintaining its official rate of about 8.3 yuan to the dollar. With the economy growing by a jaw-dropping 9 percent annually, no one thought China would have to devalue its currency the way Argentina did. Foreign investment was pouring in, and the government owed less than half as much debt, relative to the size of its economy, as the United States did. The problem was overseas, and especially in the United States.

Americans had grown used to seeing their manufacturing jobs lost to lower-cost producers in China. But the situation was getting more serious. The removal of textile quotas in January—the culmination of a ten-year phaseout—had led to a flood of inexpensive Chinese garments, and politicians were scrambling to renegotiate some controls on the market. More worrying for Americans, white-collar jobs had also started to migrate, with companies like Microsoft and Motorola employing thousands of engineers, researchers, and designers in China.

To some politicians, the competition seemed unfair. The Chinese economy was so strong, they argued, that the true value of the yuan was actually higher than its official rate against the dollar. China had picked an artificially low exchange rate so that its exports, sold in yuan, would seem cheaper to American consumers. Given the demand for Chinese products and assets, the politicians charged, the yuan would quickly gain value if allowed to float freely on international markets—and those exports wouldn't seem as cheap anymore. "We're pressing China," said President George W. Bush in April, "for floating her currency, so we can have free and fair trade."

When it came to determining the value of the Chinese currency, the United States was sending a clear message: include us out. The White House wanted the yuan's link to the dollar severed, once and for all. China did budge a little, by allowing the yuan to gain about 2.5 percent against the dollar in the second half of 2005. But the Chinese still seemed to be a long way from letting the market set the yuan's value.

Their move didn't do much for the American trade balance, either. Consumers' taste for imports failed to wane, and it wasn't as though exporters in the United States had suddenly hit the jackpot, either—China wasn't such a big customer for them. During that same six-month period, the monthly deficit grew by 11 percent, to almost $66 billion. That deficit, like the ones before it, would be paid with American financial assets. Reversing it was a tall order, in any case; for thirty years, the United States had been borrowing from and selling off shares in its economy to scores of countries around the world, not just to China. Foreign lending and investment were supporting American companies, as well as financing the federal government's budget deficits; in return, the United States was playing a big part in keeping slews of foreign exporters, from Mexico to Malaysia, afloat.

The imbalances—the U.S. trade deficits on one side, the rest of the world's investments in the United States on the other side—had grown so large that commentators and economists wondered out loud whether the world's leaders shouldn't get together and do something about them. If they didn't, there was a chance that some shock to the system, like another big terrorist attack on the United States, could send the entire global economy into turmoil. Anything that gave foreign investors the jitters could cut off a vital supply of cash to the American economy. If the American economy hit the skids, then its consumers wouldn't be able to afford all those imports, and the United States would drag the rest of the world down with it.

The suggestions for action ran the gamut. In early 2006, Clyde Prestowitz, who was a trade official during Ronald Reagan's presidency, suggested a concerted effort by central banks (and their governments) to correct the imbalances. He recommended at a meeting between officials of the world's biggest economies, the G-8, that they launch a strategy for intervening in currency markets. This kind of thing hasn't always worked, though. Early in the euro's lifetime, when it was languishing around $0.85 in September 2000, the central banks of the United States, Japan, the U.K., and the euro area worked in concert to raise its value. They bought euro-denominated securities and sold the others. Crucially, they took investors by surprise and did manage to pump up the currency by a few pennies on the day of the intervention. But after another month of trading, the euro had dropped to record depths, below $0.83.

Gadflies ranging from established academics to the fringe politician Lyndon LaRouche proposed a return to something like the Bretton Woods system, an exchange rate arrangement set up at a conference in the New Hampshire town of the same name in

1944. Under the system, the United States fixed the amount of gold for which a dollar could be redeemed, and the other Allies from World War II fixed their currencies' exchange rates to the dollar. The system required the United States to back every dollar in circulation with gold. It was abandoned in 1971, when the government chose to remove this backing, having decided it was unnecessary and restrictive.

Going back to fixed exchange rates would supposedly set the stage for some reversals in the flows of imports, exports, and financial assets. If the dollar found a new, lower level relative to other currencies, the American trade gap might start to close while, at the same time, foreign investors would find new homes for their money. After all, a lower dollar would render returns on existing American investments less valuable in the rest of the world. But the most recent experience didn't offer much hope that the strategy would actually work.

Since 1973, the Federal Reserve has maintained indexes of the dollar's value that depend on its exchange rates against the currencies of the United States' major trading partners. These rates are weighted by the volume of trade with each partner, and they're also adjusted for prices of goods and services. The highest value on record for the Fed's broadest-based index was 127, in February 1985. That number didn't mean anything by itself, but it would change along with the exchange rates.

In 1985, the United States was racking up trade deficits of a size never seen before, equivalent to about 3 percent of domestic economic activity on an annual basis. Within just three years, however, the currency index had fallen to 92—a drop of 28 percent—as the dollar plummeted relative to the world's big currencies. After three more years, the trade deficits had shrunk by more than 80 percent as foreigners snapped up cheaper American goods. So far, so good.

The index didn't come close to its record highs again until February 2002, when it peaked at 113. Again, the dollar came tumbling down, this time to 95 by December 2004. In the next year, it stabilized around 100. Yet despite the drop, this time American trade deficits continued to grow. In October 2005, partly as a result of high oil prices, the monthly deficit hit $68.9 billion, and at least one analyst predicted that the annual total could hit $730 billion—over 6 percent of the domestic economy. (He was off by only $4 billion.) The exchange rate–trade link of the 1980s seemed to have disappeared; the dive in the dollar's value hadn't led to a narrowing of the deficit.

A third idea for correcting the imbalances came from Kenneth Rogoff, another Harvard professor, who had been the top economic adviser at the International Monetary Fund. He hypothesized that the IMF could step into the breach and coordinate countries' policies to reduce the imbalances. Part of the IMF's mission was to monitor exchange rate policies and provide a forum for discussing their deficiencies. The executive director of the fund, Rodrigo de Rato, had certainly talked about the imbalances in several speeches. But the fund had abstained from taking its consultative role a step further, by trying to coordinate government actions in an effort to change global economic trends. Perhaps afraid of intensifying the existing jitters in the financial community, the fund hadn't even called for crisis talks between its members.

This wasn't too surprising, since the IMF would have had a hard time taking a bold stance without the assent of the United States, its most powerful member. And politicians in Washington showed little interest in coordinating; they were busy blaming overseas governments for the imbalances. In September 2004, John Snow, the Treasury secretary, said they were the fault of a "global growth deficit"—other countries lagging behind the United States as a result of their insufficiently liberalized economies. If their economies would just grow faster, they'd buy more American exports, and investors would be more tempted to put their money somewhere besides the United States.

For the time being, control of the dollar and its significant counterparts would remain a question of supply and demand, with central banks often operating on both sides. There would be no fixed exchange rates, and no coordination.

Meanwhile, politicians in the euro area are still free to encourage the ECB to cut interest rates. The discussion is likely to intensify as the ten nations who joined the European Union in 2004 become part of the euro area—something they promised to do as soon as their economies were ready. In short, the airspace between Brussels and Frankfurt is likely to get hotter before it cools down.

Though the politicians and economic officials may disagree, the verdict was unanimous at a newsstand on Brussels's Avenue de la Toison d'Or—the "Avenue of the Golden Fleece." Philippe Degryse, working behind the counter, said he approved of central control of the currency, rather than leaving it to be fought out between politicians.

Philippe le Maire de Warzée, an architect who stopped by for a chat, agreed. It's one decision, he said, so have one body make it by consensus to avoid the biases of individual nations. Governments come and go, he added, and they also contradict themselves: "Les gouvernements se passent et se trépassent."

NEW YORK
9:30 A.M.
JUNE 15

NEW YORK
9:30 A.M.
JUNE 15

STOCK MARKETS

At precisely 9:30 a.m. on most weekdays in New York, an assortment of business types gather on a balcony in southern Manhattan to press a button, which results in a ding-ding-ding sound heard around the world. On June 15, Andrew Puzder, president and chief executive of CKE Restaurants, owned the finger that rang the opening bell of the New York Stock Exchange—a tradition so famous that the exchange has it service-marked as The Opening Bell[SM].

Exactly six and a half hours later, Philip Shearer, group president of the Estée Lauder Companies, would ring The Closing Bell[SM]. Shearer and his colleagues were celebrating no less an occasion than the relaunch of the company's Clinique Skin Supplies for Men line. But every time these bells ring, they celebrate something much bigger, indeed one of the crowning achievements of capitalism: a place, existing in physical and virtual reality, where people from around the world can buy and trade part ownership of companies under a system that, generally speaking, protects their right to control their investments.

During that one trading day in New York, almost a billion and a half shares with a value over $50 billion changed hands. As in all of the world's stock exchanges, almost none of these trades involved shares that companies were selling for the first time. Rather, they were trades between investors—individuals, companies, hedge funds, pension systems, charitable foundations—that determined the value of existing shares. These trades, called the secondary market, are just as important as the ones where a company comes to the market for the first time. Without them, those brand-new shares wouldn't be as attractive. After all, you would want to buy an asset that you couldn't sell later on?

At almost any given moment, a stock market somewhere is open for trading. But the importance of a physical stock exchange building, like the one on Wall Street in Manhattan, has diminished of late. Though the markets started out as hives of frantic buying and selling, all carried out face-to-face, these days most trades are executed through the ether by computers—many of them according to preprogrammed reactions to changes in the market. After-hours trading, which the New York exchange has offered for several years, gives investors a chance to make computer-aided trades when the lights are out in the building. Big companies further extend the trading day by listing their shares in several exchanges around the world, a practice that also gives brokers and investors easier access to shares in their home markets.

Even before The Opening Bell^{SM} rang, however, there was action in the market. Investors were trading stock futures— contracts in which they promised to buy shares at predetermined prices during the coming hours or days. By looking at the prices investors were willing to pay to enact those contracts, one could glean their expectations of the underlying share prices during the trading day. For example, a contract to buy a thousand shares of General Motors at $25 each would be worth a lot if investors expected the stock's value to rise to $30 when the market opened. It wouldn't necessarily be worth the full $5,000, though, as long as some investors thought the stock would open lower.

There was plenty of action in the stock futures market on June 15. At 8:30 a.m., as Ashraf Laidi already related in Chapter 4, the Bureau of Labor Statistics released its monthly report on inflation. And there was other news to digest: Schering-Plough, a huge pharmaceutical company, had announced plans to test a new drug for HIV-related infections; International Flavors & Fragrances said its earnings would be hurt by a batch of Spanish paprika containing artificial color that was unsuitable for food; and of course, there was Napster's tie-in with Ericsson from Chapter 1.

By the end of the day, the major indexes of stock prices—basically different averages of the values of big companies' shares—had risen slightly. An hour later, Larry Kudlow was on the air with his financial talk show. Kudlow had made his name as an often-reliable Wall Street forecaster. Later, he parlayed his modest fame into a career as a television personality known for conservative views and fast, blunt chatter.

A few of his comments about the market's day were particularly illustrative. "Bear Stearns beat the Street and its stock went up almost a percentage point," he said. By "beat the Street" he meant that Bear Stearns, a large financial firm, had earned more than investors expected, according to its latest quarterly report to the public—a report required by law from companies with publicly traded shares. In this case, investors got a positive surprise, and Bear Stearns's shares rose. Given higher earnings, the company's future profits—the money shareholders actually owned a share of—would probably be higher than expected, too.

Later, Kudlow said, "Drillers and refiners led the way as crude oil prices rallied despite OPEC's promise to raise production." In this case, share prices rose across an entire industry along with the value of its product. If investors had already expected oil prices to rise, then it's unlikely that the drillers' and refiners' shares would have moved along with the news. But then again, if investors had already expected oil prices to rise, they probably would have bid up the price of oil until the price met their expectations. The increase in the oil price was a surprise, and surprises are what make share prices change.

"Listen, more and more I have come to believe that the low inflation, solid growth economy is ideally placed to support higher share prices as this rally broadens and escalates," Kudlow went on, warming to the subject. Here he wasn't talking about a single company or industry, but rather the entire economy. The Bureau of Labor Statistics had reported that prices for consumers had actually fallen in May. A lack of inflation was a sign that the economy was in little danger of overheating; there was less pressure on the Federal Reserve to apply the brakes by raising short-term interest rates and making credit more expensive.

Kudlow's remark was also referring to a factor besides news that can drive the stock market: psychology. A rally "escalates" when the spirit of the mob, or hysteria, mixes with investors' expectations to push the market upward. There's no doubt that this happens; just remember the heights of the Internet boom, dubbed "irrational exuberance" by Alan Greenspan, the chairman of the Federal Reserve at the time.

Kudlow continued his unintentional master class with these comments: "Look it, compared to bonds, stocks are greatly undervalued. Compared to profits, stocks are undervalued." Here he touched on the principle of supply and demand, the final factor that drives share prices. No matter how rosy investors' expectations of future profits may be, a company's stock will be worth even more if lots of people are racing to buy it. If for some reason they flock instead to another type of investment, then that first stock could be "undervalued" in the sense that Kudlow suggested. At the time, there was indeed a flood of money pouring into bonds, much of it from foreign central banks. Stocks, in Kudlow's opinion, offered a much better return at a substantial discount.

What Kudlow surely knew, though he didn't mention it, was that all of these factors would influence markets outside the United States, too. For instance, a change in interest rates in one country affects the global market for credit, because much of the market is international; companies in the United States, Europe, Japan, and dozens of other countries compete to attract financing from investors, millions of whom are willing to send their money anywhere for a good mix of risk and return. Also, a change in the economic conditions in one country—like the downturn in prices in the United States—can touch all the companies that have business interests there, no matter where they're based. In the case of the United States, at least five groups of companies could fit that description: American companies, foreign companies with branches in the United States, companies that export to the United States, companies that import from the

United States, and even foreign companies that compete with American companies in other countries.

Later in the afternoon, news outlets recounted the suspected factors behind the market's moves in more detail. Even though OPEC, the crude oil cartel of eleven drilling nations, was going to raise its daily production, the change was viewed as a token gesture. In the meantime, the U.S. government had reported an unexpected drop in the nation's oil supply, which probably led to the price increase. Investors were still pretty sure that the Federal Reserve would raise short-term interest rates at the end of June— you could judge this by looking at the current market values of short-term loans—but the drop in inflation made some of them think that the string of rate increases would end sooner rather than later. Finally, the dollar had lost value against the world's other major currencies; foreigners might have used this as an opportunity to pick up American stocks on the cheap, thus driving up the market.

There were thousands of other stories behind the 4.4 million trades that took place in the New York Stock Exchange on June 15. But the stock market is a bit like a subatomic particle; the instant you think you've got it pinned down, it has already changed. That's part of what makes it such a powerful engine of the economy, so full of possibility, so seductive, addictive, and, to the unwary, even dangerous.

CHAPTER 6

NEW YORK
9:34 A.M.
JUNE 15

PRETORIA
3:34 P.M.
JUNE 15

"ZUMA FALL SEEN AS GOOD FOR SOUTH AFRICA IN-VESTMENT" WHAT DOES CORRUPTION COST?

Near the end of Paul Kruger Street in Pretoria, a statue of the eponymous fighter for Boer independence stands atop a high pedestal, surveying a broad square lined mainly by public buildings. For years, locals have joked darkly that Kruger, who began life as a frontier farmer and ended as an exiled president, was standing on the heads of the indigenous African population. Now the view is one he wouldn't recognize: South Africans of all ethnicities relaxing and milling around on their lunch hour.

On one corner of the square stands the Directorate of Public Prosecutions, a plain building fronted in white stone and tinted windows. It is the headquarters of the National Prosecuting Authority, which began operating in 1998 and has since led South Africa's sporadic battle against corruption. Its corruption investigations have often been splattered with mudslinging and buffeted by countercharges, made worse by the uneasy relations between factions of the African National Congress, the party that dominates politics across the country.

On June 14, the NPA's investigations claimed their biggest scalp yet. Jacob Zuma was fired from his position as vice president of the Republic of South Africa after the trial of his financial adviser, Schabir Shaik, revealed some seemingly underhanded activities involving bribes and arms deals. Within a day, the international financial community had offered its verdict: the firing was a Good Thing. Investors took Zuma's fall as a signal that Thabo Mbeki, South Africa's president, had finally become serious about fighting corruption.

Some forty miles away in Johannesburg's leafy Sandton neighborhood, Geoff Rothschild watched the JSE Securities Exchange's All-Share index rise. As director of marketing for the JSE, he is the public face of a stock market that's trying to attract investment from around the world while raising the standard of corporate governance among its member companies. Anything that helps South Africa's reputation as a place to do business also helps him and the JSE.

At his office at the JSE's new headquarters, Rothschild gives the impression of being the calm in the storm. He's an older but energetic man, balding, in a crisp blue shirt and tie. Right outside the door, there's a constant buzz of activity, but he talks at a deliberate pace and considers his answers carefully.

"The action Mbeki took was the only action that was appropriate given the circumstances and what had been made public," he says. "Mbeki in many of his talks and by his actions has sent out a very clear message that corruption will not be tolerated."

Corruption is indeed a deep problem in South Africa, Rothschild continues. It begins at the lowest levels. "In our local authority, the word goes around that if you get stopped for speeding, if you give the guy enough money he'll get you off," he says, adding that this undesirable attitude is reflected in other areas as well.

Though a bribe-taking cop would be considered corrupt in many countries, other differences are more subtle and ingrained in the local culture. For example, exchanging gifts can be a traditional feature of deal making, even though it might be considered bribery in Europe or the United States. When investors from those places come to South Africa, they expect to see their own anticorruption standards upheld. Yet among South Africans, Rothschild says, there's still "a matter of people understanding just what's right and what's wrong."

To Rothschild, rooting out corruption is an important step toward attracting more investment in South Africa. But across the street from the JSE's gleaming headquarters, the link between Zuma's firing and economic growth is not so clear.

Along the sidewalk, where dust from the red earth peeks out from between paving stones, half a dozen men and women are selling everything from T-bone steak with grits and pickled vegetables to old pairs of high-heeled pumps. Sitting in an improvised open-air café is Rose Jiyane, a young dishwasher from a Sandton restaurant. Like a lot of people who work in kitchens, she has her hair pulled back, wears black-and-white checked trousers, and is tired after her work.

Rose says she follows the issues in the Zuma case and agrees with the decision to oust him, but not many other people do. "We don't read newspapers," she says. "Maybe we're just not into politics." She adds that Zuma has always drawn most of his support from the province of KwaZulu-Natal, which has the largest population of poor people. It's here in the wealthier province of Gauteng, which contains both Pretoria and Johannesburg, that Rose says people care "more about business, money."

That many South Africans don't see the Zuma case's bearing on business might worry those among them who are engaged in the fight against corruption. But it's not completely clear how much difference it makes. To figure that out, you have to decide exactly what corruption is and how much it actually costs.

In answering the first question, you might be tempted to resort to the old test that Potter Stewart, a former justice of the United States Supreme Court, used for pornography: "I know it when I see it." That's not good enough in matters of international economics, though. Corruption can take many forms, and attacking it requires not just creating a vaguely ethical culture but also setting down specific criteria. And even under those criteria, what looks like corruption can in fact be the result of more fundamental problems, and not conscious wrongdoing at all.

Most types of corruption are those related to specific actions, like Rothschild's hypothetical bribe to escape a traffic ticket. Here, one person pays another to take an action; it just happens to be illegal. Another variety is holdup or extortion, where people insist on extra, informal payments in order to do what they're legally supposed to do anyway, for example, processing a visa application. On the other side of the coin, corrupt officials may simply decide not to honor contracts or perform their responsibilities; they may look the other way as crimes are committed, if they stand to profit by them.

Corruption can also contribute to black markets, when officials sell things they're not supposed to be selling, like the arms Iran bought from Ronald Reagan's administration in the United

States, or when officials allow things to be sold below otherwise fixed prices. Then there's patronage: simply giving out contracts or jobs to one's friends and political allies. And finally, there's good old-fashioned stealing: embezzling, misappropriation, illegal perks, wastage, call it what you will—it's the hand in the till.

These activities are called corruption when they take place in the public sector, but they can also corrupt the workings of an economy in the private sector. For example, bribes offered to managers to ensure jobs go to particular people aren't punishable by law in every situation. But they still distort the choices employers and employees make, possibly pushing them away from the most efficient uses of the workforce.

Every country has some corruption. That's not a generalization; it's a statement based on the research of Transparency International, an independent organization dedicated to shedding light on corruption around the world. Every year, the group puts out a "corruption perceptions index" that rates countries on the likelihood of encountering corruption when dealing with public officials. The index is based on over a dozen surveys compiled by other agencies, universities, and businesses. The surveys compile feedback from analysts of various types, local businesspeople, expatriate businesspeople, and other correspondents.

The perfect score, 10, was achieved by exactly zero countries in 2005. Iceland came the closest, at 9.7. The United States was 17th, at 7.6. At the bottom of the list were Bangladesh and Chad, tied for 158th with scores of 1.7. Across the continents, eastern Europe, Asia, South America, Central America, and Africa were all virtually covered by medium to high levels of corruption. For them, corruption was the rule, not the exception.

In the view of some experts, the universality of corruption in these areas has cultural sources. As a result, they question its definition, and the usefulness or correctness of trying to dispel it.

"Cultural differences dictate different behaviors," Rothschild says. When it comes to deciding what's acceptable and what's not, he adds, "there are certain circumstances where it's easy to take a decision and others where it's extremely difficult."

But there are differences in corruption, even among very similar cultures. South Africa ranked 46th in Transparency International's index—better than most, better even than Greece in the EU, but not as highly as neighboring Botswana, which was 32nd. Chile was 21st; across the Andes, Argentina was 97th, though improving.

The wealthiest countries are also, for the most part, the least corrupt. But is this a cause or an effect? On the one hand, people might be less tempted to circumvent the law if their wages were already high enough to purchase life's necessities, and even a few luxuries—so high incomes could mean less corruption. On the other hand, corruption itself could be the main obstacle to rising incomes.

Economists have tried to sort out this question of causality with little success. But there is another possibility; corruption may just be a response to other problems in an economy. Let's take a hypothetical case.

Most poor countries have a hard time collecting tax revenue. As a result, a customs officer may earn a salary that's fixed at a lower level than his skills could command in the private sector. In fact, he may be expected to extract bribes in order to make up the difference, just as a waiter is expected to supplement a low wage with tips. So he makes sure that anyone trying to receive a shipment of imported goods has to pay him a little extra.

Now, the people doing the paying are not exactly the same people who pay his salary—presumably, his country's tax base is a bit broader than that—but they're likely to be middle-class at least. And some of the burden may actually fall outside the country, if foreign exporters have to lower their prices. For instance, a merchant importing fancy jams and jellies at $500 a crate might import fewer if he had to pay a $50 bribe on top of each shipment; to keep sales going, the jam and jelly maker might lower the price to $475 a crate, thus absorbing half the burden of the bribe. So, viewed through the most rose-colored glasses, paying the customs officer's salary using bribes could be a way of fighting inequality while extracting aid from abroad—fantastic!

There is a cost, however. Facing the necessity of paying bribes, fewer people might go into the importing business. As a result, the customs officer's compatriots wouldn't have the same selection of goods to buy. And that's just one side of the story. Overseas companies, in addition to sharing the burden of the bribes, won't be able to do as much business if they can't find enough importers.

There is statistical evidence to support the idea that corruption is linked to worse economic outcomes, even if the causality isn't completely clear. Some of the most definitive results come from a paper published by Paolo Mauro, a researcher at the International Monetary Fund, in 1995. In rough terms, he showed that if Argentina had a level of corruption as low as Chile's, the yearly growth rate of its average income—a simple measure of living standards—might be more than a percentage point higher. Argentina's per capita income rose by about 7 percent in 2005, which was already a world-beating rate. But 8 percent would have been that much better.

Not surprisingly, corruption is also linked to black markets— the "informal economy" of transactions hidden from the eyes of tax collectors, whether for labor, financing, or goods. Of course, black markets exist even in the wealthiest countries. A bartender in New York may ask you to pay more for a drink if you use your credit card, since the sale will be recorded electronically; it's easier to avoid paying tax on transactions made with cash. Similarly, a home owner in London may hire a housekeeper recently arrived from eastern Europe without reporting the work, or making pension contributions, to the government. Both are black market deals. And corruption can create completely new black markets directly, through illicit deals made by officials, and indirectly, through officials' willingness to turn the other cheek given a sufficient bribe, or their reluctance to do a job for which they're underpaid.

Even before Argentina's financial crisis in late 2001 and 2002, black markets made up about 27 percent of the economy. Over in Chile, the rate was 20 percent. With a bigger black market, the government collects less tax revenue. That's part of the reason why, even during a period of strong economic growth, Argentina almost never ran a budget surplus.

To make matters worse, corruption-driven markets like the one for the customs officer's labor don't usually work as well as regular markets. As some economists have pointed out, the necessity of keeping payoffs secret can cause more distortions; corrupt governments may not just extract bribes but may also change what they buy in order to hide their actions. Because of the climate of secrecy, and the lack of any formal contracts, corrupt transactions also add uncertainty that is not present in regular markets.

That uncertainty, as well as the burden of the bribes them-selves, can sometimes discourage foreign companies and in-dividuals from investing in countries. Shang-Jin Wei, another economist at the IMF, has used data on foreign investment to show that corruption can act very much like the taxes that it supposedly replaces. In 2000, he wrote: "An increase in the cor-ruption level from that of Singapore to that of Mexico would have the same negative effect on inward FDI [foreign direct in-vestment] as raising the tax rate by 18 to 50 percentage points." Wei's data were from the early 1990s. In the first of Transpar-ency International's corruption indexes, which drew on surveys from roughly the same period, Singapore ranked third out of forty-one countries, while Mexico was thirty-second.

Corruption has human costs, too. More often than not, despots solidify their positions through corruption, and use cor-ruption to exploit their positions as well. They use patronage to maintain their political power base, and they use their unrivaled power to embezzle. When threats to their supremacy finally arrive, they cling not just to the power to determine their countries' political destinies but also to the luxuries of their corruption-fueled lifestyles. In other words, the fruits of corrup-tion provide another motivation for repression and resistance to change.

They can also stand in the way of important services. It stands to reason that tax revenue or international aid diverted to Swiss bank accounts can't reach the people on whom it was sup-posed to be spent. But even when a central government decides to spend money on, for example, public health, localized corrup-tion can get in the way. That was the case in the Philippines, where an investigation by the Philippine Center for Investigative

Journalism found rampant kickbacks, patronage, and waste in the delivery of drugs and patient care. Drug prices were marked up by as much as 100 percent in some areas, with the extra cash going to local officials.

Even when they have the inclination, central governments can have a hard time trying to control local corruption, especially in big countries. Olusegun Obasanjo, Nigeria's president, has been a vocal campaigner against corruption since the dictatorial days of his predecessor, Sani Abacha. Yet even after six years of Obasanjo's administration, the passing of anticorruption laws, and the firing of openly corrupt ministers, Nigeria is still rated as a snake pit—tied for 152nd place on the Transparency International list. Making matters worse, the president himself has come under attack for corruption; in August 2002, in what was likely a political gambit, members of his own party led Nigeria's lower house of parliament in calling for his resignation.

Clearly, corruption is a tough nut for any country to crack. Yet foreign companies and even well-meaning foreign governments often make the fight against corruption still more difficult.

Businesses from wealthy countries are often asked to pay bribes when they try to sell products or open up branches abroad; by paying them, they are supporting corrupt systems. In 2002, Transparency International ranked twenty-one nations with big investments abroad by their companies' willingness to pay bribes in fifteen developing countries. (The ranking was based on a survey of "business experts" in those fifteen countries.) No nation's companies were viewed as completely unwilling to bribe, though Australia came closest. Despite a decade of legislation attempting to stop American companies from participating in foreign corruption, the United States tied for thir-teenth. China and Russia brought up the rear, but none of the twenty-one investing countries scored as poorly, on average, as the developing countries' own businesses.

Since most poor countries are home to high levels of corruption, foreign aid—whether from wealthier nations, international agencies, or private groups—always runs the risk of ending up in the wrong hands. The donors and lenders, especially the World Bank and the IMF, have tried to add some accountability through their own monitoring. But even if aid money is perfectly monitored, it can still spur corruption.

It's an argument often made by Sir Edward Clay, the U.K.'s former high commissioner (the equivalent of an ambassador) in Kenya. An outspoken critic of the Kenyan government, Clay pointed out that while aid money may be keenly watched by outsiders, tax revenue isn't. If a government receives more aid money, it may duly use the extra cash to benefit the public, but that doesn't mean it's doing anything new. The same goods and services may have been paid for with tax revenue in the past. Now, however, that tax revenue is free to be siphoned off into wasteful projects, perks, or Swiss bank accounts. Even if the out-side donors require that their money be used for new programs, older ones may simply be cut . . . with the leftover funds diverted for personal enrichment.

John Githongo, who resigned as Kenya's anticorruption czar and fled to the U.K. early in 2005 after he allegedly received personal threats from senior politicians, recalled that government money regularly flowed to nonexistent companies in exchange for goods or services that never arrived. In February 2006, he told the British Broadcasting Corporation that when he revealed a portion of his findings to the government in Nairobi, some of the money actually started coming back. But he kept investigating.

"If somebody's willing to pay back $12 million, in all likelihood it's because they're involved in other transactions of a similar and larger scale that they would not like attention to be focused on," Githongo said. "And so they pay back, so that this attention goes away. I really do not appreciate the argument that if someone steals your television and then brings it back, then a theft has not taken place. They have simply returned the evidence of a theft."

Sometimes, however, aid money is simply being thrown at a problem that a poor country can't solve. Rothschild says he's seen it happen in South Africa. Sometimes there's no one around who can do the jobs that are being created by investors, or who can follow through on the programs favored by donors. So, Rothschild asks, when funds appear to be wasted, is it wanton misappropriation or just a case of insufficient skills? "It's a very difficult line to draw," he says.

It isn't only in Africa where that line is sometimes blurry. On June 15, Willem Buiter, then the chief economist of the European Bank for Reconstruction and Development, was running into the same issues. The bank was set up in 1991, after the Iron Curtain fell, by the governments of wealthy countries in Europe and abroad; the largest shareholder is, narrowly, the United States. The bank's job was and is to encourage economic growth in the democratizing countries of the former Soviet Union and the Warsaw Pact. With the backing of its shareholding governments, it borrows money on world markets in order to finance its loans to governments and businesses in the region. Buiter had some doubts about where that money was going.

1:00 P.M. LONDON (8:00 A.M. NEW YORK)

Lunch with the bank's business group director for infrastructure. Discussed the kerfuffle last week in the Opscom (Operations Committee) meeting when I objected to a change proposed by the bankers in the permitted use of European Union–financed subsidies in loans to municipalities. I told him that while we cannot stop the EU wasting its money if it wishes to do so, we can and have a duty to stop it wasting its money in ways that harm the transition process in our countries of operation. They may wait till I leave the bank at the end of the summer before presenting this again, in the hope that my successor will be a softer touch.

The bank, which held about 10 billion euros' worth of stocks and loans in late 2005, has instituted several measures to reduce corruption in its own dealings: a hotline for reporting corruption or fraud, protection for whistle-blowers inside the organization, and a sort of ombudsman's office for complaints by people affected by the bank's operations. Yet the bank, despite the size of its portfolio, hasn't always stuck to its mission. Buiter's observation was that the bank wasn't correcting distortions in the market or greatly helping the transition to democracy through its actions. Rather, its subsidies were simply making loans by other institutions cheaper—reducing, if anything, the incentives for good behavior.

Despite fifteen years of changes in the former Communist bloc, corruption is still rife—especially in Russia. Over a dozen countries in central and eastern Europe have been trying to stamp out corruption as part of their efforts to join the European Union. But Russia has had no such carrot, and very few countries are big or bold enough to try using the stick. Buiter's day continued:

2:00 P.M. LONDON (9:00 A.M. NEW YORK)

Met with an Indian friend and former student, now working for Standard Chartered Bank, who is in town to collect some prize for the best investment project since the pyramids. The project involved prefinancing of exports by an Indian steel producer. He is now looking into the possibility of doing similar projects in Russia. I told him that he should investigate whether the EBRD can be a partner in his proposed Russian ventures, but that in any case he should talk to our Russia experts and to some bankers in the Moscow office. Our senior Russian economist, Ivan Szegvari, joined the conversation. I suspect that even to someone familiar with the economic shenanigans of India, the rough-and-tumble of Russian project finance may come as a bit of a shock.

If things in Russia are bad, then they are worse in central Asia, where the bank also invests. Georgia, Kyrgyzstan, Uzbekistan, Tajikistan, and Turkmenistan ranked among the thirty most corrupt countries in the world in Transparency International's index. On the bank's Web site, you can read that "the mandate of the EBRD stipulates that it must only work in countries that are committed to democratic principles." Those principles presumably don't include organized corruption of the sort that exists, for example, in Turkmenistan—a state that is apparently run for the personal edification of its autocratic leader, Saparmurat Niyazov, who calls himself the "Leader of All Turkmen."

Still, if the bank manages to set an example with its clean way of doing business, it may do some good. And even in a corrupt climate, its investments could encourage economic growth and help to bring about a cleaner state of affairs. There's a similar argument about foreign aid: send the money anyway—even if much is stolen or wasted, the rest will do some good. For example, in June 2005, Bob Geldof, the Irish rocker and antipoverty campaigner, castigated rich countries for holding back promised aid to Africa because of worries about corruption. "There are, of course, extremely corrupt governments in Africa, but there are very corrupt people in our part of the world—the difference is that we are rich," he was quoted as saying. "Get off the corruption thing and force our governments to get there."

If governments are supposed to put up with corruption, the question then becomes, how much wasting of aid money is acceptable? Fifty cents of every dollar? Seventy-five? If the figure were that high among investors as well as donors, there'd be little reason for countries like South Africa to try to quell corruption, no matter what people like Rothschild said—except that doing so could provide a handy excuse for getting rid of political rivals.

That charge did surface against Mbeki immediately after Zuma, a potential challenger for the presidency, got the boot. (It gained some force among Zuma's backers when a rape charge, of which he was later acquitted, was added to the accusations against him.) The stock market still rose, though, sending the signal that investors would be happy to see more of the same. They, at least, wouldn't want to kiss fifty cents of every dollar goodbye.

And that's the important part. Private investors simply have to be more discriminating than donors when it comes to sending money to corrupt countries; they can't afford to do otherwise. So what will happen over time? Countries that fight corruption will receive more investment, while those that don't will become dependent on foreign aid and all the strings that can come with it: political alliances with wealthy countries that the domestic population dislikes, carpetbagging experts receiving salaries that are outrageously high by local standards, and economic policies imposed from abroad.

CHAPTER 7

NEW YORK   **DAMASCUS**
11:44 A.M.   **6:44 P.M.**
JUNE 15   **JUNE 15**

"SYRIA AIMS TO HAVE A STOCK MARKET BY YEAR-END" HOW IMPORTANT ARE FINANCIAL MARKETS TO ECONOMIC GROWTH?

You don't have to walk along the cobblestoned alleys of old Damascus to sense the rich, pungent scent that practically suffocates the energy and ambition of all who inhale it. It's everywhere in the city, engraved deep into the brows of the men and women bustling through the dusty streets. It is nostalgia.

Nostalgia for the city's days of glory, as capital of the mighty Umayyad Empire that stretched across the Islamic world in the religion's early years. Nostalgia for its military power, as the headquarters of Saladin, scourge of the Crusaders and victor of Jerusalem. And nostalgia for its commercial importance, as the intersection of two main routes along the old Silk Road: one east to west, from the Mediterranean ports of what is now Lebanon all the way to China; the other north to south, from deep in the Ukraine down to Mecca.

Lately all that nostalgia has been mixed with another intoxicant, the underdog mentality. Trampled by an Allied invasion in 1941, finally set free by the French in 1946, trounced by Israel in 1967, and now harried by the United States and the French again with accusations of lax patrolling along the border with Iraq and complicity in the assassination of Rafik Hariri, Lebanon's former prime minister, Syria has been reminded of its fall from grace with aggravating regularity.

Damascus is also filled with reminders of where Syria's plans for a socialist, egalitarian economy went awry. On the slopes of Mount Kassioun, a litter-strewn maze of countless ramshackle homes overlooks the city center, with its scattered green patches. Down below, the wealthy elites, redolent of musky perfume and hair gel, cruise around in their sleek luxury cars.

When Bashar al-Assad succeeded his father as president in 2000, some Syrians took hope that in one area at least, things would improve. Economic growth had been slipping steadily, from 5.2 percent in 1996 to 4.6 percent in 1997, 2.0 percent in 1998, and zero in 1999. Assad promised a program of economic reforms to turn things around.

Syria's economy did start to expand, but the pace of reform was slow. Growth stalled again as dark clouds formed along its borders—the Israeli-Palestinian conflict, the invasion of Iraq, the expulsion of its military from Lebanon. Less than two months after this last indignity, however, Assad's government made its boldest economic pronouncement yet: Syria would soon have its own stock market.

It wasn't the first time Syrians had heard this kind of talk. A modern exchange was supposed to open in Damascus in the mid-1990s, but Bashar's father, Hafez, never got around to it. Bashar doesn't have as tight a hold on power as his father did, though, so he probably needs to worry a bit more about the happiness of the general population. As every politician knows, jobs and economic growth are crucial to that happiness. Yet when Syria's parliament approved the law intended to lead to a stock exchange, Syrians had mixed feelings.

For Nawar Awad, special adviser to the deputy prime minister for economic affairs, it was a long-awaited moment. "It was a joy, because we had been discussing this for two or three years," he says. "On a larger level, in Syria, between the potential investors and the potential clients of this service, I wouldn't talk about joy. I would say there was a positive reception of this announcement."

That reception was enhanced by patriotism, he adds, among Syrian investors who had to bring their business to nearby exchanges, like those in Jordan and Saudi Arabia. But Awad also notes that some people didn't take the announcement as a sure sign of good things to come: "We are in a period of change, and it's not very clear what we're doing and why we are doing it."

The government made no buts about its intentions, though. "The main objective of Syria now is to achieve a framework that guarantees us economic growth," Awad says. "For this purpose we are trying to develop our infrastructure financially." The hope, he continues, is that a stock market will bring benefits both domestically and from abroad. "We are hoping for foreign investment," Awad says. "This is one of the reasons why we are doing these reforms. But the main reason is to improve our performance, which has not been very distinguished in the last years."

Awad acknowledges the challenges his country's government

faces. American investment stopped, and other foreign investment dropped off, as a result of Syria's political situation. Furthermore, Syria's big companies aren't run in the most transparent fashion. "The rules governing the Syrian market are really complex and sometimes contradictory," Awad says, adding that businesses are a long way from complying with internationally accepted norms and regulations for public companies. "We said within one year we need to have a market operation," he recalls. "But this means nothing if we don't have tradable companies, or we were not capable of developing the necessary legal framework."

As a first step, a commission made up of the deputy prime minister, the deputy minister for the economy, the governor of the central bank, and four private individuals will draw up the legal charter for the exchange—a process intended to take a mere six months, with cooperation from foreign experts and Syrian capitalists. The government left them the task of choosing a model for the Syrian exchange. "Do we want to follow the Istanbul model, which is liberal in a way, or the Amman model?" Awad asks. "And the London stock exchange is completely different. This is how we ask ourselves this question." Then, within another six months, the exchange will launch. At least that's the plan.

Even if everything goes off without a hitch, could the stock market really prove to be the answer to Syrians' prayers? At the least, it would satisfy the requirements of some international agreements. If Syria wanted to engage further with the European Union, or to have any hope of joining the World Trade Organization, the reopening of the stock market had the potential to send a significant signal: Syria was serious about creating a healthy financial system. Yet simply having a stock market would not accomplish that goal all by itself.

Stock markets serve more than one function. First, they accomplish the obvious task of putting companies and investors together in an environment driven by supply and demand; the ability to sell shares can be vital to a company looking to finance its own growth. But the markets can also make companies accountable—which tends to help with the first function.

Not just any business can sell shares on most of the world's successful exchanges. If that were the case, there'd probably be more than a few scammers trying to hawk shares in useless or nonexistent enterprises. At first glance, that might not be so bad; investors could simply demand some verifiable proof that a business was real and profitable. If a business couldn't provide the proof, no one would want its shares. There are a few problems with this free-for-all strategy, though.

First, not all investors are savvy enough to avoid the traps set by even more savvy con artists. Second, if investors could never be sure that their money was going into a bona fide concern, they would probably hold back a bit—a move that would hamper fund-raising by legitimate companies, who could never completely escape the cloud of suspicion, as well as the shams. And finally, all those phony companies would take up the exchange's resources, not to mention the valuable time of investors trying to scrutinize their options.

To avoid these problems—or at least to try—stock markets and governments usually impose rules and obligations on companies that wish to sell shares to the general public. The companies often have to make their boards of directors accountable to the shareholders through voting, the companies have to publish their accounts, the accounts must be audited by outside firms, and more. The rules aren't 100 percent effective, of course—just witness the rash of corporate scandals that swept through the United States and Europe from 2001 through 2005, helping terrorism and impending war to push the markets to the floor, and then holding them there for a couple of years. But the rules do provide a hurdle high enough to deter basic forms of deception.

Equally important, they help to reduce the deficit of information between investors and the managers of the businesses. Not that they eliminate it entirely; if they did, thousands of corporate analysts at the big banks and at independent research firms would have to find new jobs. Still, by evening out the asymmetry a bit, the rules pave the way for more useful matches between companies and investors. Not surprisingly, the more rules exist to protect investors, the more financial markets appear to grow.

So what was the scale of Syria's ambition? It would have to go a very long way in a very short time even to come close to Western standards of corporate disclosure and discipline. But the basic idea was for the stock market to fulfill the first function: to match investors with profitable businesses looking for money. Would just having the market do the trick?

As of June 15, Syria's corporate sector was structured like an occupied seesaw: scads of tiny shops and service businesses on one end, a few huge business empires on the other, and almost nothing in between. There were a few companies with privately traded shares; some enterprising types had even set up brokerage houses to trade those shares in the 1990s. If those big businesses floated on the stock exchange, though, it wouldn't necessarily mean that millions of middle-class Syrians would be lining up to buy stock. "Middle-class" in Syria often means several generations living in an old family house, with the men—even civil servants, of which there are many—working two or three jobs to make ends meet. Then there's that pesky socialist ideology, still hanging around in the rhetoric and regulations of Syria's ruling Baath Party—not exactly the basis for a new generation of capitalists.

A substantial chunk of any new investment would likely have to come from abroad. Of course, foreigners could already invest in Syrian companies directly, if they had friends in the right places. But as Syria girded for the preparation of its securities laws, one group of foreigners who were particularly close to the process were the Turks. As ties between the two nations intensified—including a visit to Damascus by Recep Tayyip Erdoğan, the Turkish prime minister, in late 2004—Syria sought out the expertise of its financially intrepid northern neighbor.

To be sure, Turkey was not an ideal role model. It had suffered from the dual problems of inflation and unsustainable debts for more than a decade. In the meantime, however, its financial sector had blossomed. Its banks expanded into Russia and eastern Europe, where local competitors sometimes lacked sophistication in offering consumer and business credit—both are important, since one helps companies to grow and the other helps people to buy their products. And Turkey's stock market had been around since 1986, though its historical antecedents dated back to 1866.

The maturity of Turkey's financial infrastructure hadn't always allowed the country to avoid crises, but it did have one advantage: once the crises were over, the markets set the stage for the quickest possible recovery. One of the beneficiaries of Turkey's advances is Elif Bilgi, who heads EFG Istanbul Securities, a boutique investment bank based in the city of the same name.

After studies at Brown, Harvard, and the London School of Economics, and stints at Morgan Stanley and Goldman Sachs—two of New York's biggest financial firms—she returned to Turkey as a managing director in one of its leading investment banks, Iktisat Yatirim. Then she left to start her own. Her experiences on June 15, which began with an 8:00 a.m. flight from Istanbul to Milan, could offer Syria a few useful lessons.

11:00 A.M. MILAN (5:00 A.M. NEW YORK)

I arrive safely, although with an hour-and-a-half delay. I take a taxi to my hotel; turn on my phone to find many messages. I have some time before my first meeting, so I walk around the streets of this very fashionable city. I enter a shop but get called to participate on a conference call regarding the initial public offering (IPO) of a large Turkish bank.

I got connected from my mobile phone from the street. We are in a consortium with another London-based bank to win the lead manager and global coordinator role for the IPO. The issues were mostly regarding pricing of the mandate: the right price to motivate the sales team and attract a high-quality syndicate, and the correct incentive structure, positioning, etc. were discussed. I spend the next several hours on the phone talking to my clients and colleagues to secure the IPO mandate.

3:00 p.m. I visit one of the original investors in my company. This person is a famous Italian consultant and private investor whom my husband and I know from our business school days. (My husband was my classmate.) His specialty is to invest in people that he regards as business leaders. During the setup of our company, EFG Istanbul (formerly HC Istanbul), I raised funds from him and some Italian banks he has introduced me to. He is a very strong leader himself, so talking to him, especially in person, is very inspiring.

He is raising other funds in Italy and asks me if I need financing. We discuss various opportunities and I leave his office very positive and full of ideas. He is a great motivator for many entrepreneurs.

8:00 p.m.: I am back in my hotel. I call my four-year-old son to say hello, and he says, "Mommy, come," as he always does on the phone, which is still difficult to hear. I have bought delicious food from one of the delis and sit down to eat it while reading a magazine. It looks like we will be winning the bank IPO mandate, so I feel very excited and ready for tomorrow. I will also be back with my husband and son, so I feel good.

Bilgi did five things that a Syrian investor would have had a harder time doing. First, she left her native country. In Syria, that requires an exit visa, which in turn requires clearances from two intelligence agencies and the political security force. Second, she spoke on her mobile phone from Italy. Many Syrian mobile phones don't work outside Syria, and it would be a rare one indeed that worked in Italy. Third, she entertained the idea of foreign investment without thinking about the government's involvement. The Syrian government exerts tight control over foreign ownership of businesses. Fourth, she participated in open negotiations for an IPO. In Syria, large transactions rarely occur without some sort of machinations in the background, often involving the government. In a survey from 2003, almost 60 percent of companies in Syria called corruption a "very severe" or "major" obstacle to doing business. And in any case, or perhaps as a result, less than 20 percent of the surveyed companies' financing came from outside investors. Fifth, Bilgi called her son back home. Calling Syria, as anyone who's done business there can tell you, is not always a sure thing. Depending on the telephone network you use, it can take a dozen tries to get through, if you get through at all.

Clearly, a stock exchange wouldn't solve all of Syria's business-related problems overnight. But if Syria worked on those other fundamental factors as well—ease of movement, ease of communication, freedom to choose financing, freedom of foreign investment—then the stock exchange would probably multiply the benefits.

Of course, with progress comes complexity. American financial markets may be among the best developed in the world, but they are also filled with dark corners and arcane practices that are open to abuse. Monitoring them and punishing misbehavior is a full-time job for the Securities and Exchange Commission's roughly thirty-eight hundred employees—not to mention countless lawyers, analysts, and accountants in other branches of government and in the private sector—and almost every chair of the commission says that doing a thorough job would take many thousands more.

The United States broke new ground in this area when Congress passed the Sarbanes-Oxley Act of 2002. The law, named for its cosponsors in the Senate and the House, respectively, introduced a bevy of new requirements for companies' financial reporting, record keeping, and interactions with auditors. It also made executives more directly liable for any wrongdoing, to the point that the chief executive and chief financial officer of a company would have to take personal responsibility for the accuracy of its public accounting statements. Analysts and auditors were targeted as well, to prevent conflicts of interest arising from their ties to the companies they covered.

Some critics griped that the new requirements were too burdensome, and that they might keep good businesses from selling shares. But as far as investor protection went, this was the state of the art. Would it help the American economy to grow?

It's difficult to sort out the effect of one law from all the other things that affect the size of the economy. A few things did become clear, though. At first, the law caused big companies to spend a lot of cash on upgrading their internal accounting and, in some cases, their auditing services—not surprising, given that the CEOs' and CFOs' necks were on the line. The law also seemed to steady the waters for American investors, after the storms of distrust whipped up by Enron, WorldCom, Adelphia, and others. It took almost a year more for the stock markets, weighed down by the uncertainty of the impending war in Iraq and worries about the government's budget deficits, to begin their recovery. Yet in the long term, the restoration of confidence, and perhaps its enhancement beyond the pre-scandal levels, looked like it might help the economy to stay healthy and grow.

Syria could take some lessons from the American example, too. First, even if developing financial markets can help an economy to get off the ground, the job of maintaining them never stops. Second, look at the United States: it still suffers recessions, often for reasons that have nothing to do with financial markets. There's no guarantee of economic growth, even in the world's most productive economy. And not in Syria, either—even after the announcement of the stock market, local and international forecasters were predicting lower, not higher, growth for Syria in 2006 and 2007.

It's also useful to remember that healthy financial markets aren't necessarily a prerequisite for economic growth. China's economy has exploded despite the immaturity of its stock exchange. Indeed, the government is still encouraging many companies to list their shares elsewhere. But a working stock exchange also offers one more intangible benefit: it's a positive symbol of a country's place in the world—something Syria could really use.

CHAPTER 8

NEW YORK
11:47 A.M.
JUNE 15

ZURICH
5:47 P.M.
JUNE 15

"JULIUS BÄR CONFIRMS PRIVATE CLIENT DATA STOLEN" IS THE FINANCIAL SYSTEM BECOMING MORE VULNERABLE TO THE ACTIONS OF THE FEW?

It's a sunny afternoon on Zurich's Bahnhof Street, and blue-and-white trams trundle by as crowds of laid-back locals eat, drink, and shop along the tree-lined sidewalks. A flautist plays Bach's Air on the G String with a keyboard accompaniment. Other musicians, cases in hand, hustle by on their way to the city's renowned conservatory. Mixed in between the boutiques and cafés, the glass doors of modest stone mansions slide open and shut without a sound.

Without the small signs outside, you'd never guess that these buildings were the headquarters of some of the world's most exclusive private banks. Their unimposing architecture belies the hundreds of billions of dollars that lie within—stored mostly in computers these days, rather than in gold or paper. But the gray facades reflect how the banks have served their generations of wealthy clients: with discretion, not ostentation.

A ripple disturbed the calm in the spring of 2005. An envelope, postmarked from Germany, arrived at the offices of *Cash*, a finance magazine with offices just a short walk from Bahnhof Street. It quickly made its way onto the desk of Leo Müller, a reporter specializing in financial crime.

"Inside we found a CD-ROM with these 169 megabytes or so, and an anonymous letter," Müller says. "That's it." The files, however, were a treasure trove of information about the affairs of Julius Bär, one of Zurich's leading private banks: data on clients, documents, cover sheets for faxes, spreadsheets, back-office records—in short, as Müller says, "everything."

"They were some very famous institutional clients, North America–based institutional clients or offshore clients of these institutions," he adds. "Secondly, you could find from all around the world so-called ultra-high-net-worth individuals, which means that these are people with $20 million, or $160 million, or $200 million, or more than that."

Müller's interest didn't stop there, though. "Normally I'm responsible for stories about financial crime or business crime, and the first thing I was checking was if there were some clients with a problem in the background or which had a criminal background, or were politically exposed persons," he says. "At the end of the '90s, I had a CD-ROM from a very important trust company in Liechtenstein, and in this case it was a little bit of another situation—you had very shaky clients, clients from Colombia and so on." This time was different, though. "What I found in this case was that the bank was operating in a very professional way. I found some relatives, for example, of politically exposed persons who were checked very clearly and very carefully."

Müller went to Julius Bär with the CD. At first, he recalls, it took a while for the bank to understand exactly what had happened. "They gave me a wonderful presentation on what they are doing for IT security," he says, "and told me all the things they are doing in IT security, for the employees, and that the employees have to know about passwords and correct usage of passwords and all these things. This presentation was taking half an hour or so, and then I said, okay, let's talk about reality, and showed them some printouts of the CD-ROM. At first they were a little bit shocked, thinking that someone was delivering some single papers to me or to the editorial staff. Then I said, no, we have 169 megabytes of this. They were totally shocked at the situation. It even took days for the people in the bank to understand what was going on. They didn't realize immediately what was the problem."

On June 15, Julius Bär confirmed in the press that a former employee had stolen computer files relating to some wealthy clients from its branch in the Cayman Islands. The next day Müller's article supplied all the disconcerting details.

Julius Bär was hardly alone. In the previous six months, several of the world's biggest financial institutions had lost files containing personal, private data on their clients: Bank of America, up to 1.2 million government purchasing card accounts in the United States; HSBC, 180,000 credit cards in the United States; UBS, 15,500 clients in Tokyo; CitiFinancial of Citigroup, 3.9 million accounts in the United States.

Julius Bär described its incident as minor, and its stock price didn't seem to react. Indeed, at the time, individual malfeasance was just about the only way that the bank's information security could be breached. Even the bank's clients could only read about their accounts online; there was no way to dial into the computer system to trade stocks or transfer money. "Most leading banks are operating in this sort of transaction system," Müller says. "You do not dial into accounts with $20 million inside."

It may indeed have been a minor incident, but it showed once again how one person could shake up an enormous company through willful misconduct. In 1995, Nicholas Leeson destroyed a 233-year-old investment bank, Barings, by hiding over a billion dollars in losses from his derivatives trades; with every attempt to recoup his shortfall, he dug himself into a deeper hole. A similar fiasco surfaced in 2002, when Allied Irish Bank discovered the secret losses of one of its currency traders, John Rusnak. His activities may have cost the bank nearly $700 million.

But one person's destructive behavior doesn't have to be intentional, and it doesn't have to take place over years, either—or days, or hours, or even minutes. In a few seconds on the morning of December 8, 2005, a broker at Mizuho Securities in Tokyo wiped out $224 million in potential profits. The cause? A typo. He meant to sell one share of a new stock for 610,000 yen, or about $5,000. Instead, he told the firm's computer to sell 610,000 shares—more than were actually available—for one yen each. Under the stock exchange's rules, the trade could not be reversed.

In some cases, the person at fault is not a trader but a computer programmer. In early May 2006, a bug in Citibank's electronic banking system in Japan mishandled more than a quarter-million transactions. Some transactions were executed twice, while others didn't go through at all. The problem lasted for an entire week.

These incidents demonstrated the lack of effective safeguards within some enormous financial institutions and, in the last case, within a seemingly mature stock market. Like many businesses, they probably planned much more thoroughly for when things went right than for when things went wrong. The resulting tremors, though they may have convinced some banks to be more watchful, did not shake the financial system as a whole. Yet doing that is surprisingly easy, too.

It doesn't even require any errors or deliberate misdeeds—just a bit more capital. In 1998, Long-Term Capital Management, a hedge fund whose masterminds included a pair of Nobel laureates in economics, had to be rescued by the Federal Reserve and a group of Wall Street giants after its big bets on interest rates turned sour. The fund's returns had been dropping, and its traders compensated by taking on bigger and bigger risks; doing so was the only way to try to win back their losses quickly, before cash flow became a problem.

But these traders were no rogues or dabblers. Their earlier profits had attracted so many billions to the fund that its portfolio covered 5 percent of the global market in which companies traded risks among one another. And that, in the end, was part of the problem. As far as the Fed was concerned, letting LTCM go under was not an option. If it did, big banks all over the world would be affected. In many cases, LTCM had offered to pay these banks over time in exchange for risky assets that the banks were holding. (This kind of transaction, where one type of investment or loan is traded for another, is called a swap.) A collapse of LTCM would leave the banks with much more risk, and less cash, than they had expected.

Moreover, investors would likely react to news of such a large collapse by pulling their money out of similar hedge funds, leading to a contraction of the market and less liquidity in the financial system. To head off this hysteria—the equivalent of a run on banks, but in hedge funds—the Fed's officials stepped in to help LTCM sort out its obligations to its creditors, to the extent possible, in an organized fashion.

This kind of vulnerability is often called systemic risk, or risk to the entire financial system. It's the most dangerous type for the global economy, and it is by no means a new occurrence. In the early eighteenth century, the British stock market was wrecked by speculation in the South Sea Company, a firm that had shouldered the empire's war debts in exchange for trading rights in the colonies. Here the blame lay with frenzied investors and unscrupulous executives. The latter sold out before the former could learn the true value of their inflated shares, though it's not as if they were paying much attention anyway.

As markets become more complicated, however, systemic risk can increase dramatically. Even if earlier problems are ironed out, new problems spring up by the dozen. Enron's demise in 2001 showed that a runaway stock can still beguile investors, though it can no longer bring the entire market to its knees. But LTCM was a different animal altogether, using frequently complex financial contracts called derivatives, whose values change depending on all sorts of events in the market and the world at large, to make its money.

The trade in derivatives is fast-growing and barely regulated in the global economy, where it is a relatively new feature, so there are likely to be many more exotic species traipsing through the markets without catching the eye of the park rangers. The trade is not very transparent, either, since derivatives allow investors to create a tangle of connections involving just about anything that can change over time: share values, interest rates, credit ratings, crop yields, oil prices, and even the weather. In the midst of the tangle, it's often difficult to figure out who owns what, and who owes what.

Each fund makes its money by adopting a unique investment strategy—the secret formula that turns base metals into gold, through a series of predictions and occasionally intricate trades. Some funds do it by researching companies and borrowing shares of the less promising ones, which they then sell, hoping to buy back and return the borrowed shares after the price drops. Others look for tiny discrepancies in the values of currencies and securities. For example, it might be true, for just a couple of seconds, that using euros to buy South Korean won, and then won to buy dollars, would give you more dollars than simply using the euros to buy dollars directly. In that couple of seconds, a trader might borrow hundreds of millions of euros, execute the trades, and then turn the dollars back into euros in order to pay off the debt. The result, in theory, would be a small profit.

In both cases, the overall idea is to hit upon a profitable strategy and then execute it as many times as possible with as much money as possible. If investors could look at a fund's books, they'd probably be able to figure out the basics of the strategy. So hedge funds report very little information about their trading until well after the fact, and so far they've also been able to keep regulators from poking around much.

When the stock markets aren't making much headway, hedge funds become particularly tempting to investors. The funds can turn a profit even when the market is moving in a narrow range. They predict or identify small discrepancies in prices, and then funnel in huge amounts of cash—much of it often borrowed—to take advantage; a correct bet against a stock might earn only ten cents per share, but that's nothing to sneeze at if you buy half a million shares.

Between 1999 and 2005, the amount of money managed by hedge funds grew from less than $200 billion to roughly $1.2 trillion. Many used simple strategies based on research about stocks and bonds, but many others used derivatives to balance vast amounts of risk, the way LTCM did. Investments in "funds of funds," which package different strategies together, added about half that amount again.

The question is, where in this money jungle are the other beasts like LTCM, teetering on the verge of an extinction that could cause more than a ripple in the financial system? It's hard to tell without knowing how their balance sheets look. For example, say one hedge fund has predicted that long-term interest rates will rise, so it begins eagerly trading derivatives with big banks who think that rates will fall. Pretty soon, each bank stands to gain hundreds of millions of dollars if the hedge fund is wrong. And then rates do fall . . . but the hedge fund is overexposed, and it can't pay everyone at once. It implodes, and all the banks take a huge loss. The banks' investors desert them in droves, scrambling to find safer assets. The banks' own share prices take a dive, no one wants to lend them money, and suddenly they can't cover their own liabilities. Then things really start to get ugly.

If a crisis like this were to occur, the Federal Reserve and the world's other central banks might be able to rescue the financial system by lending to the hamstrung banks at low rates. But what if more than one crisis occurred in the same week? Would even the central banks' ability to add liquidity to the financial system, by flooding it with money, be stretched? It hasn't happened yet, but the recent proliferation of hedge funds makes this kind of catastrophic coincidence more likely by the day. Without regulation, or even monitoring, there may be little warning if one eventually does occur.

Hedge funds aren't the only source of systemic risk, though. Another is the machinery of the market—all those computer systems, executing millions of trades daily, linked around the world and virtually impossible to monitor in a comprehensive way.

After global stock exchanges lost about a quarter of their value on Black Monday in October 1987, several tried to limit the damage that computers could do on their own. The problem was that if computers were programmed to sell when share prices dropped, a general dip in the market could quickly snowball. To match the potential for runaway trading by these programs, the New York Stock Exchange instituted automatic circuit breakers that would halt the markets when share prices began to swing wildly.

Since then, the threats to computer systems in general have multiplied. It might be an exaggeration to say that one particularly lethal virus would be enough to cause chaos in the markets, since there are many other safeguards in place besides the circuit breakers. But a virus could paralyze the computer systems of the traders themselves, many of whom use off-the-shelf software in their offices just like people in any other business. And losing time really is equivalent to losing money—analysts regularly adjust quarterly results to account for differences in the number of trading days in the calendar, for example, during a leap year. Fortunately for the markets, the disgruntled employee who stole files from Julius Bär didn't exhibit the skills of an expert hacker.

One sign of an increase in systemic risk is an enhanced demand by investors for ultrasafe assets. Treasury bills and notes issued in Washington have traditionally occupied this role of honor, but even they could be threatened if a crisis struck the broader financial system; the United States has so much debt that it relies on its ability to issue new IOUs in order to pay off old ones. So where can investors go for a truly crisis-proof asset?

The ultimate answer, for many, is gold. It doesn't need repaying, it can't disappear from a computer's hard drive, and it's worth something all by itself—unlike a flimsy piece of paper that just promises its owner something else. And between the stock markets' peak in early 2000 and the end of 2005, the shiny yellow stuff almost doubled in value. The price for an ounce topped $500, territory unseen since the period from 1979 to 1982, when worries about conflicts involving the United States and the Soviet Union in the Middle East and central Asia roiled the markets.

Insofar as anyone—a hacker, a terrorist, a technician having a bad day—could make all the screens on Wall Street go blank, gold offers a certain peace of mind. Because of its scarcity, it can be the basis for an alternative monetary system in case the current, electronic one fails.

Yet it's unlikely that worries about a one-off catastrophe are solely responsible for driving up the value of gold and other precious metals in more recent times, since their prices changed little after 9/11 or the invasion of Afghanistan. What tends to get investors' attention most is not single events, like Al Qaeda's coordinated attack on the United States, but repeating patterns. If Al Qaeda were disrupting the financial system (and killing thousands) every six months, or even every year, investors might have second thoughts about putting their money on Wall Street—at least until the system found a way to protect itself. The same goes for billion-dollar frauds by rogue traders.

But there is a pattern in security breaches at financial institutions; to the extent one can judge from news reports, they're becoming bigger, and more frequent. Müller, who published a book on financial crime, is convinced that the system is much less safe than it used to be. "In the former system, or twenty years ago, the client relationship manager could use his papers and close them in his office or wherever, and you had only one paper and that was it," he says. Now many documents reside on central servers, and anyone with access to the server can make his or her own copy. Certain regulations, like those intended to stop money laundering, require the archiving of various types of documents. Moreover, Müller says, banks often use encrypted files for sensitive information. But it's not easy to check encrypted files for viruses, since they don't always follow commonly recognized formats. The information in a given file may be hard to decipher, but it may also be easier for a virus to worm its way into the system for other purposes. There's a trade-off, evidently, between hiding specific information and safeguarding the entire system.

Investors' concerns may be heightened by the speed with which the value of their paper-based holdings can change. Once again, the actions of just a few people could make a huge difference to the net worth of millions.

In one scenario, the few are the credit raters. The three major credit-rating agencies—Fitch Ratings, Moody's, and Standard & Poor's—all rate the bonds issued by governments around the world when they borrow money. To many investors, the assessments compiled by credit-rating agencies offer vital information about the prospects for runaway inflation and the chances of a financial crisis in the various countries. Many crises, after all, end with bondholders and other creditors receiving only a fraction of what they're owed.

Now, say one of these agencies decided that the U.S. government's budget deficits were starting to spiral out of control. Perhaps the economy had endured a series of recessions where, in each case, Congress had cut taxes to stimulate the economy without touching spending. Perhaps foreign investors were starting to prefer securities issued by other economies, like the European Union—because economic growth sped up there, or simply to diversify their portfolios. Perhaps the idea of safety wasn't enough to lure them into the Treasury bond market anymore . . . and so, the rating agency concluded, the safety had disappeared as well.

It's like a self-fulfilling prophecy; if people believe American government securities are safe, then they'll buy more, the United States will be able to roll over its debts, and the securities will indeed be safe. But if someone starts to doubt, then that chain of new loans paying off old loans could be broken. If the United States couldn't take out new loans, by selling new securities, then it wouldn't be able to pay its debts.

If that one agency, with a team of maybe a few dozen people, decided to lower its rating of U.S. government bonds by one notch, the repercussions in the financial world would be immense. It's likely that some money managers, bound by a duty to their clients, would have to sell off their Treasury bills and notes in order to maintain the quality of their portfolios. With more selling, the government's ability to borrow would erode further. For Washington, and the economy as a whole, it would be a nightmare—one that had been in the making for years, to be sure, but one that happened on a particular night because of the decision of a very small group of people.

At the moment, this scenario looks unlikely, though not solely because the American economy continues to grow at a strong rate. The thing is, when it comes to moves this important, the three big agencies are hardly trailblazers. For example, it wasn't until May 2005 that they started cutting their ratings of General Motors and Ford to "junk"—the level of risk considered inappropriate for investment by banks. By then, the writing had been on the wall for several months. For example, in January, a struggling GM had separated its mortgage-lending operation from the rest of its business in a public bid to protect the sub-sidiary's credit rating. The lending operation was profitable and needed a high rating so that investors would supply money for its mortgages. GM, noting the likelihood that its overall rating would decline, didn't want to saddle the operation with a low rating that didn't reflect its ability to repay loans.

But even if one of the smaller agencies that struggle to com-pete with the big three were to downgrade the U.S. government, the markets would start to ask questions. Investors have a bound-less willingness to believe that other people know more than they do. And when they seize on a bit of supposedly useful infor-mation, the speed with which they move the markets can be frightening.

A notorious example was George Soros's attack on the British pound in 1992. The speculator relentlessly sold the pound short, to the tune of billions—that is, he borrowed pounds in order to sell them for other currencies, assuming that he'd be able to re-pay the loans when pounds were cheaper. Investors took Soros's cue, figuring that he wouldn't bet so heavily against the pound without good reason. His actions became the trigger for a slide in value so big that the U.K. had to bow out of the mechanism that then controlled exchange rates between European currencies. On September 2 of that year, a pound bought exactly $2.00; by November 10, it was worth only $1.51. In retrospect, some experts have concluded that the pound was bound to fall, but that Soros managed to determine the timing, at a significant profit to himself. Indeed, it's estimated that he netted over $1 billion on the pound's plunge. If he made the maximum of about fifty cents on each pound he borrowed, he would have had to borrow 2 billion pounds. In all likelihood, he borrowed much more.

The currency crises that swept East Asia in the late 1990s (more on them in Chapter 14) happened even more quickly. The Thai baht fell from 23 to the dollar to 32 in just over a month in 1997. Indonesia's rupiah lost almost 40 percent of its value between November 24 and December 24 of that year—including, at one point, 14 percent literally overnight.

These things can happen not just because of the countries' fragility and investors' hysteria but also because money moves at the speed of electrons through the world's information networks. And after the experiences of the late 1990s, some people decided that it was time to slow down.

On September 1, 1998, the Malaysian government put in place a system of "capital controls" to stop money from entering or fleeing the country with such alacrity. To economists, it was a gamble: the controls could have the desired effect, by protecting Malaysia against the violence of more frenzies; or they could discourage investors from holding any money in Malaysia whatsoever—after all, why would you want to keep your money somewhere if you couldn't take it out quickly in a crisis, especially with the government apparently planning for exactly such an eventuality?

In the end, Malaysia's economy recovered without too many apparent side effects from the capital controls, and many of the controls were eventually relaxed. But talk had already begun of introducing a wider system of controls, to encompass the world's major financial markets. It just so happened that the Treasury secretary of the United States at the time was one Lawrence Summers, who, with his then-wife, Victoria, had been one of the most vocal advocates of such brakes in the late 1980s and early 1990s.

The Summerses' proposal was similar to the tax on foreign exchange trades suggested by James Tobin, a Nobel laureate, a decade earlier. Both ideas were supposed to slow large swings in the financial markets—and the resulting hysteria that could take hold among investors—by discouraging international transactions, if only a little bit. Both ideas also suffered from the same criticisms: (1) that the tax rates would have to be painfully high in order to achieve the desired effect, (2) that the scope of the tax bases would be unclear, since securities transactions can be cloaked in many guises, (3) that the taxes would create enormous black markets, and (4) that the taxes would not decrease, and might actually increase, volatility.

The talk of such a tax quieted down for several years, until, in January 2005, Jacques Chirac, the French president, proposed instituting one to pay for antipoverty programs around the world. Chirac had suggested some sort of global tax before, but this time he made a concrete proposal for a levy on financial transactions with a maximum rate of 0.01 percent—a rate he considered too

low to have the same effects, desirable or otherwise, of the Tobin tax.

By this time, however, more evidence of capital controls' dark
side had come to light. One survey article looking at the effects
of capital controls on specific industries and companies found
instances of higher financing costs, lower international competitiveness, and costly detours intended to circumvent the
controls.

In the absence of broad measures to control risk within the financial system, individual companies and exchanges will have to
rely on their own ability to create incentives for good behavior.
So far, one could argue, they've done a pretty good job. Only a
few cases like Leeson's or Rusnak's have been big enough to make
the headlines in the past couple of decades. Yet to dismiss the
risk because of low probabilities would be to miss the point: if the
size of the potential loss is enormous—as it would be in a break-
down of the global financial system—even an extremely unlikely
outcome is worth taking seriously.

And for that reason, economic logic recommends some sort
of cooperation. If a trader at one bank paralyzes an exchange for
a day—for example, by downloading a Web site that carries a
virus—his or her actions hurt all the other banks, too. As a result,
it's in all the banks' interests to assess and contribute to each
other's monitoring systems, if they can do so without appearing
to collude in other areas.

Monitoring is always difficult, however—a fact that David
Miles, the chief U.K. economist at Morgan Stanley, exploited on
June 15 in London.

7:00 A.M. LONDON (2:00 A.M. NEW YORK)

The day starts fairly early—indeed rather brutally so, since several meetings take place at about 7:00 a.m., London time, before European markets open.

In New Zealand the time is early evening. Now, New Zealand— wonderful country that it is—is not usually the focus of many people's thoughts in the London financial markets . . . except that June 15 was a day on which the British Lions rugby team were playing a key match on their once-every-twelve-years tour to play the best sides in New Zealand (and therefore the best teams in the world).

So between about 8:00 a.m. and 10:00 a.m. London time— when the match was under way in faraway Wellington—I found my attention being drawn away from global financial markets and toward the very physical battle over a funny, oval-shaped ball being waged by thirty oversized, very aggressive, and very fit men on a rainy night twelve thousand miles away. I was not alone in this. The conflict between the need to be seen to be doing work and watching the game (shown live on several large screens on the trading and research floors) was real.

I judged that the sensible strategy was not to be seen in front of the same screen for many minutes on end. So I adopted the tactic of walking from one screen to the next, inquiring politely of the group gathered there what the score was (creating the impression that I had not been watching the game), and then watching for exactly five minutes before loudly saying what a shame it was that I had to get back to work. I fear my transparent strategy is all too obvious . . . but I reckon that at least in displaying guilt about watching the game I may not be sacked as an appalling slacker.

NEW YORK
12:30 P.M.
JUNE 15

LONDON
5:30 P.M.
JUNE 15

OIL

Just how crucial is oil to the world's economy? In a word, very.

Oil is very expensive. In 2005, the world used roughly eighty-four million barrels of oil a day. The price of that oil, at an average of about $50 a barrel, was $1.5 trillion—close to 3.5 percent of all the income the global economy generated in 2005. Other consumable commodities don't even come close. You can buy the world's annual supply of wheat, for example, at the bargain price of just $100 billion. For the same price, you'd get only about twenty days' worth of oil.

Oil is also very versatile. It powers jet airplanes and provides the base material for plastic tricycles. It can be separated into dozens of individual compounds that underpin countless industries, from paint to pharmaceuticals.

Oil is very sensitive, too. The main reason for this is that supply so closely matches demand. The oil supply has risen steadily over the past quarter century, thanks to discoveries of new sources. But demand has risen, too, and the rapid growth of developing economies like China and India has only steepened the climb. Because the world doesn't have much of an oil surplus, a change in supply or demand can quickly lead to a big fluctuation in price.

Those changes can come from almost anywhere. The world's major sources of oil aren't just in the Middle East, but also in Russia, Nigeria, Canada, Mexico, Venezuela, the United States, and the North Sea. Tension of almost any kind in just one of these economies, from political unrest to extreme weather, can send prices spiraling upward. The biggest users of oil are the United States, Europe, and China. Major changes in demand don't usually happen overnight, but they do happen; China's consumption of oil, for example, shot up by more than 40 percent between 2001 and 2005, while its economy grew by roughly the same amount.

And the risks for consumers and businesses don't stop there. Since virtually nobody uses crude oil in its natural state—that is, straight out of the ground—the refiners are almost as important as the extractors. For example, the land along the Gulf Coast of the United States isn't a particularly important source of oil, but it is dotted with refiners who process crude into gasoline, kerosene, and other products. So when Hurricane Katrina tore through the area in August 2005, the damage to the refineries pushed the prices of oil products higher.

And oil is very important, even more than its 3.5 percent share of the world's income suggests. Without oil, the global economy would screech to a stop. In the world's biggest economy, the United States, oil provides 40 percent of the energy needed to run cars, heat homes, and even create electricity. In the

United States and practically every other country, the commercial infrastructure relies on trucks to ship goods back and forth. Until all those trucks are refitted with engines that take non-oil-based fuel, oil will be the essential ingredient for the global economy.

That's why oil prices matter. When they go up, it's more expensive to obtain the raw materials for hundreds of products and to move almost any products around. As a result, an increase in the price of oil is likely to lead to an increase in the price of many other things, too. Higher oil prices also lead to higher gasoline prices, which, in turn, make it more expensive for people to leave their homes and buy goods and services. When all of these things happen, consumers are likely to ask for higher wages. In order to pay for them, businesses are liable to raise prices for goods and services even higher.

On June 15, much of the global trade in oil was taking place in New York, London, and Singapore. The London market, which is the world's biggest, closes at 5:30 p.m. That's when benchmark prices for Brent crude—a blend of North Sea oils that's among the world's easiest to refine—are finalized. Afterward, trading continues around the world using other benchmark crude oils, such as West Texas Intermediate and Dubai. The oil isn't actually in New York, London, and Singapore for the taking, but those cities are home to hundreds of traders who buy and sell the black goop, alongside the legions who trade other commodities, stocks, and bonds.

For them, oil isn't just a useful liquid to be bought and sold. It's also an investment instrument that can be used for financial speculation or to hedge your bets in other areas. Like most commodities, oil is the subject of scores of derivatives—securities whose value changes in predetermined ways depending on the trend in the price or supply of oil. These include call options (contracts that allow investors to buy oil, if they want to, at a fixed price up through a fixed date), put options (the same, but for selling), futures (contracts that *require* investors to buy oil at a fixed price on a fixed date), and more exotic deals that may even depend not just on the actual oil price but on its volatility as well.

Here's an example. Say you had a hunch that Saudi Arabia was going to collapse into civil war in the coming year, thus taking its oil off the market for a while. After the gap in supply opened up, you would expect the price of oil to rise. To bet on your hunch, you might buy call options that would allow you to buy oil at *today's* price next year. If your hunch proved correct, you'd be able to buy oil cheaply after the price went up, then sell it again right away at the market price. You'd make a nice profit without ever taking delivery of all that oil.

But if you heard a rumor that geologists in Kazakhstan had discovered a deep reservoir of oil underground, you might buy put options for today's price instead. After the news broke, you would expect the oil price to drop. Then you'd buy up oil at the new, lower price and use your put options (investors say "exercise" your options) to sell it at the old, higher price. Again, you'd have a nice profit and no barrels in your garage.

You'd do these things not because you have any particular interest in oil itself but because you wanted to make money. You might even be trying to insure yourself. In the example of the call options, perhaps you had a new business venture, building luxury cars in Saudi Arabia. If the country fell apart and your factory was torched by rowdy rioters, at least your call options would allow you to cash in on the rocketing price of oil. What's more, your investors would probably thank you for preserving at least some of their return.

You could do all of this from the comfort of your armchair, with the help of a telephone or a computer and the services of a financial firm. You wouldn't even have to buy Saudi oil options; any oil options would do.

That's because oil is very international. The same grade of crude oil from different sources can have slight chemical differences, but not enough to lead to wide variation in price. Most types are fairly substitutable in the open market.

The market is not entirely open, however. About 40 percent of supply is generally controlled by OPEC (the Organization of the Petroleum Exporting Countries), which includes the bigger Middle Eastern suppliers plus Algeria, Indonesia, Libya, Nigeria, and Venezuela. OPEC is a cartel that tries to set prices by regulating its own supply. Yet lately, prices have far exceeded the $22- to $28-per-barrel band that the group has targeted for several years.

You might ask why a cartel, which presumably exists to keep prices high, would want to reduce prices to keep them within a fixed band. Long-term thinking holds the answer. If oil prices are high for long periods of time, consumers and businesses will seek out alternative fuels more actively, as well as trying to constrain their use of oil. The last thing OPEC wants to see is demand for oil drying up before its members' oil wells do. But the group simply hasn't been able to supply enough oil to make prices come down.

As a result, on June 15 oil was a very risky proposition. The price had already risen from about $33 per barrel a year earlier to more than $49 on the day. The ongoing crisis in Iraq, rebel fighting in Nigeria, the possibility of a hard-line government being elected in Iran, leftist rhetoric from Venezuela, and surging demand from around the world all threatened to push prices higher, but there was uncertainty attached to every single situation.

There was another, more enduring kind of uncertainty, as well—the kind that probably kept OPEC's wealthy potentates awake at night. What if a scientist somewhere invented a cold fusion nuclear generator that could fit under a car's hood or inside a home furnace? Oil would still be needed to make plastics and many other products, but demand would take a huge hit as people adopted the new technology.

Yet until such a day arrives, the world's most popular commodity will keep oozing through the veins of the global economy, taking a few percentage points of everything it finds.

CHAPTER 9

NEW YORK   **SÃO PAULO**
1:42 P.M.   **2:42 P.M.**
JUNE 15   **JUNE 15**

"BRAZIL MARKETS SLIDE AS POLITICAL JITTERS RISE"

WHICH COMES FIRST, POLITICAL OR ECONOMIC STABILITY?

Wend your way through the endless, high-walled labyrinth of São Paulo, and you may come across the occasional, incongruous oasis. In between the stained 1960s apartment blocks that cluster on the city's undulating hills, not far from the potholed streets where armored cars make their rounds and soccer commentary blares incessantly from open-fronted bars, a few colorfully painted, colonial-style houses still sit quietly.

On the second floor of one such building, set among the leafy trees of a gated, guarded courtyard, Reni Adriano Batista sits tapping away intently at a computer. He's a slight man in his mid-twenties who looks like a pint-sized version of Denilson, the soccer star known for his elaborate dribbling. At least, that's what everyone—even the occasional foreigner—tells him. Denilson was born near the suburb of São Paulo where Reni's family ar-

163

rived from the countryside in 1990. For decades, playing soccer was the only way that many young Brazilians from poor backgrounds, like Reni, could even conceive of becoming rich.

All that was supposed to change when Luiz Inácio Lula da Silva, a former metalworker and head of a trade union with no college education, became Brazil's president in 2003. Lula, as he is known, brought with him a mandate for change—not just political, but social and economic as well. In the previous decade, Brazil had already made startling progress in reducing infant mortality, raising life expectancy, and improving literacy. But its elected leaders had often seemed to pursue economic growth with no consideration for the fortunes of ordinary citizens. For people such as Reni, the election of Lula and his Workers' Party meant new hope.

Less than three years later, that hope is flickering. Reni still has a good shot at escaping the dire poverty of his home in Diadema, the suburb of São Paulo that spawned the Workers' Party's ideological ancestors. Yet it's more because of a chance encounter with a pile of old books—and his own initiative—than because of anything the Workers' Party has done since taking over in Brasília.

Reni's passion for reading began in third grade, when a teacher annoyed by his talkativeness shut him up in the school's closetlike library. Now a teacher trainee himself, he's part of a program of reading circles that seeks out ambitious young Brazilians who are looking for more education and challenges than their schools can offer. Sitting in the book-lined offices of the Fernand Braudel Institute of World Economics, which runs the program, he has little praise for the Workers' Party.

"The policies of the government should be so people learn

how to run their businesses, not to be a slave of the job market," he says through Virgínia Montesino, another member of the program who speaks some English. As it stands, Reni says, the education system doesn't give people the tools to strike out on their own.

Frustrated with the government's failure to spur big increases in employment, Reni even suggests lowering interest rates very gradually. With Brazilians eagerly entering into expanding credit markets, he says, lower interest rates could ease household budgets and encourage spending even if prices rose. But Virgínia interjects her own comment here: "If the people think the prices will go up, they will be frightened."

Reni agrees that Brazil's economic restraints shouldn't be relaxed too much. He explains that the Workers' Party's mandate depends on their ability to maintain low inflation and balanced budgets. "The politicians know that if they can't maintain these economic policies," he says, "the people won't give them the same trust."

And so begins the latest episode in a long debate in Brazil. Must the government ensure economic stability above all, to protect the political stability that saw it elected? Or will it endanger that economic stability—for example, by engineering a short-term boom that could result in high long-term inflation—in order to make a grab at popularity, thus solidifying its own position for a few more years?

These questions were particularly apt on June 15, when the Workers' Party was being enveloped in a fast-spreading scandal. The central allegation was that the top echelons of the Workers' Party—though perhaps not Lula himself—organized regular bribes to politicians from other parties in order to maintain their loyalty to the ruling coalition. On June 14, a representative from the Brazilian Labor Party, Roberto Jefferson, had testified in Brazil's congress that half a dozen politicians from the Workers' Party had been behind the scheme, which paid the bribe takers as much as $12,000 per month.

The next day, June 15, stocks in Brazil tumbled as worries about the stability of Lula's government dogged investors. A day later, the scandal brought about the resignation of José Dirceu, a former revolutionary who had reincarnated himself as an above-board politician in time to lead the Workers' Party's march to power. He had been Lula's behind-the-scenes enforcer and de facto prime minister.

After Dirceu's resignation, the Bovespa—Brazil's stock market—seemed to right itself. Two senators from the *opposition* actually met with bankers and business owners to reassure them that the political system would stay intact. In the background, there loomed an enigma: Was Brazil's political stability a prerequisite for its economic stability, or vice versa?

When Lula's government took office, you could have argued that only Brazil's economic stability assured a smooth transfer of power to a left-leaning, populist politician. After their election, Lula and his colleagues strove to reassure foreign banks and institutions that despite their politics, they would maintain the budgetary and monetary policies that had reduced inflation and spurred foreign investment in Brazil. Without those reassurances, the vested interests that supported Brazil's previous center-right government might have tried to derail the succession.

It wasn't that economic stability was somehow necessary for the simple functioning of the political process (though it probably helped). It was more that economic stability was such a valuable prize that no sane politician would have done anything to jeopardize it.

This logic was at work again during the time of the scandal. At first, it seemed like the scandal could grow into a rupture capable of torpedoing Brazil's nascent prosperity, and investors sent stocks spiraling. But rather than fanning the flames in order to improve its chances of breaking up the ruling coalition, the opposition in the congress sought to calm the market's fears. In other words, the politicians knew that they could harm the economy's stability, but the very existence of that stability prevented them—it was too valuable to risk losing.

The immanence of economic stability works both ways, according to Norman Gall, a former journalist from the Bronx who is now executive director of the Braudel Institute. Lula's promises for big changes in social programs have gone largely unfulfilled, Gall says. Part of the reason is that the president can't bump up the federal budget, at least not in the same way Hugo Chávez, the populist leader of Venezuela, has.

"If he started screwing around with big increases in government spending," Gall says of Lula, "he would be out the door in two weeks." The same goes for lowering Brazil's high interest rates, he adds, which have kept inflation in check.

On the other hand, the opposition is also toothless, Gall says. It could have demanded the firing of Antonio Palocci, Lula's finance minister, who reportedly asked to leave the government on his own at least three times after being accused of running money from Cuba to the Workers' Party. Yet it did not. "The opposition has not asked for his resignation, because they know this would compromise stability," Gall says. Stability, he adds, has been the only "big plus" of Lula's presidency.

Indeed, it seemed like the political stalemate might only come undone if the economy took a turn for the worse, in which case the stakes—and the possibility for blame if things turned ugly—would be lower. In Brazil at least, economic stability seems to have the power to force political stability, if an uneasy form thereof. The corresponding question may then be asked: Must political stability precede economic stability? Judged by experience and history, the answer is yes.

For starters, foreign investors, who can play a crucial role in a developing country's growth, look for political stability when they choose where to put their money. Credit ratings can provide an indirect indicator of expectations for stability. The California Public Employees' Retirement System, which controls pensions and health benefits for the state's 1.4 million government workers and retirees, takes the exercise a step further. CalPERS, as it's commonly known, puts out a list every year of countries where it will consider investing $4 billion earmarked for emerging economies.

The list is made public, so other investors can free-ride on CalPERS's research. And according to one strategist quoted by the *International Herald Tribune*, investors do take note. "If they put a country on or take it off the list, it can move a market by a few percentage points, so you have to pay attention," said Wim-Hein Pals, the chief investor in emerging markets for Robeco, a leading fund manager in the Netherlands.

Political stability is just one of the factors CalPERS considers in making up its list. But the lack of it can turn any country into a no-go zone. The worst absence of political stability is civil war, and civil war has usually brought economic development to a standstill, or reversed it, in countries at all income levels. One need only look across sub-Saharan Africa for evidence of this point.

Yet even when the political *system* is stable, it may help to have stability in political *leadership* as well. In Brazil, it took eight years of single-minded, market-friendly reforms under Fernando Henrique Cardoso, Lula's predecessor, to usher Brazil out of an era of financial and budgetary crises.

To be sure, a similar package of reforms could have taken hold under a series of governments with different political stripes. But it's hard to find examples in recent history where this has happened; India, where three parties have formed governments over the past few decades, may be the only one. The enormous value that different political parties may assign to economic stability, once it has been achieved, is not always uniformly attached to the policies needed to achieve it.

Stability in political leadership can be taken to the extreme as well, and economic stability is often complicit. People tend to vote for governments who keep the economy growing and inflation under control. Singapore and the United Arab Emirates have become very wealthy under authoritarian regimes. Kazakhstan and Vietnam, where the ruling autocrats have become entrenched, may be heading in the same direction. It's worth noting that the United Arab Emirates and Kazakhstan have been able to rely on exports of oil to ease the vicissitudes of budgeting. Still, the citizens are probably less likely to complain about their essentially one-party states as long as their living standards keep rising.

To some, it's a trade-off worth making. In September 2005, Helmut Schmidt, the former chancellor of West Germany, appeared at a forum in Beijing to discuss China's economic and political outlook. Here is an excerpt from his remarks:

Some Western politicians and intellectuals believe they are morally entitled to reproach or even castigate the Chinese in regard of democracy and human rights. But they lack respect for Chinese civilization, which has evolved over several millenniums. They also lack an awareness of the terrible shadows that historically hang over the laborious development of Western civilizations . . . I do believe that the stability provided by the present political system is expedient and beneficial for the Chinese nation—and for its Asian neighbors as well.

There can be no doubt that human and civil rights do not receive the same respect in China that they do in many wealthier countries. Schmidt claimed that could change with time, though, and that the development of China's markets would ensure that it did.

Economic growth is no guarantee of political freedoms, however. In Singapore and the United Arab Emirates, where average living standards are as high as in parts of western Europe, there are still limits on basic rights. Amnesty International cited Singapore for restricting the press and civic groups in its 2005 annual report; the United Arab Emirates came under fire for persecuting people with allegedly "Islamist" tendencies and for failing to give legal protection to migrant workers against abuse by their employers. In fact, it sometimes seems like citizens of these countries are willing to trade off some civil rights in return for prosperity. Their flavor of capitalism is quite different from that of the United States, where individual freedoms and prosperity are assumed to go hand in hand.

Prosperity can also be taken for granted, though. In some countries in the West, citizens seem to have become so confident of their economic security that they feel free to engage in the kind of politics that would destabilize a less mature economy. That's what Joyce Chang, the head of emerging markets research in global currency and commodities for JP Morgan, found out on June 15 while on a fellowship sponsored by the German Marshall Fund.

BILBAO, SPAIN (SIX HOURS AHEAD OF NEW YORK)

I am on day fourteen of a Marshall Memorial Fellowship that lasts for twenty-five days and have been traveling throughout Europe with a group of leaders, all aged under forty, from different walks of life. It's the longest that I have been away from Wall Street for sixteen years (including maternity leave) and a rare opportunity to spend time away from other professionals in the financial services industry. The other fellows work in education, nonprofits, and media for the most part. It's also a chance to set aside market prices, spreadsheets, and number crunching to see what is really going on in Europe following the failure of the referendums in France and the Netherlands over the EU constitution.

Today, I am in Bilbao, Spain—my first visit to Basque country—a part of the world that I would probably never travel to apart from this fellowship. I've started the day by checking BlackBerry messages and calling London. The dollar continues to strengthen against the euro and we've revised our dollars/euro forecast to $1.15 at the end of this year (one of the most bullish dollar views on the Street). It's timely to be in Europe in the aftermath of the French and Dutch rejections of the EU constitution. I was in Amsterdam before arriving in Bilbao, and the general mood was very pessimistic, given the country's commitment to integration and its liberal stance on so many issues. There seems to be a massive change in the way the European

Commission and the EU see themselves relative to self-perceptions three months ago.

Bilbao is a surprising contrast to the rest of Europe. EU integration is a completely marginal issue here, and there is little evidence of immigration, social tensions, or some of the other challenges facing the rest of Europe. Bilbao is also more prosperous than any other part of Europe that I visited, and the standard of living is higher, with incomes 25 percent higher than the rest of Europe. Of the 700,000-plus immigrants in Spain, only 13,000 are in Basque areas, and 9,000 of these immigrants work as nannies. After going through a difficult period in the 1980s when heavy industry declined and unemployment reached 25 percent, Bilbao rebuilt itself, and the Guggenheim museum is the centerpiece of the city.

The city coordinators are enthusiastic, warm, passionate, and very intent on indoctrinating us in Basque culture. We have a meeting with the principal Basque political parties today. We spent yesterday at the Gernika [Guernica] Museum of Peace and touring the Tree of Peace. We also learn that 98 percent of the families in Basque country choose to learn the Basque language in schools even though most of the parents do not speak Basque, since it was banned under Franco's dictatorship. Our hosts tell us that even reading a Spanish-language newspaper at a bus stop would provoke negative public harassment.

This is definitely a part of the world that is frozen in time and seemingly in denial that it is a part of Spain. There is no mention of economic issues or an economic agenda by any of the seven political parties that brief us. They are 100 percent focused on the issue of independence and self-determination. To the extent that they are focused on the EU constitution, it is centered on the desire to be represented at the same level as other European countries. The leaders of the opposition parties all have bodyguards accompanying them, although the parties all point out that the ETA [a terrorist Basque separatist group that announced a permanent cease-fire in March 2006] has not successfully carried out an assassination for two years. The parties struggle to articulate a model that they wish to emulate, citing Québec and Bavaria as examples.

Québec and Bavaria are also sometimes-wayward regions in wealthy countries—Canada and Germany, respectively. Around the world, though, most of the civil conflicts, especially the "hot" ones, are in poor countries. It's hard to tell whether the countries are poor because of their political unrest or vice versa. In most cases, the pretense for conflict is ethnic, religious, or political, even if the true cause has something to do with economics. But there is one illuminating way of looking at the evidence.

By focusing on the economic conditions that preceded recent instances of unrest, you can gain some relief from the chicken-and-egg problem. By seeing the order in which things happen, you might be able to sort out what causes what. And you don't need to look only at countries where conflict erupted; the other countries, examined over the same time period, provide a sort of control group. You could also try to separate out those other factors like religion and ethnicity.

That's exactly what two Stanford professors did. James Fearon and David Laitin created a data set detailing almost all the world's civil wars between 1945 and 1999. They found that lower incomes, and also greater size and rougher terrain, are all correlated with violent conflict inside a country. Ethnic and religious splintering weren't, by themselves, terribly important.

From this perspective, it's not surprising that the Basques,

Bavarians, and Québecois haven't been engaging in much violence lately. Spain, Germany, and Canada have been getting steadily wealthier over the last few decades. More people have opportunities to look forward to, and more people have something to lose—a house, a car, a business—if violence breaks out. They can still pursue their desire for independence through politics, however. In sum, it's "cool" conflicts for the rich and "hot" ones for the poor.

That leaves middle-income countries with stable economies as islands of relative calm: virtually all of eastern Europe, most of Latin America, and much of East Asia. Among those middle-income countries where conflicts are still active, the affected regions are almost invariably poor: the jungles of Colombia, the south of Thailand, the Kurdish parts of Turkey, and Russia's Chechnya. Even these countries have been able to make economic progress, though, thanks to the peaceful conditions in their business centers.

Brazil is one of the biggest of the middle-income countries. And though its corruption scandal rolled on into 2006, with Palocci finally resigning successfully in March, any economic damage was somehow contained.

The Ibovespa, the main index of the values of shares in Brazil's stock exchange, lost just over 1 percent of its value on June 15, closing at 25,481 and change. But six months later, the index stood at 33,193, after a gain of 30 percent. Over the same period, the Brazilian currency—the real—appreciated in value by about 7 percent against the dollar and the euro; by contrast, prices in Brazil rose by about 3 percent. Unemployment had started to fall, and so had interest rates. By February 2006, Lula's popularity among Brazilians had risen back to its pre-scandal levels.

This turn of events was not to be taken for granted. The scandal, though it spared Lula, claimed many other scalps from the top of the Workers' Party, known in Brazil as the PT: its secretary-general, president, treasurer, and communications secretary, among others. In addition, several top officials, including the finance minister's chief of staff, resigned their posts in government.

"We work in the periphery of São Paulo in a municipality run by the PT," Gall says. "We knew that it was not squeaky clean. But the dimension of the scandal and these operations surprised everyone."

Had the economy not ticked upward, beating some forecasters' predictions, Lula might not have survived his party's travails so easily. But were the travails less torturous because Brazil's opposition, perhaps reflecting its population in general, was reluctant to rock the boat? It's hard to believe that politicians wouldn't try to squeeze through any opening they saw. More likely, they simply couldn't present economic policies different enough from those of the PT to sway voters' preferences. Spending restraint and relatively high interest rates had contained inflation, reduced fears of a financial crisis, and attracted foreign investors. To diverge from this successful recipe would not be an easy sell.

As the Brazilian summer of 2006 drew to a close, the nation began looking forward to the World Cup, where its soccer team was favored by the oddsmakers to improve its record tally of five triumphs. With a wealth of new talent on offer, Reni's look-alike hadn't featured in the coach's squads during the qualifying. A win would probably have lifted the economy through to the elections in October, with its likely by-products of widespread optimism and consumer confidence. Brazil played bizarrely unin-spired soccer and lost in the quarterfinals, but Lula won his elec-tion anyway. If anything, the hangover from that soccer loss may have been more destabilizing than one of the most insidious cases of corruption Brazil had ever seen.

CHAPTER 10

NEW YORK
2:46 P.M.
JUNE 15

PARIS
8:46 P.M.
JUNE 15

"U.S. TREASURY SECRETARY URGES EUROPEAN FINAN-CIAL REFORMS" CAN THE UNITED STATES SET THE GLOBAL ECONOMY'S RULES?

The United States didn't invent capitalism, but sometimes it sure acts like it did. Back in 1776, the American Declaration of Independence asserted that people had rights no one could take away, and that among them were "Life, Liberty and the pursuit of Happiness." The framers borrowed that phrase from John Locke, a British philosopher who penned the words almost a century earlier, with one not-so-subtle change: where they claimed "the pursuit of Happiness," Locke had written of man's right "to preserve his property, that is, his life, liberty and estate."

These days the American urge to export democracy is matched only by its desire to export capitalism. In the minds of some politicians, the two missions are apparently synonymous. It makes sense, in a way; the United States is perhaps the only country in the world where you can buy class. In fact, some of the most admired people in the United States are those who've built their fortunes up from nothing. But in plenty of other countries, people with the wrong name, the wrong skin color, the wrong hometown, or the wrong accent would never have gotten through the front door.

Just as there are several brands of democracy, there are several brands of capitalism. The American brand has been selling well lately in some parts of the world, like eastern Europe and Southeast Asia. More broadly, the American model—companies free from government ownership, largely self-organizing markets, and protection for consumers and investors—has been the driving force behind many changes in global regulation of trade, accounting, and financial markets. Is it because the system works, or is it because other countries don't have a choice?

There's one country that always thinks, at least, that it has a choice: France. On June 15, that's where John Snow, the U.S. Treasury secretary, was meeting with the country's newest finance minister, Thierry Breton. For a while, after the rupture between the United States and France over the invasion of Iraq, the trip would have been akin to a foray into enemy territory. Relations had improved a bit since then, but Snow still had his work cut out for him—especially since he was, like so many of his predecessors, going to try to offer the French some helpful hints.

Snow had been barnstorming across Europe for a week, bringing a message of economic and financial reform. Of course, the secretary probably wasn't doing this for the good of the Europeans. His job was to represent his government's interests, and he was doing just that: a stronger European economy would be good for the United States, too, if it meant more demand for exports and more foreign investment back home. It could also cut into the value of the dollar, if investors decided to move some of their money by buying securities there. Both factors could help to close the nation's yawning trade deficit—a record number that, in the eyes of some economists, was hanging over the economy like a grand piano tied up with fishing line.

Not by coincidence, however, "reform" could have been translated as "be more like us." What would help the American economy would also do a world of good for its ego, since the secretary's prescription was to follow his nation's lead: fewer restrictions on hiring and firing in labor markets, lower tax rates, and smoother flows of investors' money into and out of each country.

When he spoke, Snow framed his agenda as a bunch of stuff the Europeans had heard before and already agreed with. The first part was probably true, but the second part most definitely wasn't. The reason why these changes hadn't happened yet was simple: in France, Germany, and Italy—the major economies that Snow targeted in his speech—politicians and populations were divided about how to move forward. Some wanted to embrace American-style free markets; others preferred to keep policies aimed at job security and social welfare, even at the cost of new jobs and economic growth.

In most cases, the latter group was in the majority. If 90 percent of the labor force was employed and happy, it would be difficult to loosen up the labor markets, potentially threatening their job security, in order to help the 10 percent who were unemployed. Violent reactions by the 10 percent, as seen in France in late 2005, were the only risk.

Yet Snow made it clear that he expected action. Though he was careful to say, "I am not here to tell you what to do," he also said, "Europe and Japan have a critical role to play in maintain-

CONNECTED: 24 HOURS IN THE GLOBAL ECONOMY

ing global economic strength, but they have not been doing their part of late," "Much hard work remains for Europe," and, "The ball is in Europe's court to make this a reality."

One of the people who wrote the speech with Snow was Mark Sobel, who joined the Treasury Department in 1978 at the age of twenty-three. He had been a graduate student in international relations who liked economics. In 2005, he was the deputy assistant secretary for international monetary and financial policy.

"It's been a revolutionary period, for sure," Sobel says from the Treasury, a pillared, foursquare pile that sits just a block from the White House. "I started my Treasury career doing foreign exchange. I'd go to New York and I'd sit in a trading room. There'd be a table, kind of a round or ovular structure with fifteen or twenty people. Now if you go to HSBC in London or somewhere like that, there is a trading floor, and there'll be six or seven hundred people there.

"It's just truly incredible," he adds. "Basically, the markets truly are twenty-four-hour, they truly are global, and so the regulators are always having to adjust."

Sobel is a believer in convergence of global financial regulation. That means he wants to see progress toward similar rules for buying and selling securities, plus the way companies prepare their balance sheets, anywhere that an investor might consider doing business. And he makes a logical economic argument for it.

"If businesses are operating everywhere in the world, and every place in the world uses a different set of rules and regulations, then there's just an enormous welfare cost—a higher cost of capital, and all kinds of burdens that make it more costly for consumers," Sobel says. "Two countries are never going to be alike. They have their own cultures, histories, legal traditions. But to the extent that there can be convergence toward high-quality global standards, that's a good thing."

So what should those standards be? Not surprisingly, to Sobel they look a lot like the regulations in place in the United States. It's not just that the United States says it wants other countries to adopt its rules; sometimes, their companies have to.

Snow may say that he doesn't want to tell Europe what to do, but the regulations say otherwise. Foreign governments have offered to recognize American standards for corporate accounts and transactions, but the United States won't reciprocate. For example, if a company from Germany wants to list its shares on the New York Stock Exchange, then it must adhere to the Securities and Exchange Commission's reporting rules—Germany's own standards, however high they might be, are not enough.

Moreover, American regulating agencies—the Securities and Exchange Commission, the Federal Reserve Board, the Commodity Futures Trading Commission, plus others that are independent from the government—don't seem to feel like they have much to learn from foreigners. "I'm not sure you'll ever find a U.S. regulator that will ever say, 'Country X's system is better than ours, and we will do it that way,' " Sobel says.

Yet that is exactly what the United States expects foreign regulators to say, time after time. It's hard to change the political reality in Europe, though, especially as other American policies become less and less popular. Left-wing politicians in Germany, for example, scored points in the 2005 election by emphasizing their hostility to American influence. U.S. foreign policy, one could argue, has started to become an obstacle to U.S. regulatory policy.

Regulators aside, the United States also expects representatives of foreign governments to follow its lead in a variety of other settings. Just three blocks away from the Treasury sit the headquarters of the World Bank, the biggest provider of multinational loans and aid for economic development, and the International Monetary Fund, whose job is to maintain international economic and financial stability. Why are they in Washington? You might as well ask why the United Nations is in New York. Though both of the organizations operate on their own, their management boards are composed of representatives from the countries that back them. Voting power on those boards depends on the size of each country's stake. In the World Bank's two major loan agencies, the United States holds 16 percent and 13 percent of the voting power (Japan has the next-biggest shares, at about 8 percent and 10 percent). At the IMF, it's 17 percent, compared with Japan's 6 percent.

The United States also has de facto power to appoint the president of the World Bank—witness the installation of Paul Wolfowitz, the controversial mastermind of the invasion of Iraq—and what amounts to a veto over the managing directorship of the IMF. Those voting shares translate directly into policy, too. Perhaps most important, the United States can influence the general tenor of the conditions set by the bank and the IMF for their multibillion-dollar loans to foreign governments. But it can exert its power in very specific instances, too.

For example, in 2002 the first deputy managing director of the IMF, Anne Krueger, introduced a proposal that promised to ease the problems associated with defaults on debt—that is, bankruptcies—of national governments. The proposal would have given the IMF a role much like a bankruptcy court, by which a country's debts would be frozen while its obligations were settled in an orderly manner. The plan also called for the IMF to be the lender of last resort in these situations, which made it the equivalent of the interim owner of a bankrupt company, except for a country. That last part wasn't too popular, but the proposal still received some favorable reviews. It went nowhere, though, for one main reason: the United States preferred a different solution, which involved changing how bond contracts were written.

It's only in consensus-driven groups like the World Trade Organization that the United States is cut down to size, at least on paper. At the WTO, which is located in Geneva, the United States has one vote and one veto—the same as every other member in a constantly growing group of about 150. But the nation finds other ways to exert its influence.

Because of its size and wealth, the United States can represent its interests in ways that only the European Union and Japan can really match. Its activities in the WTO have offered ample evidence. The organization doesn't just exist to set global trading rules; it also serves as a forum for resolving disputes. Fighting a dispute takes years of work by skilled lawyers, of which the United States happens to have an enormous supply. In the first eleven years of the WTO's existence, from 1995 through 2005, the United States was the plaintiff (or complainant) in 81 such cases; it was the defendant (or respondent) in 90. There was a total of 335 cases, so the United States was involved in just over half. Only the EU comes close, with 70 cases as complainant and 53 as respondent; the next highest total is Canada, with 26 and 13, respectively.

That the United States should lead on both sides of the ledger stands to reason. It's the most aggressive trader and has the great-est capacity to defend its own interests, but, as the world's biggest market for exports, it's also the most important target for other members of the WTO. Ecuador wouldn't necessarily sue tiny Cape Verde for dumping cut-price shrimp on world markets. (Cape Verde does sell a lot of cheap shrimp . . . for a nation of 400,000 people, anyway.) But Ecuador certainly did go after the United States for that offense in November 2005.

And trade is an area where the United States doesn't always get its way. Though it can force a series of appeals to any decision that goes against it, some countries have eventually been able to call the United States on the carpet. Even then, however, getting results can take time—a lot of time.

For example, the Foreign Sales Corporation provision of the U.S. tax code gave American companies an unfair advantage in trade for years. The provision contained tax breaks that became more valuable the more a company exported; in essence, it al-lowed companies to charge lower prices when they shipped their products abroad. But the tax breaks also seemed a lot like the kinds of export subsidies that were illegal under the WTO's rules.

The EU, cheered on by other nations, filed a complaint in the WTO in November 1997. It finally won an appellate decision more than two years later, in February 2000. The United States enacted legislation that supposedly repealed the tax breaks in November, but the EU wasn't convinced; pointing to the in-completeness of the law, it complained again. It won another appellate decision in January 2002. In August, the WTO's arbitra-tor concluded that the EU could levy up to $4 billion worth of punitive tariffs. The EU started to draw up a list of American products, from cheese to fishing rods, on which it would slap tariffs of up to 100 percent. But the EU didn't use this big stick right away, for fear of igniting a trade war.

After about eighteen months, in March 2004, the EU began to use a small one: tariffs starting at about $16 million a month, rising to over $55 million monthly if the United States still failed to obey the WTO's ruling. The strategy seemed—that's right, seemed—to get results. In October 2004, the United States enacted new legislation to change the tax code, claiming compliance with the WTO's decision, and the EU celebrated by promising to drop its tariffs on January 1, 2005.

Within a couple of months, however, the mood had soured. The EU judged that the tax breaks still hadn't been completely removed and threatened to keep the tariffs in place when the new year came. Then, in January 2005, the EU asked for yet another WTO panel to discuss the case. It also decided to lift its tariffs while the case went forward. In September 2005, the WTO again agreed with the EU. The United States promised, yet again, to appeal.

Almost eight years after the dispute began, the matter still wasn't closed. In the meantime, the United States and the EU were slugging it out on other issues, too, some with the potential for equally vast transatlantic tariffs. Things might just have resolved themselves sooner if the EU had finally fired its multibillion-dollar tariff cannon. But it just couldn't bring itself to pull the trigger on the biggest export market in the world—perhaps because of that old saying that starts, "Let the trading bloc that is without sin . . ."

Clearly, the United States is well equipped to defend itself in formal disputes with other countries. In addition, American workers are among the most mobile in the world, and they bring their influence with them whenever they travel to and invest in other countries. On June 15, the members of CommonAngels, a venture capital firm based in Boston, provided a good example. Here's how James Geshwiler, the firm's managing director, described their day:

BOSTON (SAME TIME AS NEW YORK)

One of Boston's largest networks of business leaders is Common-Angels, a formal organization that coordinates business leaders' advice and pools their capital to support new high-tech companies. More than a hundred people contribute their time, capital, or both to CommonAngels, and as its managing director, I coordinate evaluating investment opportunities and managing its portfolio.

Everyone else in the CommonAngels network has another job or set of responsibilities in the business world, including chief executives of public companies, board members of nonprofits, university faculty, and retired executives. These individuals travel the globe working on projects that apply their expertise and contribute to their collective understanding about markets, company formation, and technology. Over the course of today and in the coming weeks and months, these people will apply these skills and lessons learned as they evaluate and assist new ventures. They will do this by e-mail, phone, fax, and in person. Some of these interactions will be with the companies they are considering for investment; others will be with prospective customers, employees, partners, industry analysts, and other investors. Today, June 15, these activities include the following:

Ken Morse, managing director of the Massachusetts Institute of Technology's Entrepreneurship Center, is in Damascus, Syria, coaching 450 women entrepreneurs from all over the Middle East on how to address the challenges of globalization, and how to quantify the value proposition for their companies and to develop their sales strategies accordingly. Bob Frankston, coinventor of the spreadsheet, is in Zaragoza, Spain, participating in the "Innovate! Europe '05" conference, fostering entrepreneurship on that continent. Don Mitchell, CEO of industrial sensor and encoder company MicroE, is in Poole, England, working with a partner company defining several generations of products for electronic assembly equipment.

American influence spreads in other informal ways, too. Innovations in policy and governance are often adopted simply because they work. For example, the conservative anti-inflation stance first taken by the Federal Reserve Board under chairman Paul Volcker at the end of the 1970s has become a model for central banks around the world. Even the inflation-rule-based strategies adopted by the European Central Bank and others have their roots in American academic research.

In addition to all these factors, there is a bottom line that explains why many countries follow the American example of their own accord. Over the past couple of decades, the United States has enjoyed the highest average growth rate among the world's wealthy economies. This growth rate matters to investors; the faster the economy is growing, the more profitable opportunities there are likely to be for companies. It matters to politicians, too. If the economy is growing, there's more income to spread around. That usually makes voters happy. And attracting more money from investors, both at home and abroad, helps to *keep* the voters happy.

Here, too, though, there is a hidden fallacy. For starters, living standards only rise—on average—when the growth rate of the economy outpaces the growth rate of the population. A better way to look at these figures is on a per capita basis—that is, how fast is the average income of one person rising? Already, things start to change. The U.S. economy expanded by about 3.5 percent in 2005, but the population also grew, by about 0.9 percent. That means the per capita growth of the economy was just 2.6 percent. Meanwhile, Spain's economy grew by 3.3 percent in 2005, but its population barely increased at all; the per capita increase was 3.1 percent. So, based on just one year of data, whose example should aspiring countries follow, that of the United States or that of . . . Spain?

You can make the analysis even more complicated by looking at the distribution of income. Watching how the size of a country's economy compares to its population can give you some idea of changes in average income, but you'll be missing an important part of the story: economic growth rarely lifts the income of every citizen at the same rate. So even when a country's average income is rising quickly, the gains may be helping just a select few.

That's become a problem for the world's other economic darling, China. At 8.6 percent, its per capita growth rate was the highest on Earth for an economy of any substantial size; indeed, it was the highest of all economies except for a few petroleum-producing countries lucky enough to ride the wave of higher oil prices. China's growth has brought hundreds of millions of people out of poverty in the past couple of decades. But for hundreds of millions of others, especially farmers and migrant laborers, little has changed.

Since the fall of Marxism, no country has set the absolute flattening of the income distribution as a main goal of economic policy. Sometimes countries have used the tax system to make incomes somewhat more equal; Tony Blair's government in the U.K. is one recent example. But even making equality a goal, in addition to or instead of the overall size of the economy, still assumes that incomes are the most important indicator of overall well-being.

And that's not necessarily true. You can take two people with exactly the same incomes, facing exactly the same prices, and they might not be equally happy. Moreover, giving someone more money won't always make him happier. If Microsoft paid Bill Gates $1 more every year, would he be skipping to work? Probably not. Still, in his case you could argue that his increase in happiness is just too small to measure. That's not so in the case of Turk Wendell, though.

Wendell, a baseball pitcher known for wearing an animal-tooth necklace, is apparently obsessed with the number nine. In December 2000, he signed a three-year contract with the New York Mets that paid $9,399,999.99, or $9,999,999.99 if he pitched especially well. Surely, the Mets would have been happy to round these figures up by a penny. But Wendell, with his thing for nines, preferred to leave the penny on the table. Then, in February 2004, Wendell passed up money for another, more common reason. He could have signed a deal for a guaranteed $900,000 from the Florida Marlins, but instead he chose $700,000—a figure he'd receive only if he made the team—from the Colorado Rockies. He wanted to work nearer to his children, who lived in suburban Denver.

Money may not be everything, and yet much of American economic policy—the kind used at home and the kind exported abroad—is focused on increasing incomes. Each generation in the United States is expected to earn more than the previous one, and data detailing the growth of the economy—that is, the increase in the nation's annual income—always make the headlines. Through the 1980s, the U.S. government used its influence in the World Bank and the IMF to encourage poor countries to adopt pro-growth strategies. Higher incomes, once again, were not merely a means to an end; they were an end in themselves. Even in this decade, as American policy has shifted toward improving the productivity of individuals through medical care, public health, and education, outcomes are still measured primarily by incomes. The United Nations' most broadly cited measures of poverty, for example, are the percentages of people in a country who live on less than $1 or $2 a day.

There's no doubt that higher incomes can help to buy important things like vaccines and textbooks, and money may be a good proxy for human satisfaction in some cases. In fact, one could argue that by stopping with money—by not trying harder to figure out the subjective matter of what actually makes people happy—the United States is taking a correctly cautious approach to the problem. But exactly what problem is that? Is it poverty? Or is it the inability of people to live a happy, long, full life?

The two do not always go hand in hand. Indeed, the single greatest threat to the American policy model could be an emerging field in economics: happiness studies.

Economists have always been interested in happiness. Every first-year economics student learns that maximum happiness, not money, is the correct goal for policy. Yet somehow, by the time those students have turned into policy makers, they've thrown up their hands and decided to use money as shorthand—just as the American model does.

Recently, however, some economists have been going back to their roots. Together with experts from other fields, they've been surveying people around the world to find out how happy they are, and what makes them happier. How puzzling it must have been, to some of those American policy makers, to find that people in many poorer countries were, on average, happier than Americans.

Ruut Veenhoven, a professor at Erasmus University in Rotterdam, keeps a database of rankings compiled from those surveys. In a ranking of ninety countries, the United States comes in eighteenth for its population's overall satisfaction with their lives. Mexico, its significantly poorer neighbor, ranks eighth. The scores for Guatemala, Honduras, and El Salvador—all relatively poor countries in Latin America—are almost the same as that of the United States. And there are other riddles: Why does booming South Korea (55th) lag so far behind Nigeria (39th), where the average person's purchasing power is just one-twentieth as large?

You could be forgiven for asking whether poverty is really such a problem. Surely it is, when it takes lives. But even where that happens, the differences in happiness persist. In Veenhoven's rankings of how many happy years of life people can expect, the Latin American trio perform far worse. But Mexico, where higher happiness offsets lower life expectancy, still finishes right behind the United States.

Once a country has obtained a basic level of economic security, higher incomes may not be the key to greater well-being. In at least one country, this empirical fact has turned into policy. It is one place where the American model falls on deaf or, shall we say, otherwise engaged ears.

It is the Himalayan kingdom of Bhutan, a land of perhaps a million, perhaps two million people—no one seems to know exactly how many—that sits sandwiched between China and India. It's not clear whether Jefferson was the inspiration, but shortly after taking the throne in 1972, King Jigme Singye Wangchuck rejected the pursuit of property and began gearing his government's policies to maximize *gross national happiness*.

The Bhutanese, whose ideas probably owe more to Buddha than to Aaron Burr's boss, don't measure happiness the way other countries measure gross domestic product. But they do try to focus their policies on four areas that they think will lead to bliss: sustainable and equitable socioeconomic development, conservation of the environment, preservation and promotion of culture, and promotion of good governance.

Bhutan limits visits by foreigners, and the fairly theocratic government has kept its citizens' way of life much the same for centuries. In the meantime, the United States has transformed itself through rising incomes, and continues to do so. But if you had to bet on whose citizens' happiness will have improved the most a century from now, it might not be such an easy call.

CHAPTER 11

NEW YORK
6:44 P.M.
JUNE 15

CALGARY
4:44 P.M.
JUNE 15

"ALBERTA AIMS TO ATTRACT SKILLED OIL WORKERS"
IS IMMIGRATION A LUXURY OR A NECESSITY?

Calgary is a rich city, and it's getting richer. You wouldn't necessarily know it from walking the streets downtown, though. On
almost every corner stands a man in his forties or fifties, silently
holding a cup or a baseball cap in front of him. These guys look
healthy enough, and they're dressed pretty well for the chill. But
despite Calgary's boom, they can't get jobs. Sure, the oil and gas
companies who are pulling riches out of the Alberta frontier, and
points farther north, are hiring—in fact, they're desperate for
people. But the people they need have skills that these men lack.

To hear Cheryl Knight tell it, some of the energy companies
are just as bemused as these unfortunate men. For years, they relied on a labor force of young white male employees to do dirty
jobs in cold climates, either in Canada's vast oil sands or on its
offshore drilling platforms. Now the way the industry works has
changed, and so have its needs for workers.

That's where Knight thinks she can help. A vivacious middle-aged woman with a broad grin but a serious mien, she's the executive director of Canada's Petroleum Human Resources Council, one of about three dozen nonprofit agencies funded by the government to help industries find the workers they need.

"The industry right now is not very diverse," Knight says in the council's windowless conference room, where images of an offshore rig caught in a storm and an oil-splattered wellhead hang on the walls. "They've relied on traditional sources of supply, primarily young men. I don't believe industry will do a really great job of attracting more diverse workers without our help. And they're not doing any promotion to young people."

Knight's council estimates that the petroleum industry currently employs about 120,000 people directly and maybe two or three times that number indirectly, in jobs like construction and local services. Over the next ten years, she says, the industry will have to bring in about 43,000 new employees—and their indirect counterparts—just to keep up with the potential for production. That huge turnover doesn't just represent the people running the drills, either. There are engineers, programmers, network managers, and countless other occupations to fill. The boom means companies can pay more, but that may not be enough.

"That's traditionally how industry has attracted and retained people in the past—through compensation," Knight says. "That doesn't work for all types of people. Compensation attracts more significantly than it retains." The petroleum sector is behind— perhaps decades behind—other industries in the tools of workforce strategy, such as offering flexible schedules and family-friendly leave policies, she adds. "There's some catch-up to be done."

But in addition to these changes, the sector needs to get the word out. Alberta and its neighboring provinces can't provide all the necessary workers by themselves. Some will have to come from elsewhere in Canada, or elsewhere in the world. In April 2004, the council put out a report offering tips for attracting and retaining new workers, especially immigrants.

It pointed out that immigrants aren't always ready to jump right into the jobs that the industry has to offer, and that they don't always come straight to Alberta, either. Even immigrants with the right credentials and experience "do not assimilate easily into the Canadian upstream oil and gas industry," the report said. It suggested reaching out to them through local associations in big cities, streamlining the recognition of foreign work and education, and assisting them with adaptation to the language and culture.

Doing these things can be costly, but the petroleum sector is facing a crisis. It is not alone. There's a shortage of engineers and technicians in several industries—so much so that the Canadian government has started offering to exempt immigrants from some visa rules if they fit the bill.

Canada is not alone, either. All over the world, governments have started making exceptions for immigrants who can work in industries with labor supply problems. In the United States, it's high-tech whizzes. In the U.K., it's nurses. In much of Southeast Asia and the Arabian Peninsula, it's domestic help. In China, it's scholars and scientists.

In increasing numbers, people can freely trade their labor around the world, just as financiers trade securities and businesses trade goods and services. But the trade in labor doesn't flow quite as smoothly, and it can have some profound economic effects that aren't always obvious.

One obstacle to the trade is information. As Canada's oil and gas companies have found out, some of the people whom they'd like to hire don't even know that the jobs exist. Or, even if they do, they have an outdated conception of what working in the petroleum sector can imply.

Contrast that with other markets. If you want to buy shares in an oil company, you have thousands of options at your fingertips: all different combinations of brokers, exchanges, companies, and even types of stocks. If you want to buy a new oil furnace for your house, you only have to look in a telephone directory or on the Internet. But if you want to hire a skilled oil pipeline technician, where do you look? There are job agencies and Web sites, sure. But these tools are nowhere near as comprehensive as in the financial and product markets, where almost all of the relevant purveyors are within easy reach.

International labor markets still rely heavily on word of mouth. That slows them down, and it also leads to bad matches between jobs and workers. Workers migrate by choice, in most cases, but they don't always find what they expected in their new homes. One of them is Zhang Rongde, who works on a Web site for footwear suppliers in Jinjiang City, in the Quanzhou region of Fujian Province, on China's eastern coast. Here's what he wrote about his life in 2005, at the height of China's growth:

I was born in a village in Guanghan County, a small town thirty miles away from Chengdu, the capital of southwest Sichuan Province. Before China's massive economic reform nearly thirty years ago, in my village, there is no electricity, no TV, no refrigerators, no use of toothpaste. People there lived a very traditional way of life resembling lives of our ancestors several hundred years ago. Very few people ever went out of the county except that they joined the army or entered into colleges to study . . .

The city where I live is a manufacturing base for textiles and footwear in China. The sneaker production according to the local statistics occupies two-fifths in China and one-fifth in the world. And many are exported to Western countries. The world's largest retailer, U.S. company Wal-Mart, already set up a logistic center here for purchasing shoes . . .

The labor here is extremely cheap. And the price of labor remains unchanged for a decade while the local economy increases at the double digit every year. Generally speaking, the working time of factories here is more than twelve hours and without weekend to rest. The monthly salary for workers is from 500 yuan to 1,000 yuan a month [about $60 to $120] . . .

Thousands of migrant workers as well as me from inland China come to this coastal city and seek their fortune. Most of them work in the so-called sweat factories. World-famous footwear producers like Puma, Skechers, and Nike have contract factories here. But for most of them what awaits them is not heaven but hell.

The reason that Chinese textiles are so cheap is not mainly because Chinese are so efficient, but mainly because the rights of workers are overwhelmingly ignored and the environment is seriously polluted. The situation in Jinjiang exactly proves it. Many people should buy bottled water to drink since the river is heavily polluted, and even the tap water doesn't conform to sanitary standards and [is] poisonous to health. The migrant workers, who seek their fortune in a strange place, where they don't know the local dialect, can only earn a little more than *their basic expenditure on food, while they risk their health and lives in very poor conditions.*

The migrant workers bring serious problems [while they] bring huge profit to China. For example, the sexually transmitted diseases here are extremely rampant, because they need to release the physical and psychological pressure. To visit a prostitute here just costs about 20 to 30 yuan—about $2.50 to $3.50—because migrant workers can only pay such a low price.

This sort of thing has happened before, of course. The millions of people who moved to the United States in the late nineteenth and early twentieth centuries believing the streets were paved with gold, as the old saying goes, more often found hard work in unsafe factories and cramped homes in tenements or row houses. Today, the hazards can be just as bad, or worse. For example, human rights groups annually detail widespread physical and sexual abuse of women who leave the Philippines, Malaysia, and Indonesia to be domestic servants elsewhere in Asia.

Illegal immigrants are particularly at risk of acting on poor information. In Europe, they often find themselves in a sort of indentured servitude as they work off supposed debts to people traffickers. In the United States, scores of people entering from Latin America die in the desert borderlands of the Southwest, unprepared for the rigors of the journey.

But when buyers and sellers of labor do have good information about each other, the trade in labor is like any other kind of trade; both sides gain, with some good and bad side effects.

The basic gains are the same as in any kind of employer-employee relationship; person A would rather work and receive wages than be at leisure, and person B would rather pay for person A's work and its output than use the money for other purposes. They exchange, and they're both better off. The fact that person A has to move in order to complete the deal is part of the calculus, for better or for worse.

Migrants bring more economic effects with them than regular workers, however. When they leave their countries, they take with them all the skills that could have contributed to economic growth at home. In some countries, those skills are direly needed.

For example, the World Bank released a report in October 2005 stating that 84 percent of Haiti's college-educated citizens did not live in Haiti—a country that ranks 153rd out of 177 in the UN's index of human development, a holistic measure of living standards. The 84 percent figure may be inflated by people who left the country as children, but their parents may have taken the family abroad for the same reason that many adult graduates emigrate: better opportunities abroad, or little chance for advancement at home. Haiti is poor and corrupt. People who invest in their own education may doubt that they'll receive a decent return—either because of patronage or because there are too few good jobs. Even if they can earn a good wage, they may decide that protecting the rewards of their labor is too difficult.

As a result, Haiti finds itself in a trap. It can't hold on to its best workers without improving living conditions, but improving living conditions will be much tougher without its best workers. There is one saving grace, however: remittances.

When goods and services move from one country to another, money or securities move in the opposite direction to pay for them. When people move, they often choose to send cash back to their relatives and friends. In Nicaragua, these remittances accounted for 18 percent of national income in 2004. Elsewhere in Latin America and also in Southeast Asia, the percentage is not quite as high, but still substantial.

Research in various countries has shown that remittances can be essential for buying household necessities, to the extent, for example, that they can even reduce infant mortality. (One might ask, though, whether some children would exist without the remittances.) As well as supporting families, the remittances can provide hard currency—dollars, euros, and the like—to countries that would otherwise have trouble supporting their exchange rates and importing goods and services.

In the long term, however, the remittances may still be less useful to the receiving countries than the skilled labor that produced them would have been. If a college-educated person earns $40,000 abroad and sends $5,000 home, his or her home country is still missing out on the products of at least $35,000 worth of work.

Though migrants are often the subject of xenophobia or discrimination in their new homes, they do bring some extra economic benefits with them. In addition to taking jobs that local people either can't or won't fill, they bring new ideas and techniques to the workplace. And for many wealthy countries, they bring an extra bonus by contributing to the local pension systems.

In the United States, most of Europe, and Japan, retired people are outnumbering workers by a greater ratio every year. With lower fertility rates, each generation isn't replacing itself with enough new workers to pay for its pensions. Migrants ride to the rescue by jumping straight into the labor force and, when they do so legally, paying into social security and private pensions right away. Elderly migrants are rare, and children are, in some ways, even better than migrants of prime working age. They can be educated in their new countries, and chances are that they'll earn more than their parents. By the time they start working, the pension systems will need contributions more than ever.

This point is sometimes overlooked in debates about offshore outsourcing. The call centers used by American and British banks in India and the Philippines, for example, are just a way to import labor without actually moving any people. Migrants, on the other hand, not only pay into pension systems but also funnel most of their income back into the local economy by paying for food, housing, and other necessities. Offshore workers don't; the only benefit to the country of their employers comes when shareholders receive higher profits, as a result of lower labor costs.

As with any kind of trade, however, there are losers as well as winners. If a migrant worker can do a job more cheaply than a local person, then that local person may soon have to find a new line of work. Moreover, the migrant may be bringing his or her cheap labor to an industry that, in the most efficient use of the economy's resources, would die off. For example, it would be possible to keep the American textile industry running in its current state for much longer if tens of thousands of low-paid Bangladeshis were brought over to work in the factories. But it might make more sense simply to buy textiles from Bangladesh while using the American industry's land, factories, and financing for something else.

These issues have been particularly contentious in the European Union, where the joining of ten new countries in 2004 created new pathways for workers, who have mostly moved from east to west. Despite the ability of EU citizens to live in any of the twenty-five member countries, expanding their businesses across borders is not always so easy. A chiropractor certified to practice in Slovenia, for example, may have to obtain new certifications or licenses before opening up shop next door in Austria.

Evelyne Gebhardt is on the front lines of this debate. She's the member of the European Parliament—the union's legislative body—who's responsible for working behind the scenes to forge an agreement on the mobility of workers in services. On June 15, she was being torn between domestic politics and the interests of the union as a whole. It was a volatile time; in the past few weeks, both France and the Netherlands had rejected the proposed EU constitution, which would have paved the way for closer economic ties between the members. The next day the heads of government from all twenty-five members were meeting in Brussels to discuss the union's future.

BRUSSELS (SIX HOURS AHEAD OF NEW YORK)

Today will be a hard day. I have got up at five in the morning to catch my plane from Stuttgart, Germany, to Brussels, because I have to attend my first meeting of the day at 9:00 a.m.—the meeting of the committee on internal market and consumer protection of the European Parliament.

The main subject of the day certainly is the services directive, a very exciting issue. It is a proposal for a legislative text drafted by the European Commission that aims at improving the freedom of services within the European Union. I welcome the general approach of the commission, but in my opinion, the draft text is far from being perfect.

Today the president of the competitiveness council of the European Union is attending our committee meeting, and it is funny that all members of parliament seem to agree on the good work he has done on the services directive, though among themselves the members are constantly arguing about the issue. Basically, the conservatives are aiming at more competition, whereas we Social Democrats want to protect the European social model and workers' and consumer rights.

Here in Brussels, we are all fighting for a good European legislation—that is why I was shocked to hear today that my own political group in the German national parliament wants to reject the whole legislative proposal! For me, one thing is certain: I will continue on my way in order to obtain, at the end of the procedure, a services directive that both opens the markets and respects workers' rights. That is important, that's what I am fighting for in this European Parliament!

Finally, the committee meeting is over, and I am having a nice lunch break sitting in a restaurant with a colleague and a French journalist. Obviously, we discuss the services directive and the political options after the French "non" to the European constitution.

Now back to work. Together with my colleagues from the German Social Democrat delegation I am meeting the vice president of the European Commission—another intense discussion on Europe's future after the negative outcome on two referenda on the constitution and on Europe's financial perspectives.

Later, discussions continue, but this time it's lobbyists who are coming to see me in my office in order to explain their point of view on various legal projects. It is very important to meet these people and to listen; they can give us members of parliament an expert view on complicated topics—but of course, between all the different positions you are confronted with, you always have to make up your own mind!

Just as in export markets, there is a fine line in international labor markets between protection and protectionism. Extra licensing requirements for service businesses have the same effect as stringent sanitary regulations for crops. At moderate levels, they can protect the public; at extreme levels, they serve mainly to prevent trade.

To European politicians devoted to the "social model," preventing trade is not always a bad thing. By stemming the flow of migrant workers, they preserve job security for their constituents. Yet this strategy also deprives their constituents of lower prices and wider choices in markets for everything from advertising to zoo keeping.

It is possible to garner the gains from trade in labor and take care of the local population at the same time, but doing so requires more thought. First, government has to figure out how to compensate workers who lose their jobs to foreign competition—with things like cash payments, retraining, and educational opportunities for them or their children. Next, government has to figure out how to pay for this compensation, preferably by skimming off some of the gains from trade.

For example, let's say the EU decides to create an open market for house cleaners. As a result, thousands of Italian house cleaners will lose their jobs to migrants, let's say from Poland, who are willing to accept lower wages. At the same time, the price of housecleaning will drop significantly. In order to compensate the Italian house cleaners, the government could impose a lump-sum tax on people who purchase housecleaning services—the main beneficiaries of the trade. The tax wouldn't be enough to erase the benefit of lower prices, but it would generate some money to compensate the Italian house cleaners. As the unemployed house cleaners reached the retirement age, and Italians stopped going into the housecleaning profession, the tax could be phased out.

This is a simplification—and one likely to create a black market, at that, since people would probably try to avoid the tax by paying house cleaners under the table—but it does address the problem at the center of most disputes about expanding trade. Economic theory tells us that the benefits to the winners outweigh the costs to the losers, so it must be possible to redistribute the benefits so that everyone is at least as well off as before. But how? Governments haven't come up with too many ingenious mechanisms yet. Even in the United States, where the federal government has spent billions trying to help people laid off by industries rendered unprofitable by foreign competition, retraining programs receive poor reviews.

If more attention were directed toward managing the transition toward open markets, rather than trying to protect against them, that might change. An immigration policy directed purely by economic considerations would strive (1) to fill shortages in the labor market, (2) to recruit as many bright or entrepreneurial people as possible, and (3) to help locals who lose their jobs to find new ways to earn a living.

Policies that put restrictions on immigration don't necessarily help the economy. One example is quotas for immigrants from certain countries, like the United States has; the labor market doesn't really care where someone's from, as long as he has the right skills for a job. Another is the denial of government health benefits, as in the United Arab Emirates; if the economy needs the workers, then surely the economy needs healthy workers. In many countries, migrants must leave immediately when their services are no longer wanted by employers; if they had some time to look for new jobs—rarely an instantaneous process, even for natives—they might continue to help the local economies.

Migrants pay a heavy cost, not just in terms of the tough jobs they do. Though many send money back to their families, those ties can be stretched to the limit, as Zhang relates:

> To migrant workers, to return [to their] hometown is a very difficult thing. Their inland home is at least hundreds of miles away from Jinjiang. It will cost much for them to return home once . . . Many of them even don't go back to home to see their parents and wives and husbands and children for more than three years. Another difficulty for migrant workers to return home is that they fear they will lose the current jobs if they leave.
>
> They can stay here. But they can't be formal inhabitants if they can't buy houses here, even if they [came] here more than a decade ago. For example, I already stayed in Fujian since 1997, while my hukou (permanent residence permit) is still in Guanghan County, Sichuan Province. Without a local hukou, it means that you lose many advantages that local people have, such as the allowance on education, health, communication, and the entry condition for better job in government and public organizations. Migrant workers, in the words of the government, have to live temporarily in their motherland.
>
> I never heard that migrant workers in Jinjiang started a family here. For most of them they can only seek spouses in their hometown. Many conditions prevent them starting family here, including the economic conditions, the discrimination by the locals, and the language barrier, etc. They maybe find their spouses here, while they have to marry in their hometown.

Even this happens very little because they have little free time to communicate with others. Most of them toil to work a long time every day like a machine in factories and construction zones.

Though the pay of most of migrant workers in Jinjiang is below 1,000 yuan [$120] a month (at least 500 yuan of that they should spend on food and other necessary expenditure), most of them send money to their relatives at home. Generally speaking, migrant workers remain with the strongest Chinese traditional ethics: How can a man forget his family responsibilities? They have the responsibilities to feed old parents and children and their younger brothers and sisters and take care of their lives.

China's involvement in global economy greatly changes the lives of peasants. Young people, wherever they come, cities or rural areas, they want to watch TV, own their own mobile phones, their own modern houses . . . That is to say, after thirty years' economic reform, when China becomes an important global player, everyone's life is changed and confused . . . however, can all achieve their dreams? Few, probably very few for the peasants can do this, while many will pay heavy cost for these great changes I believe.

If migration were easier within China, and around the world, then these social costs might be somewhat reduced. Markets for labor, however, are likely to be the last ones where trade becomes truly free. Despite migrants' strong reputation for helping economies in the long term, xenophobia and racism have given them a bad name. It's understandable that people in country X might not want a bunch of poorer people from country Y to come along and hang out until they can find jobs. But millions of people aren't even allowed to try, in large part because it can be hard to find and send back the ones who fail.

Faced with these problems, some countries are trying to bring back their own expatriates. In November 2005, in the midst of severe labor shortages in several service industries, New Zealand launched a program designed to make coming back easier and more attractive for its far-flung citizens. A Web site supplies everything from mortgage rates to job leads for the expatriates, who make up about 10 to 15 percent of New Zealand's native-born population. And expatriates have several advantages over other migrants: they have no legal or language problems, they settle down easily, and they usually have families to fall back on.

Canada probably has about a million expatriates, the vast majority of whom live in the United States, to judge by figures from 2001. Luring them north may not be easy. Knight's council has an idea for one part of Canada's petroleum sector, though. Oil rigs off the country's eastern coast are facing a shortage of underwater technicians. The solution? "Robotics may play a larger role . . ."

CHAPTER 12

NEW YORK
7:26 P.M.
JUNE 15

CARBONDALE
6:26 P.M.
JUNE 15

"FORMER SIU AVIATION STUDENTS SUE HOOTERS AIR OVER BUSINESS PLAN" DOES IT HELP THE ECONOMY WHEN IDEAS HAVE OWNERS?

Ideas drive the global economy forward. Everything we make and consume came from an idea. Our instincts tell us that we want food, warmth, safety, and the rest, but ideas tell us how to find, create, and keep those things. In the production of goods and services, there are ideas, and then there's replication—end of story.

Well, almost. Ideas sometimes hit us like lightning bolts from the blue, but more often they're the product of focused thinking: brainstorming, problem solving, call it what you will. And ideas don't always pop into our heads fully formed. Most of the time, the best ideas need a bit of fleshing out. That takes work. So to keep the ideas flowing, it's probably a good idea to reward people for putting in the time required to develop the good ones.

Back in the fall of 1997, a trio of students at Southern Illinois

University's Carbondale campus were pretty sure that they had a good one. Sean Peirick, Michael Watts, and James Johnson had been students in Bob Kaps's airline management class. That may sound like an atypical part of a college curriculum, but SIU is a somewhat atypical university. The rambling campus sits on the edge of the Shawnee National Forest, with the usual collection of high-rise dormitories, low-rise offices, parking lots, and classrooms. But on the outskirts of the campus is the university's own airstrip, proud home to a Boeing 737, a McDonnell Douglas DC-9, and a few dozen Cessnas.

Since 1979, SIU has offered classes in aviation management. Professor Kaps, who was once the director of personnel at TWA, has been teaching undergraduate students how to run an airline for most of that time. It was in a square classroom in building 9-D, a brick bunker erected with a grant from the Federal Aviation Administration, that he assigned the trio and their classmates the same final project that he poses every year: Imagine that your wealthy uncle leaves you three DC-9s, a couple of Canadair regional jets, and several million dollars. They're all yours, on the condition that you use them to start an airline.

Broken up into small teams, the students have always dived into the project with gusto. Visit Kaps at SIU, and he'll show you shelf after shelf of spiral-bound business plans, some running to over a hundred pages. There are videocassettes, too, where the students recorded their own advertisements and promotional presentations.

The trio was no exception. They thought they had lightning in a bottle—a revolutionary idea that would combine air travel and entertainment for a very, let's say, discerning audience. What better way to soften the bumps of in-flight turbulence, they thought, than by staffing the cabins with the bustiest waitresses in America? Their plan was to combine the amenities of Hooters, a chain of casual dining establishments lately known by the slogan "Delightfully tacky, yet unrefined," and a low-cost regional carrier. The result was to be known as . . . Hootair.

That Hootair could jump from the pages of a business plan into real life was not so far-fetched a notion. A few years earlier, some of Kaps's students had played a starring role in the launching of Vanguard Airlines, which operated out of Kansas City until 2002.

"We had a group of students who were all pilots," Kaps remembers. "They put together an airline, and they wanted a hub in Kansas City. So they got on planes and flew up there to talk to the airport manager. He introduced them to the mayor. All of a sudden these kids are working together very closely with the city."

The Hootair trio was so enthusiastic, Kaps says, that they started advertising in the local Hooters franchise for flight attendants. Calls in response began coming into the aviation management department's office. And once the trio had finished their business plan, they sent it to the company's offices to see if they could hook the management—and the payoff.

In November of that year, they received a letter back from Sal Melilli, a vice president at Hooters in Chicago. "It appears as you have all the bases covered for establishing Hootair airline," he wrote. "We will be forwarding this proposal on to the board of directors . . . we look forward to being part of your inaugural flight."

So far, so good. But it wasn't until March 6, 2003, that an airline called Hooters Air started plying the skies between

Myrtle Beach and Atlanta. And Messrs. Peirick & Co. were not on board.

"I remember getting a phone call from Sean Peirick at my home in St. Louis, and he said he felt slighted," Kaps says. "The next thing I knew, he was looking for an attorney."

The group picked up their original presentation, videotape, and Kaps's grading materials from SIU. On June 15, the lawsuit became public. Hooters headquarters said that Melilli was part of a company that owned several Hooters franchises, and that he was not involved in corporate decision making. The suggestion was that the real bosses of the company, based down in Atlanta, would never have seen the students' business plan. Nevertheless, the case went ahead.

The students in Kaps's class know they have to come up with a good business plan—their grades depend on it. But the chance that a plan could turn into a job, or maybe even a real business, probably drives them a little bit harder. If companies like Hooters can wangle away ideas with impunity, then that incentive will disappear.

The same is true in the global economy as a whole. Some people try to come up with ideas that will make their daily lives easier, and others just sit in their garages and think up new inventions for the fun of it. The potential for profit often overtakes both groups, however. At the moment, it also happens to be under attack.

There are two wars going on in the marketplace for ideas. One is over the usage of ideas in contravention of the laws that protect their owners. The other is over the question of whether these laws should exist at all.

In the first war, the battle lines are drawn by patents, copyrights, trademarks, and other ways of stamping ideas with owners' names. In each case, an idea can only be used for profit—or sometimes in any way at all—with the owner's permission.

The flouting of these rules has become a regular feature of the global economy. Manufacturers in poor countries buy new gizmos developed by companies in wealthy countries, and then reverse-engineer them, taking them apart to unlock their secrets and then producing identical versions on the cheap. Electronic media of all kinds—music, films, software—are easily duplicated en masse, in rich and poor countries alike. Books are photocopied by students at Ivy League universities and street merchants in Vietnam.

Brands are applied with impunity, whether to fake Prada handbags sold on the avenues of Manhattan or to fake 7 For All Mankind jeans sold in Beijing's crowded markets. Sometimes, it's just the *look* of the brand that's stolen. Inattentive tourists who think they've picked up a red-and-white can of Coke in Syria will probably find that they have, in fact, purchased a local tipple called Master Cola.

These rip-offs can damage companies in several ways. The most obvious is lost business; if cheap DVD players with pirated parts hadn't existed, the people who bought them may well have stumped up for a slightly more expensive one. A subtler cost comes in lost reputation; someone who buys a fake Prada handbag for $20 might never have dreamed of buying a real one for $400, but the real ones might be devalued in consumers' minds if everyone knows that fakes are flooding the market. Worse, if you erroneously think that you've got a real Prada bag, only to watch it fall apart after a few days, then your opinion of the brand is likely to plummet.

The most subtle cost has to do with the possibility of future sales. At the time of this writing, American companies were forbidden to do business directly with Syria, so Coca-Cola only arrives there when it has been smuggled from other countries. Yet if the United States ever drops its sanctions against Syria, sheltered consumers might incorrectly see the newly imported Coca-Cola, not the familiar Master Cola, as the rip-off artist.

These costs can detract from companies' bottom lines, but they can also stop new companies from being formed. For example, it's a lot harder to break even as a software company if most of your clientele isn't paying for your programs. In China, up to 90 percent of all software may be pirated. Facing this handicap, a promising Chinese coder might opt to work for a big, established company like Microsoft rather than developing his or her own ideas. And even Microsoft has estimated that a third of all copies of its programs are pirated.

When piracy is rife, legitimate competition can suffer. Ultimately, that means consumers are trading choice for price. Only the companies that can hang on to a sufficient number of paying customers, at a sufficiently high price, will be able to stay in the market while pirates are operating. People who buy the pirated goods will get away with bargains, but there won't be as many products to choose from. The problem is that the consumers who buy pirated goods are forcing this trade-off on everyone else.

Of course, consumers don't always weigh all the effects of their actions. A prime example is Tim Green. He's a Christian evangelist from Day Heights, Ohio, and he made his fortune selling religious films all over the world. He's a man of high morals whose wealth was built on intellectual property, but one day he found himself sitting in a business-class lounge in the Beijing airport with a suitcase full of DVDs—the *Indiana Jones* trilogy, the *Band of Brothers* television series, episodes of *CSI: Crime Scene Investigation*, and more, all for about fifty cents per disc.

"I didn't even think about it when I got them," he said, referring to the likelihood that the discs were pirated. "It didn't even enter my mind."

Nowadays, Green avoids the ownership issue by reprinting old books on religion and history whose copyrights have expired. But he said he didn't think the Chinese pirates were knowingly breaking the law, if the copyrights even existed in China. "I don't know what the laws of China are," he said. "I'm sure they don't know what the laws of America are."

In the most extreme cases of piracy, the number of products being invented could decline to zero. Take a product that's expensive to develop, like a new prescription drug. A drug company needs to recoup the cost of developing a new treatment by selling the product at a profit. With unlimited piracy, anyone could copy the new drug, so it might be impossible to cover the cost of developing it. In that situation, the drug companies would have no incentive to create new treatments.

The current situation is different, though, because drugmakers can rely on patents to protect their chemical inventions. Patenting their drugs around the world gives them temporary monopolies, allowing them to sell their products at a profit and cover the billions of dollars they invested in research. Most patents elapse after a certain number of years, though, so there's limited time for the companies to earn back their investments.

This system has run into controversy in two situations: when drugs are needed by developing countries whose citizens can't afford them, and when drugs are needed in quantities too vast to be produced by the owner of the patent. The first problem is exemplified by the cocktails of drugs that can keep AIDS patients alive, which cost thousands of dollars a year in wealthy countries. Manufacturers in India managed to copy some of the drugs, but doing so became illegal in March 2005.

The issue was a centerpiece of the World Trade Organization's ministerial conference in Hong Kong, in December of the same year. On December 17, the United States became the first of the WTO's members to accept a rule that would allow poor countries to import generic versions of patented drugs for treating diseases like AIDS, malaria, and tuberculosis. The rule awaited the approval of the full WTO.

At about the same time, the second problem had also been brewing in the market for Tamiflu, a drug purportedly capable of protecting people from the H5N1 "bird flu" virus. Roche, a Swiss pharmaceutical company, owned the patent. But worldwide demand, stoked by fears of an epidemic, far outstripped the company's ability to produce the drug. As outbreaks were reported in Asia, governments started to play dirty. Taiwan began to develop a copy of the drug in October 2005, before receiving permission from Roche. Other countries, including Thailand and Argentina, threatened to do the same.

Roche soon began cooperating rather than trying to defend its potential for profit. The company stopped selling the drug in China and turned over its stocks to the central government for distribution. In some countries, like Indonesia, Roche had no chance of making money, anyway; the drug was not patented there, and the government could do what it wanted. The big question, though, was whether Indonesian Tamiflu would be smuggled and resold in countries where the drug was still under patent.

Most incidents that stretch the patent and copyright system don't have to do with urgent needs or the health of millions of people. They're more likely to concern digital media, as in Green's case, or new technologies for electronics and machinery, uncovered by reverse-engineering or stolen by industrial spies. And yet some very intelligent voices have argued for scaling back the patent system.

One argument suggests that patents actually get in the way of innovation by stifling the exchange of ideas. It's hard to figure out how much damage the system can do this way, since it would be a bit like figuring out which great inventions were never invented. But economists, bless them, have tried.

In one study, Fiona Murray, of the Massachusetts Institute of Technology, and Scott Stern, of Northwestern University, looked at innovations that were introduced in scientific papers and later patented. They compared scientists' citations of those papers against citations of other papers whose central innovations were not patented. Once the patents were granted, the citation rate for papers in the first group fell. The economists concluded (ultimately paraphrasing Bernard of Chartres), "Rather than simply serving to facilitate a 'market for ideas,' intellectual property may indeed restrict the diffusion of scientific research and the ability of future researchers to 'stand on the shoulders of giants.' "

A second argument contends that the patent system is open to abuses that may prevent good ideas from entering the economy. A recent episode has added force to this point of view.

Research in Motion is the company that invented the Black-Berry—the wireless e-mail device that is, depending on how you look at it, the salvation or bane of several million workers in the global economy. It turns out, however, that a business called NTP had registered patents on a kind of wireless e-mail network start-ing in 1995, years before BlackBerry hit the market. (Under the law, you can patent a "process" as well as a machine or product.) NTP, which was cofounded by a patent attorney, never tried to build the network or any wireless devices in volume. BlackBerry became a hit using its own proprietary technology. But NTP still sued Research in Motion on the grounds that NTP owned the original idea. In March 2006, after a lengthy litigation, Research in Motion paid NTP over $600 million outside of court to resolve all of NTP's claims against the company.

This practice—squatting on useful processes or products with-out actually investing anything in bringing them into reality—flips the patent system upside down. The idea of patents is to *create* an incentive to build new products, in the knowledge that their sales will be protected from imitators. But in this case, the effect is the opposite: it *destroys* the incentive to build an actual product, for fear of the legal consequences.

According to some worried observers, this practice is growing. Yet that doesn't necessarily mean the patent system should be re-vamped or dismantled. Doing so would run the risk of throwing out the baby with the proverbial bathwater.

Here's why. If squatters were a government's main concern, then it might get rid of the ability to patent ideas without actu-ally putting them into practice. That wouldn't be a problem, as long as anyone with an idea could find the money to put it into practice. And that wouldn't be a problem if the world's financial markets were thorough and meritocratic enough to seek out and reward every single useful thought. The true situation is a bit more slipshod. People who don't have the money to bring their own ideas to life can't always get it. There's usually some uncertainty in the development of new products, and investors—assuming they're sophisticated enough to know where to look for these prospects—won't always take the risk.

So if the bathwater is made up of the squatters, the baby in this case is the innovative underdog—a role played aptly by Messrs. Peirick, Watts, and Johnson. They could come up with the idea for an airline in a class. They could plan it down to the last detail. But they didn't have the money or the connections to actually get Hootair off the ground.

It's unlikely that they could have patented their idea, since patents generally involve technical processes (such as wireless e-mail transmission) or physical products (such as BlackBerrys). But say they could have. Then they wouldn't have needed to show that Hooters actually stole their idea; all they would have had to prove in court is that Hootair and Hooters Air were pretty much the same thing.

Is that too low a hurdle? It probably is, when you think about it. At the moment, there aren't any airlines offering supersonic flight in the stratosphere. Yet that might change sometime in this century, given the way technology is moving. So if you could, you'd obviously draw up a business plan and patent the idea of an airline offering supersonic flights in the stratosphere. After all, you'd know that it would happen eventually. And when it did—cha-ching!—you'd sue and cash in.

Or not. If the bar was set low enough for that sort of behavior to be legal, the patent offices of the world would be inundated with applications from every Tom, Dick, and Harriet with an active imagination. And the real scientists and engineers would have little incentive to invent. There's a reason why, at some point, you have to put in the money and time to make your ideas work.

Sometimes you need to do a little convincing, too. For example, when a supplier tries to sell a new idea to a big company, it must often find an advocate inside the company itself—an intermediary between the inventor and the buyer. Edward Sprock, director of logistics at DaimlerChrysler, was taking on that role on June 15. His position is a powerful one, but he must still sell the biggest and costliest new ideas to his bosses before he can act on them.

AUBURN HILLS, MICHIGAN (SAME TIME AS NEW YORK)

This afternoon I attended a meeting to review a new application of an existing technology. An independent organization is proposing the use of a private monorail to connect supplier/production facilities, thereby eliminating the cost of transportation and enabling material delivery to workstations without the use of fork trucks.

The concept has merit, but the payback might be an issue. As is often the case, the preparation of the business case in a manner that will make sense to all members in our approval chain will be a challenge. The concept solidly supports our objectives of reducing transportation cost and hours per vehicle, but does require significant lead time and a lengthy contractual commitment to allow the proposing organization to build the monorail.

After the meeting and a subsequent one, I ran into these folks in the hall and encouraged them to generate a "virtual video model" of their concept to aid me in selling the proposal.

The trio from SIU spent long hours on their business plan, and many more in their unsuccessful efforts to get Hootair off the ground. Just as making a videotape in 1997 required real resources, so does making a "virtual video model" in 2005. So it's back to the original question: Would that team from the outside company have come to see Sprock if there was a good chance that DaimlerChrysler would turn around and construct the monorail by itself?

The ability to own the fruits of one's ideas is a strong driving force in the global economy. The lack of protection for intellectual property—and of financing to develop it—is one reason for the stubbornness of poverty in much of the world. Without protection for ideas, there's less incentive to innovate, and fewer small businesses are born. Some countries are cottoning on to this situation . . . often when it's shoved in their faces by businesses from other, wealthier nations who are trying to protect their own ideas.

India, for example, was the subject of two disputes in the World Trade Organization, one filed in 1996 by the United States and the other in 1997 by the European Union. Both dealt with India's failure to implement the WTO's agreement on intellectual property rights—in this case, to protect the novelty of foreign pharmaceuticals and agricultural chemicals. Without a remedy, so to speak, generic drugmakers in India would have had open season on medicines developed in the United States and the EU.

The Indian government asked for enough time to implement a patent-protection system, an effort that culminated in major new legislation in 1999. In the meantime, however, it started to throw around the weight of its own intellectual property, for example, the traditional plant-derived medicines that sometimes provide the precursors for mass-market drugs in the West. Before the meeting of WTO ministers in Hong Kong in December 2005, India joined with other developing countries to demand recognition and royalties when traditional products—everything from plant extracts to yoga positions—were used abroad.

As Messrs. Peirick & Co. waded through litigation—even after Hooters Air shut down in April 2006—and India slogged through the never-ending quagmire of WTO negotiations, their chances of success looked about even. But it will take many more decisions, domestically and internationally, before the rules on intellectual property are anything close to black-and-white.

CHAPTER 13

NEW YORK
7:38 P.M.
JUNE 15

DILI
8:38 A.M.
JUNE 16

"EAST TIMOR NOT READY TO HANDLE OIL, GAS REVENUE, GUSMÃO SAYS" CAN A POOR COUNTRY GET RICH TOO QUICKLY?

The young nation of East Timor, or Timor-Leste, started life on the bottom rung of the economic ladder. Indonesian militias made sure of it when they left the territory in 1999, withdrawing to the western part of the island of Timor after a twenty-four-year occupation. A referendum sponsored by the United Nations had given Timor-Leste a path toward independence, but the militias, in a vengeful orgy of destruction, stripped the nation of almost everything else.

There was one thing that the militias couldn't take away, though. It was buried deep under earth and water, and it was Timor-Leste's birthright: oil. When the UN administration finally handed over control to the Timorese in 2002, the world's then-newest democracy devised a plan to guarantee the nation's future using this precious but limited resource. Sell the oil and invest in the nation's productive capacity and its people, and poverty would become a thing of the past.

If only things were that simple. Take a walk on the strip of land between Timor-Leste's rarely used international airport and the beach, and it's clear that little has changed in the past few years, or perhaps in the past few centuries. Families live in thatched huts set between thick-trunked palm trees. Goats loll inside pens that are almost identical to their owners' homes. Naked children, skinny dogs, and skinnier chickens run between the palms. Mosquitoes buzz by menacingly—malaria and dengue fever are very real risks here. The ground is muddy in parts, where the rain from a recent downpour has yet to soak into the sandy soil. Running water and electricity don't exist.

Closer to the main road, a few families have managed to build cinder-block boxes instead of huts, and an occasional car meanders along the pitted dirt track. It's unusual to hear a radio, though, and televisions are nonexistent. The kids are clothed, but the clothes have holes. The adults are sitting around, even on a weekday afternoon. Occasionally one asks hopefully if a visitor is bringing work, rather than just passing through.

Though the air is gorgeously clear over most of this hilly, verdant land, a pale gray haze hangs over Dili, the capital. No one needs heating here, but most people still burn wood for cooking.

That last observation comes, with a sigh, from José Teixeira, Timor-Leste's vice minister for energy and mineral resources. His family fled to Australia after the Indonesian invasion, when he was still a child. But he worked hard to qualify for a free university education, and then became involved in the Labour Party. While he kept up with politics, he studied law and opened a practice dealing with commercial litigation, labor relations, and administrative cases. Then he ran for a seat in the state legislature from Brisbane, but lost in the primary.

"I must confess that after my failure I had fairly well decided that I was never going to be involved again in politics," says Teixeira. But that changed after the Indonesians left. "This is my country," he says in a ringing Australian drawl that contrasts with the soft voices of many Timorese. "It's a dream that some of us grew up with. Being the oldest in my family, I always carried around the ethos of coming back and somehow contributing to the development of this nation. I always believed that there would be an independent country at the end of our struggle."

Teixeira came back to work for the UN, using his Australian passport, and was placed as a bureaucrat with Mari Alkatiri, then the minister of economic affairs. Eventually, he thought he'd move into the private sector, reprising his role as a corporate lawyer. But when Alkatiri became prime minister, he surprised Teixeira with an invitation to join the government. "He told me that he believed that all those of us who truly were nationalists, we should at least give two or three years' service to the nation," Teixeira says. "It's coming up to four already, and by the time we've finished with this, it will be five."

Now Teixeira, whose gray-flecked, closely cropped hair belies his youthful face, sits in a plain white room where, in places, the paint is blistered and cracked. A colorfully woven Timorese cloth stretches across his conference table. The drapes are in another bright pattern, and Timor-Leste's red, black, yellow, and white flag stands proudly in the center of the room, next to his desk. Still, these are modest surroundings for the point man in the biggest economic challenge of Timor-Leste's short history: the development of its oil industry through partnerships with foreign companies.

"What you pay is based on the production, and all payments are transparent," Teixeira says. "The production-sharing contracts themselves are public documents, and all payments made by the companies to the petroleum fund are audited." The government eventually receives about 40 percent of the companies' production, after they've recovered their investments. In addition, the companies pay an income tax for their operations in Timor-Leste.

This may sound like a fantastic prospect for such a poor country—like money dropping from the sky. But other countries that have struck it rich have found that their oil, gas, and mineral resources could become a curse as easily as a blessing.

The bad examples are more numerous than the good ones. Venezuela's economy has become dependent on oil after almost a century of developing the industry. Its people have ridden the waves of oil prices, often accompanied by political instability, without gaining much in return. Between 1976, when the government took over the oil industry, and 2000, the average purchasing power in Venezuela actually dropped by more than 1 percent a year. Even between 2000 and 2005, as oil prices skyrocketed, per capita purchasing power was stagnant.

Starting in the 1970s, Nigeria reaped hundreds of billions of dollars in oil revenue, the World Bank reported in 2004. Yet living standards dropped by about a fifth in the next few decades. In communities where the oil companies operate, protests have broken out among frustrated locals unable to see any benefits from the massive profits collected by the companies and the government. The oil revenue accounts for almost a third of Nigeria's economy. But without transparency in management, it's easier for the money to disappear into private perks, wasteful projects, and overseas bank accounts.

In Sudan, the story is sadder. Exports of oil, which began in 1999, literally added fuel to the fire of the country's decades-long civil war. The government used oil revenue to buy more weapons, and the rebel factions tried to seize control of oil fields and infrastructure in order to gain the money and power that oil promised. According to a report published in 2003 by Human Rights Watch, the fierce fight for oil led to mass displacement of Sudanese, with atrocities committed along the way. Perhaps mercifully, the oil fields that were most productive were expected to become much less valuable, with yields cut by over 80 percent, by 2020.

In the meantime, São Tomé and Príncipe—a country consisting of two fish- and coconut-dependent islands off Africa's western coast—was gearing up for its own production, the result of an underwater windfall much like Timor-Leste's. But first it had to satisfy a couple of big brothers: neighboring Nigeria and the United States, whose Chevron oil company won the right to develop much of the offshore oil resources.

To resolve the issue of territorial waters, São Tomé's government agreed to give Nigeria a share of the revenue in 2001. In the following year, it said it would allow the United States to build a military base on its shores, ostensibly to protect the oil. By 2005, however, locals watching the nation's elite building fancy new houses and driving swish new cars were beginning to doubt whether the money would help to lift them out of poverty. The discontent rose sufficiently to prompt a reshuffling of the government, which the president apparently preferred to the alternative of early elections.

Chad was supposed to set a new example. By the time its oil revenue started to flow in 2004, the country had pledged to use 80 percent for education, health care, and basic infrastructure. The money was to be held in an escrow account in London until a citizens' committee decided how to spend it. People in the extraction areas were given money, too, though there's some evidence that many of them, never having had cash to save before, splurged it all away within days.

The World Bank had garnered these promises of good behavior by lending landlocked Chad money to build a pipeline to a port in Cameroon—a necessity for selling the black ooze. But problems started early. First, the citizens' committee complained that it couldn't get enough information from the government or from the foreign oil companies to do its job properly. Further questions arose when the government placed the president's brother-in-law on the committee. Then, in December 2005, the government moved to wrest control of some revenues from the committee, in order to deal with fiscal problems. The World Bank responded angrily, but its threats to cut off funding may have been difficult to hear over the pipeline's noisy rush. Within a month, the bank followed through on its threat; it froze the account in London and suspended up to $124 million in planned lending to Chad. But the government, saying it needed money to buy arms and fight rebels, warned that it would cut off oil shipments if the World Bank didn't reverse itself. In April 2006, the two sides reached a deal, and the oil kept flowing.

As Teixeira will tell you, Norway is one of the few countries that has dodged oil's slippery bullet. Major deposits of oil were discovered in its waters in the late 1960s, and the price spikes of the 1970s, together with further finds of oil and natural gas, turned a modest industry into a cash cow. Luckily for the Norwegians, their country hadn't been plagued by corruption or civil war in the same way as Nigeria, Sudan, and others had. The government set up a ministry to formulate oil policies and, later, a fund to collect oil revenue and invest it for the future; only 4 percent of the annual revenue can be spent rather than saved.

In the meantime, the rest of Norway's economy developed apace with western Europe. Now the fund's managers prefer to invest abroad, for fear that the country would otherwise end up with a bloated private sector and runaway inflation. The fund itself will help to cover the pension benefits of Norway's aging population—a relatively easy solution to a difficult problem faced by many wealthy nations.

Despite the differences between them, Norway is the example that Timor-Leste's government hopes to follow, with a couple of twists. Timor-Leste has recruited advisers from Norway, some who used to work with the petroleum fund there. But it's also brought in people from the United States, Canada, Portugal, Indonesia, Malaysia, Australia, and the U.K., Teixeira says. And unlike Norway, Timor-Leste has an explicit process for spending oil revenue, with no specific limits. "All the government ministries make a budget, we take it to the parliament, it's debated in the parliament, then the parliament passes a law, and that law tells the government how it's going to spend that money," Teixeira says. "We've got a law that says all the money that comes out of the petroleum fund has to go through that process."

Like Chad, Timor-Leste has a consultative council that's supposed to advise the government on how to spend the oil money. But Timor-Leste lacks the same kind of safeguards that exist in Chad and, less controversially, Norway. "Nowhere in that legislation does it prohibit the parliament from taking more than the council says is advisable or sustainable," Teixeira says. "Some international NGOs [nongovernmental organizations] wanted us to put it into law that the parliament may not spend any more, but we couldn't do it—the constitution says we couldn't do it."

Timor-Leste is already spending some of its existing revenue, which comes from oil fields jointly developed with Australia, on sanitation, the water supply, education, public health, and housing. But it is also saving, Teixeira says, contrary to the advice of the International Monetary Fund and others, who have been encouraging Timor-Leste to spend its money on development as it comes in.

"If we don't start to save this money now, then it will be all the harder for us to teach people to save in the future," Teixeira explains. The petroleum fund's operational management agreement, which is available online at www.transparency.gov.tl, states that the money is being held for the central bank at the Federal Reserve Bank of New York.

Some Timorese have been puzzled, though, by the publicity surrounding the country's apparently imminent wealth. Tony, a construction worker who didn't want to give his last name, could be among Timor-Leste's winners. He already drives a snazzy pickup truck and sports shiny sunglasses along with his neatly trimmed goatee. Driving into Dili one afternoon, he said the situation was still less than transparent to him.

"They told us that the money is coming, but we don't know when, and we don't know for what," Tony said. He also said that he'd heard the revenues would be deposited in New York but that he didn't know if it was true. But Tony was quick to add that he wasn't looking for a handout.

"We don't need the government to give us money," he said. "We need the country to go up," that is, to grow. "When the country goes up, then there are more jobs."

If nothing else, Timor-Leste is committed to charting its own path toward that growth. The government has even turned down loans from the World Bank in order to avoid any preconditions on its economic policies. It's a gesture that many other poor countries, without the luxury of oil, probably couldn't bring themselves to make.

So, with a top-of-the-line system for managing oil revenue in place and, as a young democracy, the backing of many powerful countries, what could possibly go wrong? Xanana Gusmão, Timor-Leste's president, thought he knew on June 15.

Gusmão, who was a rebel leader during the Indonesian occupation, holds a largely ceremonial post. But he has sometimes tried to play the role of the country's conscience, or at least its wise older brother. And to him, things were moving too fast. He was particularly concerned that a debate over Timor-Leste's sea border with Australia was being pushed aside while the two countries agreed to split some of the profits from their joint holdings. He had broader concerns, too.

"Why are we rushing?" he said in a report by Bloomberg News. "Having billions of dollars to rest in the bank? We already have the institutions, but we don't yet have people who can assure that we will stand on a culture of transparency, a culture of effective handling of problems."

Timor-Leste wouldn't be the first country with a new government to get carried away by a nascent capitalism. Under Boris Yeltsin's leadership, Russia sold off many of the state's economic crown jewels, including much of its big oil and gas companies, in a rash wave of privatization. The sell-offs were poorly orchestrated, and a few well-connected financiers managed to buy the companies on the cheap. For years, Vladimir Putin's government has been trying to claw back those assets, sometimes using tactics that could euphemistically be described as unconventional.

A more distant example is that of the United States. Though founded on a charter of individual rights, the nation had its period of runaway enterprise in the so-called Gilded Age, from the late nineteenth through the early twentieth century. At that time, the richest financiers had the power to single-handedly move markets, and they often exploited that power at the expense of ordinary investors. The biggest tycoons monopolized markets for steel, oil, and other commodities with impunity. Mills and factories soaked up migrant workers—including many children—by the hundreds of thousands, but they worked and lived in horrible conditions. For the first time, the United States also had a class of super-rich: bona fide billionaires.

It was a period of unusually fast growth for the American economy: gross domestic product expanded by about 3.8 percent per year between 1870 and 1913, compared with 3.4 percent since the end of World War II. But the excesses of the Gilded Age were ultimately curtailed in favor of individual and commercial rights: abolition of child labor, protection of unions, transparency in securities markets, outlawing of monopolies. Tycoons became philanthropists, endowing universities and art museums—perhaps to salve their consciences, perhaps to improve their legacies.

Lately, this pattern has been repeated in places that have shot from low- or middle-income levels into the ranks of the wealthy within only a couple of decades: Taiwan, Singapore, the United Arab Emirates, and Hong Kong. They have sucked in millions of migrant workers, many of whom live in conditions that their bosses would find appalling. Income inequality has risen to levels that countries of long-standing wealth would find distasteful. And discussions of greater regulation and civil rights—not to mention conservation of the natural environment—are just starting to get off the ground.

Could these economies have grown as quickly had they stopped along the way to control the side effects? Perhaps not. But their growth had costs for the workers and families who suffered, as well as for the consumers and investors who received raw deals along the way, through uncompetitive markets and rigged share prices. If Timor-Leste shoots forward as quickly, or more so, it may face some of the same trade-offs.

Gusmão identified another basic reason for uncertainty, if not necessarily for doubt. Even with its legislative framework, Timor-Leste still couldn't be sure that all its officials would act properly. It was a bit like trying to create life in Dr. Frankenstein's lab; you added all the ingredients together, and then hoped that the spark did the trick. But as Chad's experience showed, sometimes the ingredients—in this case the government officials and the oil company bosses—didn't do what you expected.

There was also a question of skills. Propelled into negotiations with experienced diplomats and businesspeople by its oil, did Timor-Leste's government have the right stuff to manage everything? Their outside consultants would help, but ultimately the buck would stop with people like Teixeira, of whom the country had precious few. And even he came under political pressure, as a highly placed official who largely avoided the hardships of the Indonesian occupation, from Timorese whose families had stuck it out.

Timor-Leste's officials were on a very steep learning curve. But since they're essentially starting from scratch, it will take years before their number includes someone like Carlos Steneri. He represents Uruguay's economic interests, including its government's borrowing, in Washington—and he has done so for sixteen years. On June 15, he was preparing to return to Montevideo, a trip he makes several times a year, to give personal updates about his activities to the minister of finance, the governor of the central bank, and others.

WASHINGTON, 12:15 P.M. (SAME TIME AS NEW YORK)

As the financial representative of the Ministry of Finance and the central bank here in Washington, D.C., we have some matters to discuss about the International Monetary Fund program and the lending program of the World Bank. So the idea is to figure out some strategies for the program and the conditionalities that we have to comply with.

I am in this position since 1989, so I have quite a strong relationship with these institutions and also with agencies of the government of the United States, like the U.S. Treasury and the Federal Reserve Bank of New York—agencies that are connected to the lending position of this country.

I am in charge of issuing bonds, so I am with one foot in Uruguay and one foot here in the United States, close to the street. That's the idea of being here.

To Steneri, developing personal relationships, through his shuttling back and forth between Uruguay and the United States, is as important to his job as his own skills.

234

You have the flavor. You can better approach the matters that you have to solve . . . I have other meetings with people there, for example, economists, people from the central bank and other ministries who are directly engaged with the problems we are dealing with . . . You can do a lot of things through an e-mail, but the personal touch, there is no substitute for that.

Uruguay is a developing country, but it's nowhere near as poor as Timor-Leste. Even with grant money, it's not easy for Timor-Leste's fledgling government to send diplomats around the world several times a year. For starters, there was just one commercial airline flying into President Nicolau Lobato airport in the fall of 2005. Timor-Leste's revenue base and its links to the outside world will have to develop in tandem with the skills and experience of its officials.

Teixeira probably won't be around for that process. He says he plans to return to private life after the contracts are signed and the petroleum program is well on its way. Still, he adds that he's already learned a lot during his years in government—even things he didn't learn during his stint in Australian politics.

"People can alienate themselves, by their actions, by their words," he explains. "You can be forceful, achieving many of the things you want to achieve, including changing mentality and culture, without being in people's faces all the time."

Despite Teixeira's attitude, Timor-Leste's government may indeed have alienated its population. In May 2006, Timor-Leste announced that Italy's Eni and India's Reliance Industries had won the first auction for rights to develop its offshore oil fields. Within hours of the announcement of the winning bidders in the oil rights auction, groups of disillusioned veterans and jobless young men attacked government forces in and around Dili. Australian troops rushed to the capital to try to head off a civil war. Not everyone, evidently, could be patient when it came to developing the young democracy's economy.

CHAPTER 14

NEW YORK
10:41 P.M.
JUNE 15

BANGKOK
9:41 A.M.
JUNE 16

"THAI AIRWAYS WILL OMIT INTERIM DIVIDEND AS COST OF FUEL RISES" DO DISRUPTIVE SHOCKS HELP THE ECONOMY IN THE LONG TERM?

In 2005, almost thirty-nine million passengers traveled through Bangkok International Airport, making it the eighteenth busiest hub in the world and the second busiest on Asia's mainland. Stroll through the terminal on a random day, and you'll see flights leaving for everywhere from Amman to Zurich. As well as being a popular target for tourists, Thailand is a natural pivot point between the population centers of southern and northern Asia, the Middle East, Australia, and the Americas.

One of the main beneficiaries of this geographical accident is Thai Airways International. Being the national carrier of a country with sixty-five million people is not always enough to guarantee worldwide recognition or clientele; just look at Vietnam Airlines, a few hundred miles away in a country of eighty-four million. But THAI, as it's usually known, has been able to take advantage of Bangkok's positioning and Thailand's growth.

Take the forty-minute ride into town on the elevated airport highway, above a man-made plain dotted with ever-taller sky-scrapers, and it's clear that the country is growing fast . . . if a little chaotically. Down in the gridlock, the taxis are brand-new Toyota sedans. Boutique hotels are popping up all over. Roadside snack stands are being crowded out by indoor food courts in spotlessly clean malls.

This growth emerged from a crisis, the financial panic that ravaged Southeast Asia in 1997 and 1998. The Thai economy had already been leaping forward for several years. Though the value of the Thai currency, the baht, had been fixed to the dollar, interest rates were much higher than in the United States. Foreign capital flooded into Thailand, and Thai companies borrowed extravagantly.

But by 1996, some investors suspected that the debts were unsustainable. There would have to be a reckoning, and the only way out would be to lower the international value of the debts by letting the baht slide. Anticipating this move, the investors sold the baht by the billions, causing its informal value on world markets to plummet.

In July 1997, faced with the difficulty of propping up the baht (which might have required exhausting Thailand's reserves of foreign currency), the government abandoned the link to the dollar. The official exchange rate sank, and Thai companies saw the value of their baht-denominated assets plunge in parallel. The financial system foundered across the region as other countries came under the same cudgel.

In the aftermath, the Thai government strove to put its books in order by selling off state-owned businesses and fighting inflation. A painful price was paid, but the country emerged with a stronger currency and a more market-oriented economy.

Looking back, one could argue that many of Thailand's problems in the late 1990s were of its own making. It took foreign investors to upset the applecart, but the wheels were already swiveling dangerously. After Thailand righted itself, things stayed pretty quiet for six years—until another crisis arrived.

The tsunami that hit Southeast Asia in December 2004 extracted a massive toll, both human and economic. Though many lives might have been saved by a better warning system, the sheer force of the wave meant that extensive material damage—especially to Thailand—was unavoidable.

At the vanguard of the recovery effort was THAI. As the beachside resorts raced to rebuild, the government asked the company to take the lead in bringing tourists back to Thailand. Indeed, it had no choice. Sure, the airline needed the tourist trade just as badly as the hotels. But there was something else: though the government had sold stakes in THAI sporadically since the early 1990s, more than half of the shares still belonged to the Finance Ministry.

And so began a crucial time in THAI's history. Until the tsunami, the government's support and Bangkok's fortuitous location had been enough to carry it through any challenging times, even though its services weren't always up to the standard of the world's other big carriers. While airlines in Europe and the United States struggled under increasing costs and competition from budget airlines, often being forced to merge or declare themselves bankrupt, THAI always managed to make a small profit. It served four times as many destinations abroad as it did in Thailand.

The tsunami stretched THAI close to the limit, though. After supplying free flights to rescuers and the rescued, the company began a marketing blitz to lure holidaymakers back to the country's cool clubs and warm waters. Profits narrowed accordingly. Then a mere tidal wave turned into the perfect storm.

From December 2004 to June 2005, the price of jet fuel rose by almost a quarter, after rising by 44 percent in the previous twelve months. Oil prices were mainly to blame. And as John Olson of 2003 Houston Energy Partners was finding out on the morning of June 15, things would probably get worse for companies like THAI before they got better.

8:30 A.M. HOUSTON (9:30 A.M. NEW YORK)

I run an energy hedge fund in Houston, and the markets are about to open. Houston is the largest smokestack economy in the world. It is home to hundreds of oil and gas companies, not to mention hundreds of oil field service companies. Because of the latest worldwide upsurge in oil and gas prices, Houston is the place to be.

The markets have opened higher for both stocks and oil and natural gas prices. The portfolio is climbing in value; but unfortunately some of our short positions are going up as well. In an energy bull market, the incoming tide lifts all the boats, including the shipwrecks. My trader and comanager duly note all of this as well. Hedge funds are noisy affairs. Any incremental news is piped up almost immediately. Bad news is often yadda-yaddaed by everyone, with no small amount of trash talk following after. As I think about it, good news gets about the same treatment. Hedge fund culture is probably

240

about the same level as a fraternity or sorority. Everyone has a voice and is not shy about making himself heard.

At market openings, there is usually a flurry of phone calls back and forth with traders and salesmen to see about any reactions to overnight developments. I'm right in the middle of them. The news is good: OPEC has been meeting in Vienna, and no real change in output is foreseen. Crude oil is trading up to $55 per barrel, and has risen 30 percent this year.

With no more production from OPEC, oil prices were unlikely to fall anytime soon. That might have been good news for Olson, whose fund had invested in oil companies, but THAI's cosseted existence had left the airline ill prepared for this kind of crisis. Unlike many other big airlines, it did not make very extensive use of the financial markets to hedge against rising fuel costs—for example, by buying options to purchase oil at fixed prices in the future. (The oil could be sold at a profit if prices rose, which would offset correspondingly higher costs of jet fuel.) In May 2005, THAI reported that it had used hedging to lock in prices for less than a third of the fuel it needed for the year.

By June 15, the airline was experiencing some very severe turbulence. The answer to one question hung in the balance: Could THAI imitate Thailand, and emerge from the crisis stronger than before?

Then the ax fell, and the first to suffer were shareholders. The company decided not to pay a dividend for the period from October 2004 through March 2005, instead opting to save the cash in case fuel prices climbed even further.

Customers were the next to feel the pinch, when THAI announced that it would raise its fuel surcharges, already implemented in the midst of rising prices in the summer of 2004, by as much as $5 per flight. As a way to deal with higher oil prices, the surcharges were supposed to be a direct substitute for the hedging—something THAI presumably expected its customers to understand.

And then the unthinkable happened. Rumors began to fly that THAI would record a huge loss for the period of April through June. On August 12, Thailand's prime minister, Thaksin Shinawatra, announced that THAI's president had been suspended. Thaksin cited the expected losses but also suspected accounting problems. It wasn't at all odd that the prime minister was making the announcement; half of the board of directors were members of his government. Kanok Abhiradee had been in the job for little more than three years when the board pushed him aside and installed one of its own as acting president: a permanent secretary from the Finance Ministry named Somchainuk Engtrakul.

"The president still remains as our president, Mr. Kanok," said Vasing Kittikul, executive vice president of the airline's commercial department in late August 2005. He asserted that Somchainuk was truly a temporary boss, only for three or six months. "The situation is getting back to normal," he said, "to make THAI more proactive in its operations."

A few days later, the bell tolled: the losses amounted to $114 million. The fuel surcharges increased again after Somchainuk took over. Taken together, the dropped dividend and the increased fuel surcharges may have had some of the same effects as hedging. Had THAI paid to guarantee the price of its fuel supply, it would likely have passed the costs on to consumers and investors in similar fashion, through higher ticket prices. But hedging would have been a more elegant, likely cheaper, and less embarrassing solution; few signals sour the market as much as missing a dividend payment.

"Our president [Kanok] clearly mentioned that since we are not hedging—we are hedging only 25 percent of the oil—that it's not enough to cover the cost," Vasing said. Indeed, Kanok had said just after his suspension that the share of THAI's fuel supply that was hedged had fallen as low as 16 percent. "So that's why we have to adjust the fuel surcharge, to cover some of the cost," Vasing concluded.

THAI learned its lesson. By October, the airline had decided to hedge as much as 50 percent of its fuel supply on a regular basis. And it had made other changes, too. Just like carriers across the United States and Europe, THAI dumped low-margin domestic routes onto its low-cost affiliate, Nok Air.

"Because the domestic airfare is not profitable," Vasing said, "we are going to pass some domestic destinations to Nok Air to fly on behalf of us. We're going to have a codeshare with this low-cost Nok Air, and for the frequent fliers the privileges will be the same. It's a good change because we had been thinking even before the oil price increased, to promote tourism to Thailand and within Thailand, the low-cost carrier should help us."

To hear Vasing tell it, THAI just needed a little kick in the rump to make these changes happen. And by the end of 2005, the airline was starting to look very much like foreign carriers facing more competitive pressures had for several years.

There are plenty of other kinds of kicks in the rump, and some of them can help companies in the same way. For example, say a travel agency's offices are flooded, destroying all its computer equipment and filing systems. The agency has to buy all new stuff, but its insurance foots the bill. Gone are the slow, ob-solete computers and clunky monitors, gone are the filing cabi-nets with sticky drawers and that funny smell. In come the superfast computers with the flat-screen monitors, plus a new set of ergonomic office furniture that makes everything easy to find. Sure, the loss of records is painful, but the agency manages to complete a badly needed clear-out that it might not have been able to afford on its own.

Now, think of a bigger company, like an airline. A flood in one of its offices won't result in the same kind of overhaul, but other things might. For instance, if the airline declared bank-ruptcy, it might also be able to shed a lot of old stuff that's been making its business more difficult to run: hefty loans, promises to pay generous retirement benefits, strict contracts with its unions, some highly paid employees, and even a few unprofitable routes.

Bankruptcy has a dark side, though, and not just for the lenders, investors, employees, and retirees who are left holding the bag. Like flood insurance, the bankruptcy process—which has, at times, been accompanied or replaced by direct aid from the government in the United States, the European Union, and elsewhere—acts as a safety net. But unlike flood insurance, this safety net can create some bad incentives.

There's only so much you can do to protect your business from a flood, and you certainly can't determine the flood's tim-ing very easily. The same is not true for bankruptcy. If you're an executive who knows that the bankruptcy process is there to catch you, you might be more likely to jump.

So you go ahead and take out those big loans, promise those pensions, agree to those pay raises, and fly everywhere you can without worrying about cash flow or strikes. If you still make a profit, great. If not, bankruptcy will give you a chance to start again—assuming you can hold on to your job. Just ask Continental or US Airways; they've both been through bankruptcy twice.

It's a strange state of affairs. Though the Thai government's support cushioned THAI from competition before the perfect storm blew away its complacency, the very promise of a different sort of crisis—bankruptcy, and its forgiveness of previous sins—could re-create that complacency.

But there are other kinds of shocks to the system that can still help companies. One example is a buyout. And plans for buyouts often start when corporate executives, like Kanok, go astray.

Thousands of pages have been written on what drives corporate executives. Shareholders might hope that the executives' main motivation would be making money. Employees might hope that it's keeping the company in business, and their jobs safe. But there are other possibilities. The executives themselves might be trying to build the biggest corporate empire they can, or to see through some pet projects, or to accumulate the most perks, or simply to drive some guy they hated in high school out of business.

In every case except the very first, there's a strong chance that a company won't be geared for maximum profit—the thing the shareholders presumably care about above all else. And when profit seems to be too low on the executives' list of priorities, or when they just don't seem to have a plan, a buyout becomes a possibility. New owners can get the company over the hump, instituting the painful changes that the old executives failed to make. Sometimes, however, they decide that the best thing to do is to sell off the company's assets, on the theory that the whole is worth less than the sum of the parts. That was the case with the purchases by Kohlberg Kravis Roberts—a company whose business was buyouts—of giants like RJR Nabisco and Beatrice, as well as dozens of other companies.

So, to recap, there are at least three reasons why businesses in a changing environment might not make changes that would benefit them in the long term: THAI didn't adapt to the changing market until the crisis came, because it was protected. The hypothetical travel agency didn't adapt until the flood, because it couldn't afford to. And some companies, like the American cigarette manufacturers now paying hundreds of billions of dollars in damages from class-action lawsuits, don't adapt because their managers don't want to. After all, doing so might require admitting some wrongdoing or even firing themselves.

Yet there's a fourth reason for the failure to evolve: not realizing that there's a problem. This accusation has been leveled at American automakers, especially the Ford Motor Company. When it announced tens of thousands of job cuts in January 2006, along with the closure of some old plants, experts suggested that some of the layoffs could have been avoided. Ford had bet too big on thirsty sport-utility vehicles, without realizing that a jump in oil prices could change consumers' preferences. When that jump came, Ford was left as vulnerable as THAI. Unlike THAI, however, Ford's inaction wasn't a result of being coddled; its executives just failed to read the writing on the wall.

Again and again, companies don't catch even a whiff of the proverbial coffee until a crisis squirts some of the steaming liquid up their noses. And it's not just individual companies in this predicament; it can pervade whole sectors and even entire economies, too. Like the corporate scandals discussed in Chapter 2, or the hedge fund meltdown described in Chapter 8, or the workforce deficit that suddenly hit the petroleum industry in Chapter 11, a crisis can sometimes be the only way to see the shortcomings in regulations, monitoring, or strategy. In Argentina's case, as in Chapter 5, a crisis demonstrated the flaws in the monetary system itself.

It's tempting to think of crises in a Darwinian sense. A dry summer or a cold winter weeds out some of the weaker animals in the wilderness; periodic crises in industry could do the same, perhaps even improving the corporate gene pool. Most companies already have an incentive to detect problems and deal with them before they result in catastrophe; even if managers don't have a craving to increase the value of their shares, they probably want to keep their jobs. If they still can't react, a crisis could be the only way—short of a hostile takeover—to slap them into shape.

Yet crises probably shouldn't be welcomed with open arms, no matter what. In the midst of Argentina's financial crisis, its unemployment rate shot up from 15 percent at the end of 2000 to 25 percent at the end of 2001, just before the government was forced to devalue the currency. Within a year, an extra million and a half people had joined the unemployment line. In retrospect, some analysts blamed the United States and the International Monetary Fund for keeping Argentina, with its unsustainable system, afloat for too long. But the country could have worked on its fiscal and monetary missteps earlier as well.

At the national level at least, it may be worth trying harder to detect problems and deal with them. In the financial world, this role has been assigned to the IMF by the world's wealthy countries since its conception during World War II. The fund is supposed to warn countries of crises by assessing their financial situations and, where practical, to use its billions of dollars in re-sources to stave them off. Yet it's hard to tell how many crises the IMF's advice has actually averted, since, after all, those crises didn't happen. What is known is that its advice has often been ignored and has occasionally been misguided from the start.

Even with the right advice, it's hard to deal with problems be-fore they turn into crises. For example, what if a country is start-ing to look like it can't pay its bills tomorrow? As soon as someone points this out, investors will stop lending money to the country's government—and then the crisis happens today.

The same thing can happen to companies. It didn't happen to THAI right away, though. In February 2006, the company an-nounced that it would start a new airline especially for high-end passengers on domestic routes. At the time, THAI was also inter-viewing four candidates to take over the job of president after Kanok's planned departure in April, a month before his term was due to expire. Of course, Kanok wasn't actually in charge; despite what Vasing had said, Somchainuk was still hanging around after six months had passed.

All four candidates were internal; the eight outsiders, who re-portedly included the head of the Thai stock exchange, never made the short list. Why not? According to Somchainuk, they didn't have enough experience running a big organization. Yet the insiders were arguably even less experienced. So who would run THAI if they didn't make the cut? Somchainuk, of course. Only time would tell whether any real lessons were learned.

Clearly, a lot can happen in a day. Actually, June 15—a day cho-
sen almost at random—had enough going on for several books.
Australia's government refused to allow Singapore Airlines to fly
between Sydney and Los Angeles, thus protecting profits for Qan-
tas and United. The world's biggest Internet poker business announced its initial public offering in London. In Qatar, delegates
from 132 developing countries met to discuss a new fund for
fighting poverty.

Those stories flashed around the world on countless computer
screens as trillions of electric impulses passed back and forth
across wires and air. People don't move quite as quickly, but it's
safe to say that most of those delegates in Qatar arrived at speeds
above five hundred miles per hour. Better technology for transport and information greases the wheels of the global economy,
and also draws it closer together. But will the ease of moving
information ever make it unnecessary to move people?

The more people can communicate across long distances—
by e-mail, broadband telephone, videoconferencing, and the
like—the more opportunities there are to cut off face-to-face human contact. Some types of contact can't be replaced so easily,
though, like the meeting Cathy Owen, sales manager of Langs
Hotel in Glasgow (and now an independent style and image consultant), had on the evening of June 15.

5:00 P.M. GLASGOW (12:00 P.M. NEW YORK)

I met a regular client for some drinks in the bar, one of the nicer aspects to my job role. Meeting clients in this informal situation is very important; it builds a relationship and you get to know a customer better when it's not so formal. To other staff it can look like a "jolly" but it is in fact work. I have learned a lot about clients and their expectations and as a result been able to provide the service they require. This particular client wanted to look at our furniture as she is in the process of decorating new offices. They have a very grand event booked with us at the end of the year, which we also discussed, and they required a small meeting venue for Friday, which we were able to provide. It was very productive and I certainly enjoyed the chilled glass of wine.

Owen clearly couldn't do that kind of work by e-mail; even if her client's computer could display three-dimensional holograms of the furniture, there'd still be the thorny issue of the white wine. In fact, there are millions of jobs that can't be done through the ether—like cutting hair, cleaning houses, fixing pipes, or slicing sushi.

Of course, more and more people are using e-mail and other tools to work at home. But improvements in technology have made business travel easier, too. And according to some people who were at work on June 15, there's still no substitute for real, human contact. That's why Andrew Ertel was in Slovakia, Elif Bilgi was in Milan, David Dodge was in Winnipeg, and Carlos Steneri was about to catch a flight to Montevideo.

Sharon Stark was on the road, too. As a managing director and the chief fixed-income strategist at Legg Mason Wood

Walker, an investment firm in Baltimore that is now part of Stifel, Nicolaus & Co., her job is to take the broadest possible view of the global economy. She could theoretically sit in her office all day analyzing numbers and trends. Some of her competitors probably do. Yet she travels all over the United States as the human face of her research, and of her company. Why? Let her explain:

BALTIMORE, MARYLAND (SAME TIME AS NEW YORK)

I had to be up at 5:00 a.m. to leave for a flight to Austin, Texas, where I am supposed to meet up with a colleague from our Dallas office and then on to a morning meeting with a client. The trip to Austin was set up by two of our salespeople in Dallas, Bill Fry and John Pruser. I travel to various U.S. cities quite often to share my views on the U.S. economy and interest rates and also to ask clients in different parts of the country their views. To be asked to meet with clients by a salesperson is a form of validation that I can add value to our clients. Today is the third day of a five-day tour through four cities: Houston, Austin, Albuquerque, and Santa Fe.

"Face time" with clients is very important for a market economist/fixed-income strategist like me, whose only prior contact with clients is likely through written articles. This assumes the salesperson forwards my articles to their clients. While I do not sell securities and do not receive direct compensation from client transactions that may result from my visits and/or comments, the ability to provide an objective opinion on the markets does bring value to some clients and also credibility to our sales force. The biggest challenge for me is to be different from all the other market economists on Wall Street.

Other salespeople from our Minneapolis and Houston offices also have clients in Austin, so we decided to host a luncheon at Louie's

106, where I could deliver my comments once, instead of multiple times. Speaking on the economy after lunch can be a real snoozer, especially if one doesn't offer an opinion different from the "consensus." Graphs and pie charts along with a dialogue of data are a sure way to put an audience to sleep. As a result, my presentations are intentionally different; some may say "light," others describe it as conversational. My spin is to discuss the U.S. and global economies, and then the local economy in the context of what is happening nationally. I then conclude with where I believe interest rates may be in the next year to eighteen months.

Bill picks me up at the Austin airport and tells me he was unable to secure our morning appointment. We proceed to have breakfast and discuss the latest rumor involving the potential merger of our company with another and its potential impact on the fixed-income group. These conversations can be dangerous for a manager, but I believe in being up-front and telling others what I think. Since I don't know if the rumor is true or not, we commiserate over various what-if scenarios and agree that we can't control what we know but really enjoy working as a group and hope that we can stay together no matter what the outcome. I myself am concerned, given there are few positions for managing directors in research these days. However, I paint an upbeat picture for Bill, who certainly has many options as a salesperson.

We arrive at the restaurant to set up for the presentation, and of course the LCD projector does not work. The annoying "searching for signal" continues to flash on the screen despite a maze of cables connected between the projector and the laptop that houses my PowerPoint presentation. After the invitees begin to arrive and colleagues from various cities come to greet their clients, I give up and tell Bill we have to do it the old-fashioned way—use my handouts. I am a believer in technology, but a paper backup is always helpful in these situations. This has happened more than it should, so I don't let it unnerve me.

There are approximately eight clients in attendance, quite low for a presentation, but okay for a first attempt. I am a bit disappointed, but grateful our private room is cozy. I also know that since two of my colleagues have not seen me speak, they were likely cautious in "marketing" this luncheon. The audience is comprised of finance officers from various state municipalities, university fund managers, and investment advisers. I encourage the group to ask me questions while I speak, not at the end, since that gives me direction with regard to what I need to emphasize and what to skip if needed. As you can tell, I don't have a script when I speak. Since we are all seated at a long table, I speak at one end of the table, which allows me to make eye contact and "engage" the audience.

This was a terrific group in that they followed my direction and did ask questions, which made for great conversation and a one-and-a-half-hour presentation that was only supposed to be forty-five minutes. It's a great feeling to know someone is listening and processing my thoughts to the point where they actually have questions and opinions about what I have said. The discussion of local conditions is very well received, and I am pleased that they also offer their perspectives and observations that I can plug into my database. I still have no read on how my colleagues are feeling about now . . . it is going on too long!

I skip over my last two slides and stop after one more question. I then stay and address other questions individually, while my colleagues say goodbye to clients. After everyone leaves, two of my colleagues stay and watch me wolf down a Caesar salad and a slice of cheesecake and coffee and review the presentation. They both say they are pleased with the interaction and note they will "talk it up" more next year—I told you they were cautious! Nonetheless, it is a good feeling. The sales force is as much my client as the clients themselves.

We head back to the airport, where I will fly on to Albuquerque and meet another colleague from Minneapolis and visit with other clients in the city. The downtime at the airport is most welcome, for I can answer e-mail messages on my BlackBerry and return phone calls as needed. This is one of those times where I am grateful for technology and the ability to type my morning report and review e-mails now instead of doing so when I arrive at my hotel room at 9:00 in the evening.

The flight to Albuquerque is the most hair-raising I have ever had. I actually looked at the directions for the exit door, since I was seated next to it. The woman behind me is threatening to "toss her cookies" if we don't land on the third attempt. Thankfully, after two attempts, we finally land. I am sure we looked like a drunken plane as we approached the runway. Apparently, the winds were strong, and we had two wind shear warnings in the first attempts. An exciting way to end a day on the road. I am met by my Minneapolis colleague, who has a bright smile. (All salespeople do, that's why they sell and I don't.) My face is probably as green as my suit, but he nicely asks if I'd like to get a bite to eat. I went to sleep as soon as I arrived at the hotel.

Minutes later, the clock touched midnight again in New York. Twenty-four hours in the global economy were over. Billions of people made the decisions that drove it, creating more than $100 billion worth of goods and services, plus much more emotion, experience, and memory.

The effects of those decisions flowed, and would continue to flow, through every possible conduit. Some decisions would be reflected in products rolling off assembly lines, others in the prices of securities, and still others in personal interactions. Each decision would cascade around the world and then forward through time. You can just imagine an updated version of the old nursery rhyme: "For want of an oil price hedge, the profit was lost; for want of a profit, the dividend was lost; for want of a dividend, the investors were lost; for want of investors, the financing was lost; for want of financing, the airline was lost; for want of an airline, the tourism industry was lost; for want of a tourism industry, the economy was lost—and all for the want of an oil price hedge."

The global economy's connectedness is what makes these flights of fancy not so fanciful. But connections also give the big machine its energy. Sure, we work for ourselves, but we also work to provide for our families, to help our friends, and even, it must be said, to upstage the people we don't like.

We can't just think about those people, though. The day when you could sit at home and think only of your own little circle, your own work, and your own neighborhood has clearly passed. Take that attitude now, and the global economy is likely to hit you from behind.

If you want to cope with connectedness, you have to be as connected as you can—in other words, you have to pay attention to what's happening in the rest of the world. Then you'll start to feel your cog or wheel getting a bit more purchase on the big machine. In short, you'll be making connectedness work for you.

ATTRIBUTION OF ARTICLES WHOSE TITLES WERE USED FOR CHAPTER TITLES (ALL JUNE 15, 2005)

1. Aiko Wakao and Young-Sam Cho (Bloomberg News)

2. Yoshifumi Takemoto and Masumi Suga (Bloomberg News)

3. Anonymous (Agence France-Presse)

4. Doug Young (Reuters)

5. Marcin Grajewski (Reuters)

6. Marius Bosch (Reuters)

7. Suleiman al-Khalidi (Reuters)

8. Anonymous (Dow Jones)

9. Walter Brandimarte (Reuters)

10. Jocelyn Gecker (Associated Press)

11. Tamsin Carlisle (*Wall Street Journal* via Dow Jones)

12. Mike Colias (Associated Press)

13. Beth Jinks (Bloomberg News)

14. Beth Jinks (Bloomberg News)

The author thanks the prolific Beth Jinks.

SOURCES OF USEFUL DATA

The World Bank's country information:
econ.worldbank.org

The U.S. Central Intelligence Agency's *World Factbook*:
www.cia.gov/cia/publications/factbook/

Older editions of *The World Factbook*:
www.umsl.edu/services/govdocs/alpha_list.html

OANDA's currency exchange rates:
www.oanda.com

The Bank for International Settlements' data on financial transactions: www.bis.org/forum/research.htm

The U.S. Department of Energy's market information: www.eia.doe.gov

The Oxford Latin American Economic History Database's time series data: oxlad.qeh.ox.ac.uk

CHAPTER 1: WHEN DOES WORKING TOGETHER REALLY WORK?

6 rationale was to insulate investors: Karl Taro Greenfeld, "Voracious, Inc.," in *Time 100: People of the Century* (2003).

6 executives sometimes used profitable businesses: David S. Scharfstein and Jeremy C. Stein, "The Dark Side of Internal Capital Markets: Divisional Rent-Seeking and Inefficient Investment," *Journal of Finance* 55, no. 6 (Dec. 2000).

6 In July 2002, eBay: Matt Richtel, "EBay to Buy PayPal, a Rival in Online Payments," *New York Times*, July 9, 2002.

6 in September 2005, eBay: Ken Belson, "EBay to Buy Skype, Internet Phone Service, for $2.6 Billion," *New York Times*, Sept. 13, 2005.

7 If, one day, they decided to offer auction services: This insight came out of a conversation with Rocky Lee, a lawyer working in Beijing.

7 Yet the corporate cultures were jarringly different: Bethany McLean and Andy Serwer, "Brahmins at the Gate," *Fortune*, May 2, 2005.

8 a well-known investors' rights advocate said: Klaus Nieding, president of the Deutscher-Anlegerschutzbund, quoted (as Klaus Dieding, erroneously) in BBC News, "DaimlerChrysler's Woes Grow," Nov. 30, 2000.

14 One of the most notorious disappointments: Nikos Valance, "Sorry, Wrong Number," *CFO Asia*, April 2000.

14 some big banks and investors were losing interest: Keith Bradsher, "Appetite for Stocks Slackening in China," *New York Times*, June 8, 2005.

CHAPTER 2: CAN GOVERNMENTS MAKE GLOBAL MARKETS MORE COMPETITIVE?

19 The Japanese government was influencing trade: Andrew G. Brown, "The Turbulent Decades of the 1970s and 1980s," in *Reluctant Partners* (2003); and further material on trade restrictions.

19 even MITI was starting to worry: From the Web site produced in 2002 for the PBS series *Commanding Heights: The Battle for the World Economy*, which in turn was based on the book of the same name by Daniel Yergin and Joseph Stanislaw.

20 Laws ensuring competition were bolstered: This passage is based on Nanbu's comments.

21 the scheme may have been around for decades: Kenji Hall, "Tokyo Prosecutors Charge 26 Companies, 8 Executives in Japan's Biggest Bid-Rigging Scandal," Associated Press, June 15, 2005; and further material on scope of bid rigging.

21 The charge was that former bosses: Michael Gormley, "Marsh & McLennan Executives Indicted," Associated Press, Sept. 16, 2005.

21 His initial sally against Marsh & McLennan: Thor Valdmanis et al., "Marsh & McLennan Accused of Price-Fixing, Collusion," USA Today, Oct. 15, 2004.

24 It took more than ten months: BBC News, "US and China Sign Textiles Deal," Nov. 8, 2005.

24 tens of millions of sweaters: Xinhua News Agency, "EU Trade Chief Urges Unblocking of Chinese Textiles," Aug. 30, 2005.

24 the chairman of Mauritius's Export Processing Zone Association: Stephane Saminaden, "Mauritius Welcomes EU-China Textile Pact," Reuters, June 15, 2005.

24 When the World Trade Organization reviewed: World Trade Organization, Trade Policy Review: Japan (2005), including Japanese rice prices and other trade barriers.

25 compared with world prices: U.S. Department of Agriculture, "Rice: World Situation and Outlook," Quarterly International Trade Report, Feb. 2004.

28 The accusations surrounded big issues: Wired News Report, "US v. Microsoft: Timeline," Wired, Nov. 4, 2002.

29 a total amount that could reach $9 billion: Désiré Athow, "Microsoft's Lawsuit Payouts Amount to Around $9 Billion," Inquirer/theinquirer.net, July 14, 2005.

29 The accusation then was: Paul Festa, "Microsoft Inspected in Japan," CNET News.com, Jan. 13, 1998.

29 Again, Microsoft desisted: BBC News, "Microsoft Ends 'Unfair' Contract," Feb. 27, 2004.

29 the European Union had begun probing: European Commission, "Commission Opens Proceedings Against Microsoft's Alleged Discriminatory Licensing and Refusal to Supply Software Information," press release, Aug. 3, 2000.

30 Singh's motivation is: Ajit Singh, Competition and Competition Policy in Emerging Markets: International and Developmental Dimensions, United Nations Conference on Trade and Development G-24 Discussion Paper Series, no. 18 (Sept. 2002).

31 dozens of Hong Kong's business leaders: Andy Cheng, Ben Kwok, and Simon Pritchard, "Competition Law Is a Bridge Too Far for HK," South China Morning Post, Oct. 31, 2005.

NOTES

CHAPTER 3: DO MULTINATIONAL COMPANIES BRING PROGRESS OR PROBLEMS ABROAD?

36 Phuc left Ho Chi Minh City: Some supplemental details are from Agence France-Presse, "Asian Lives: Vietnam Refugee Returns to Find a Country Transformed," May 4, 2005.

42 according to its chairman, Dick Filgate: D'Arcy Doran, "Nigerian Women Agree to End Weeklong Standoff, Free Hostages at Oil Terminal," Associated Press, July 16, 2002.

42 in an interview with *The Prague Post*: Lisa Gonderinger, "Wolfensohn Unbound," *Prague Post*, Sept. 13, 2000.

43 When Skoda, the Czech carmaker: Roger Blanpain, "European Works Councils in Multinational Enterprises: Background, Working, and Experience," International Labor Organization Multinational Enterprises Programme Working Paper, no. 83 (1999).

43 and later all over the world: Martin Kempe, "Workers' Representations at the International Level Need the Local Organization's Support," *World of Work*, no. 36 (Nov. 2000).

43 The intent, according to officials: Janet Ong and Matthew Miller, "China Opens Further to Foreign Capital," Bloomberg News (republished in the *International Herald Tribune*, Nov. 8, 2005).

43 the official in charge of supervising China's state-owned businesses: Reuters, "China Says State Firms Should List at Home and Abroad," Dec. 22, 2005.

48 buyers of commodities must pay suppliers a premium: According to the Fairtrade Foundation's Web site, www.fairtrade.org.uk, in May 2006.

49 Gap Inc., which was once criticized: From a dossier compiled by the Responsible Shopper Web site, www.responsibleshopper.org.

INTERLUDE: CREDIT MARKETS AND CURRENCIES

52 a set of bonds that would help poorer Islamic countries: Massita Ahmad, "IDB's Multilateral Islamic Bond Can Be Done, Says CIMB," *Pertubuhan Berita Nasional Malaysia: Malaysia Economic News*, June 15, 2005.

53 The Federal Reserve: Cheryl L. Edwards, "Open Market Operations in the 1990s," *Federal Reserve Bulletin*, Nov. 1997.

56 Foreign exchange traders buy and sell: Gabriele Galati and Michael Melvin, "Why Has FX Trading Surged? Explaining the 2004 Triennial Survey," *BIS Quarterly Review* (Dec. 2004).

NOTES

CHAPTER 4: WHAT DETERMINES THE GLOBAL ECONOMIC PECKING ORDER?

61 owned almost as much of Tsingtao: Jeremy Grant and Andrei Postelnicu, "Anheuser Sees Profits Decline in China," FT.com, April 27, 2006; the government's stake had earlier been reported as 31 percent.

61 If you don't know about Haier: A similar formulation is used in Todd Crowell, "Ever Heard of Lenovo, Haier, CNOOC? You Will," *Christian Science Monitor*, June 30, 2005; the author discovered this after writing the chapter, and believes that the formulation is good enough to share.

63 a market Haier now controls: Qingfen Ding, "Made in China—The Brand Matters," *China Business Weekly*, April 4, 2005.

64 allowed Haier's sales to grow by an average of 68 percent: Haier, *Innovation Without End: Haier, 20 Years of Success* (2004).

65 Those companies chose to believe the illusion: Kunio Okina and Shigenori Shiratsuka, "Asset Price Fluctuations, Structural Adjustments, and Sustained Economic Growth: Lessons from Japan's Experience Since the Late 1980s," Bank of Japan's *Monetary and Economic Studies* (Dec. 2004).

66 the tortuous ownership structures of Japan's biggest businesses: Mitsuhiro Fukao, "Japan's Lost Decade and Its Financial System," in *Japan's Lost Decade: Origins, Consequences, and Prospects for Recovery*, eds. Gary R. Saxonhouse and Robert M. Stern (2004).

66 China Construction Bank: David Lague, "Betting High on Risky China Bank," *International Herald Tribune*, Oct. 20, 2005.

67 Just look at how Japan's economy grew: Department of National Accounts, Economic and Social Research Institute, Cabinet Office of Japan, "Referential Series of Quarterly Estimates of Former GDP on SNA68, 1990 Basis," n.d.

67 Compare that with how the American economy developed: U.S. Council of Economic Advisers, *The Economic Report of the President* (2005).

67 researchers at Goldman Sachs: Dominic Wilson and Roopa Purushothaman, "Dreaming with BRICs: The Path to 2050," Goldman Sachs Global Economic Paper, no. 99 (Oct. 1, 2003).

68 In 2005, material living standards in Japan: Central Intelligence Agency, *The World Factbook* (2006).

69 the World Bank ranked China: World Bank, *Doing Business in 2006* (2006).

69 the International Monetary Fund used an "economic freedom index": International Monetary Fund, *World Economic Outlook: Building Institutions* (2005), using methodology from James Gwartney and Robert Lawson, *Economic Freedom of the World: 2004 Annual Report* (2004).

70 Researchers and politicians in Brazil: Daniel Altman, " 'China Model' Is Tough to Copy," *International Herald Tribune*, July 30, 2005.

261

71 China was second only to the United States: World Resources Institute, "Emissions of Common Anthropogenic Pollutants" and "Greenhouse Gas Emissions by Source," from EarthTrends Data Tables (2003).

71 China made enormous strides: Martin Ravallion and Shaohua Chen, *China's (Uneven) Progress Against Poverty*, World Bank Policy Research Working Paper, no. 3408 (Sept. 2004).

71 Tens of millions of Chinese have gone: Center for German and European Studies, University of California, Berkeley, "China: Migrants, Economy," *Migration News* 12, no. 4 (Oct. 2005).

71 hundreds of millions by 2020: Center for German and European Studies, University of California, Berkeley, "China, Hong Kong, Taiwan," *Migration News* 11, no. 4 (Oct. 2004).

71 Official figures reported: Howard W. French, "Land of 74,000 Protests (but Little Is Ever Fixed)," *New York Times*, Aug. 24, 2005.

72 there were eighty-seven thousand in 2005: Joseph Kahn, "Pace and Scope of Protest in China Accelerated in '05," *New York Times*, Jan. 20, 2006.

72 migrant workers were owed: Xinhua General News Service, "Surveys Find Unpaid Wages Still Haunt Migrant Workers in China," Xinhua News Agency, Aug. 17, 2005.

72 The government in Beijing was sufficiently worried: Joseph Kahn, "China Hopes Economy Plan Will Bridge Income Gap," *New York Times*, Oct. 12, 2005.

72 China may already feel like the world's most influential economy: Daniel Altman, "China: Both a Powerhouse and a Pauper," *International Herald Tribune*, Oct. 8, 2005.

73 the world produces about $40 to $45 trillion: World Bank, "Key Development Data and Statistics," www.worldbank.org, n.d.; and further data.

78 it will risk falling into what Paul Kennedy: Paul Kennedy, *The Rise and Fall of the Great Powers* (1989).

79 Chevron stepped in to buy Unocal for about $700 million less: Associated Press, "China's CNOOC Drops Bid for Unocal," Aug. 2, 2005.

80 almost one and a half times the value of the business's assets: *People's Daily Online*, "China-Kazakhstan Energy Cooperation Reaches a New High," Oct. 20, 2005.

83 A well-known Chinese professor: Howard W. French, "Letter from China: A Scholar's Prescription for Getting to Next Level," *International Herald Tribune*, Oct. 14, 2005.

CHAPTER 5: WHO REALLY CONTROLS THE WORLD'S MONEY SUPPLY?

85 a small but non-negligible share: According to figures from the U.S. Geological Survey, compiled by Kenneth E. Porter and Earle B. Amey, annual gold production ranged from about four hundred to five hundred metric tons during the Belgian colonial period; an anonymously authored article called "Africa Geologically Under Exposed" from *Mining Review Africa*'s February 2004 edition states that mines in the northern part of Belgian Congo produced about fifty metric tons of gold at that time; in addition, rubber exports were extremely profitable, helping to earn Leopold II a personal fortune of over $1 billion in today's terms, according to *King Leopold's Ghost*, a book by Adam Hochschild published in 1998.

88 "Many ministers want to persuade": AFX News, "Euro Group's Juncker Says 'Many Ministers' Want ECB to Cut Rates," June 15, 2005.

88 "The bank has to remain": This and subsequent quotations in this paragraph are from Marcin Grajewski, "Euro Group Must Be More Forceful with ECB —Juncker," Reuters, June 15, 2005.

88 The euro area's trade surplus in goods and services: From European Central Bank figures at www.ecb.int.

91 The most vocal of these: Daniel Altman, "Keeping Politics out of the Fed," *New York Times*, Nov. 28, 2004.

92 That target is: According to the bank's Web site; see www.bankofcanada.ca/en/monetary/inflation_target.html.

94 The situation moved Anand Chandavarkar: Anand Chandavarkar, "Towards an Independent Federal Reserve Bank of India," *Economic and Political Weekly*, Aug. 27, 2005.

95 Inflation in Argentina had reached 200 percent: World Bank, *Argentina: Country Assistance Review* (1996).

95 according to various calculations: For example, see Ned Schmidt, "Money-ization #11," from www.gold-eagle.com, May 27, 2005; Schmidt is a fund manager based in Florida.

95 Argentina grew strongly for six or seven years: Miguel Sebastian, "Two Propositions on Argentina," presentation at Inter-American Development Bank seminar in Fortaleza, Brazil, March 10, 2002; and further material.

96 the value of their incomes and savings: The exchange rate fell to 3.65 pesos to the dollar by early June 2002, according to www.oanda.com.

99 "We're pressing China": The president made this comment at the American Society of Newspaper Editors convention in Washington on April 14, 2005.

100 Clyde Prestowitz, who was a trade official: "Prestowitz urges Koizumi to call for 'Plaza Accord II' at G-8," Japan Economic Newswire, March 28, 2006.

102 at least one analyst: Nigel Gault of Global Insight, quoted by the Associated Press ("Trade Deficit Hits Record $68.9 Billion") on December 15, 2005.

102 A third idea for correcting the imbalances: Daniel Altman, "IMF Chief Draws Fire over Style as Leader," *International Herald Tribune*, July 27, 2005.

103 John Snow, the Treasury secretary: In a speech made at the National Press Club in Washington on September 20, 2004.

103 the verdict was unanimous: These comments came from the author's impromptu interviews.

INTERLUDE: STOCK MARKETS

105 Andrew Puzder, president and chief executive: From New York Stock Exchange press releases and further material on the closing.

107 And there was other news to digest: Steve Goldstein, "Stock Market Futures Higher After Economic Data," *MarketWatch*, June 15, 2005.

107 A few of his comments about the market's day: Larry Kudlow, *Kudlow & Company*, CNBC News Transcripts, June 15, 2005.

110 news outlets recounted the suspected factors: Rick Babson, "The Closing Bell: Stocks Rally at the Close," *Kansas City Star*, June 15, 2005.

CHAPTER 6: WHAT DOES CORRUPTION COST?

112 after the trial of his financial adviser: BBC News, "South African Leader Sacks Deputy," June 14, 2005.

113 which has the largest population of poor people: Craig Schwabe, "Poverty in South Africa," *Human Sciences Research Council Fact Sheet*, July 26, 2004.

115 based on the research of Transparency International: All of the data cited, plus a complete description of the index's methodology, are available at www.transparency.org.

117 Some of the most definitive results: Paolo Mauro, "Corruption and Growth," *Quarterly Journal of Economics* (Aug. 1995); Mauro has written a useful summary for the International Monetary Fund's *Economic Issues*, no. 6 (Feb. 1997).

118 Even before Argentina's financial crisis: Friedrich Schneider, "Shadow Economies of 145 Countries All Over the World: What Do We Really Know?" mimeo (2005); the data used are based on 1999 and 2000.

118 As some economists have pointed out: Andrei Shleifer and Robert Vishny, "Corruption," *Quarterly Journal of Economics* (Aug. 1993); full disclosure: Shleifer was one of the author's doctoral dissertation advisers.

119 In 2000, he wrote: Shang-Jin Wei, "How Taxing Is Corruption on International Investors?" *Review of Economics and Statistics* (Feb. 2000).

119 That was the case in the Philippines: Avigail M. Olarte and Yvonne T. Chua, "Up to 70% of Local Health Funds Lost to Corruption," Philippine Center for Investigative Journalism report, May 24, 2005.

120 the firing of openly corrupt ministers: See, for example, Craig Timberg, "In Nigeria, Where Money Talks, Reform Is the Word," *Washington Post*, May 1, 2005.

120 the president himself has come under attack: BBC News, "Nigeria's President Told to Resign," Aug. 13, 2002.

121 an argument often made by Sir Edward Clay: For example, in an interview broadcast on the BBC World Service on November 23, 2005.

121 he told the British Broadcasting Corporation: Githongo was interviewed by the BBC's Fergal Keane in a report broadcast on February 9, 2006.

123 The bank, which held about 10 billion euros' worth: European Bank for Reconstruction and Development, "Interim Financial Report," Sept. 30, 2005.

124 a state that is apparently run for the personal edification: CBS News, "Turkmenbashi Everywhere," Jan. 4, 2004, calls Niyazov "a dictator who runs his country like it's his own private Disney World."

125 Bob Geldof, the Irish rocker: BBC News, "Geldof Warns over Africa Failure," June 10, 2005.

CHAPTER 7: HOW IMPORTANT ARE FINANCIAL MARKETS TO ECONOMIC GROWTH?

127 the intersection of two main routes: According to the map drawn by the Silk Road Project, available at www.silkroadproject.org/silkroad/map.html.

128 A modern exchange was supposed to open: U.S. Trade Compliance Center, *Country Commercial Guides: Syria* (1998).

132 the more rules exist to protect investors: A lengthy academic literature on this subject exists, consisting primarily of cross-border studies by Andrei Shleifer, Robert Vishny, Florencio López-de-Silanes, and Rafael La Porta; full disclosure: Shleifer was one of the author's doctoral dissertation advisers.

132 some enterprising types had even set up brokerage houses: James Whittington, "Syrians Turn to Entrepreneurs for Big Returns: Frustration at the Slow Pace of Economic Reform Is Forcing Investors into the Private Sector," *Financial Times*, May 10, 1994.

135 that requires an exit visa: Farid N. Ghadry, "Syrian Reform: What Lies Beneath," *Middle East Quarterly* (Winter 2005); Ghadry describes the entire process in detail.

135 In a survey from 2003: World Bank, "Enterprise Surveys: Syrian Arab Republic" (2003), available online from www.worldbank.org.

136 the Securities and Exchange Commission's roughly thirty-eight hundred employees: According to the U.S. Office of Personnel Management's November 2005 figures.

137 forecasters were predicting lower, not higher, growth: According to a series of articles and summaries posted on SyriaComment.com in February and March 2006.

CHAPTER 8: IS THE FINANCIAL SYSTEM BECOMING MORE VULNERABLE TO THE ACTIONS OF THE FEW?

141 several of the world's biggest financial institutions: Finextra.com, multiple articles: "Bank of America on ID Theft Alert After Computer Tapes Go Missing," Feb. 28, 2005; "HSBC Credit Card Data Exposed in Security Breach," April 14, 2005; "UBS Loses Customer Records," June 1, 2005; "Citi Customer Data Lost in Transit," June 6, 2005.

142 In a few seconds: Takahiko Hyuga, "Mizuho Says Typing Error Sparked $3.5 Billion in J-Com Trades," Bloomberg News, Dec. 9, 2005.

142 a bug in Citibank's electronic banking system: Associated Press, "Computer Glitch at Citibank Japan Fixed," May 10, 2006.

143 The fund's returns had been dropping: Alan Greenspan, "Private-Sector Refinancing of the Large Hedge Fund, Long-Term Capital Management," testimony before the Committee on Banking and Financial Services, U.S. House of Representatives, Oct. 1, 1998.

143 earlier profits had attracted so many billions: ERisk Case Studies, "LTCM—Long-Term Capital Management," n.d. (online at www.erisk.com).

146 the amount of money managed by hedge funds: Statistics are from the Barclay Group's research database, at www.barclaygrp.com.

148 the shiny yellow stuff almost doubled: Gold price data are from Finfacts Ireland at www.finfacts.com.

151 GM had separated its mortgage-lending operation: David Welch, "GM Is Losing Traction," *BusinessWeek*, Feb. 7, 2005.

152 In retrospect, some experts have concluded: See, for example, Paul Krugman, "Currency Crises," presentation to the National Bureau of Economic Research, 1997, available at web.mit.edu/krugman/www/crises.html.

152 he netted over $1 billion: Eric Heyl, "Soros Pumps Millions into Global Change," *Pittsburgh Tribune Review*, May 6, 2006.

152 To economists, it was a gamble: As stated succinctly in Ethan Kaplan and Dani Rodrik, *Did the Malaysian Capital Controls Work?* National Bureau of Economic Research Working Paper Series, no. 8142 (Feb. 2001).

153 one of the most vocal advocates: See, for example, Lawrence Summers and Victoria Summers, "The Case for a Securities Transactions Excise Tax," *Tax*

Notes, Aug. 13, 1990, or Lawrence Summers and Victoria Summers, "When Financial Markets Work Too Well: A Cautious Case for a Securities Transactions Tax," *Journal of Financial Services Research*, no. 2 (1989).

153 tax on foreign exchange trades: James Tobin, "A Proposal for International Monetary Reform," *Eastern Economic Journal* (July–Oct. 1978).

153 suffered from the same criticisms: See, for example, Kenneth Kasa, "Time for a Tobin Tax?" *Federal Reserve Bank of San Francisco Economic Letter*, April 9, 1999; and Robert Aliber et al., "Some Evidence That a Tobin Tax on Foreign Exchange Transactions May Increase Volatility," working paper (June 2003).

153 Jacques Chirac, the French president: Jacques Chirac, "Special Message," transcript of broadcast message delivered to the World Economic Forum, Jan. 26, 2005.

153 Chirac had suggested some sort of global tax before: Gerard Bon, "France's Chirac Backs Tax to Fight World Poverty," Reuters, Sept. 4, 2002.

154 One survey article looking at the effects of capital controls: Kristin J. Forbes, *The Microeconomic Evidence on Capital Controls: No Free Lunch*, National Bureau of Economic Research Working Paper Series, no. 11372 (May 2005).

INTERLUDE: OIL

157 eighty-four million barrels of oil a day: U.S. Department of Energy, *International Petroleum Monthly*, March 2006; and further information on prices and world production from the department's Web site, www.eia.doe.gov.

157 world's annual supply of wheat: U.S. Department of Agriculture, *Grain: World Markets and Trade* (May 2005).

158 oil provides 40 percent of the energy: Pace University, "Power Scorecard: Electricity from Oil," www.powerscorecard.org (March 1, 2005, revision).

159 closes at 5:30 p.m.: Platts, *Methodology and Specifications Guide: Crude Oil* (Feb. 2006 update).

CHAPTER 9: WHICH COMES FIRST, POLITICAL OR ECONOMIC STABILITY?

163 Reni Adriano Batista: Reni's story is culled from his own reminiscences in "Diadema," *Braudel Papers*, no. 36 (2005); his quotations come from the author's interview.

165 The central allegation: Ignacio Ramonet, "Brazil's Soiled Hero," trans. Barry Smerin, *Le Monde diplomatique*, Oct. 2005.

166 On June 14: Alan Clendenning, "Brazilian Stocks Sink Again on Scandal," Associated Press Financial Wire, June 15, 2005.

166 Two senators: Jean-Marc Poilpre, "Brazil Opposition Meets Bankers, Business-men to Assuage Fears over Scandals," Agence France-Presse, June 16, 2005.

167 reportedly asked to leave the government: Leila Seradj, "Brazilians Mourn a Wounded President and Consider the Prospects of a Major Political Upset," *Council on Hemispheric Affairs Memorandum*, Dec. 5, 2005.

168 consider investing $4 billion: Rick Smith, "Making the Cut: Lists and Black-lists," *International Herald Tribune*, Aug. 20, 2005; the quotation from Wim-Hein Pals is also from this article.

169 Helmut Schmidt: The transcript is from China's official Xinhua news service ("Forum Hears Voices for Sustainable Development," Sept. 7, 2005). It was checked against the text provided in advance of the speech. The ellipsis, which does not appear in the Xinhua transcript, has been placed where the advance text includes this fragment: "In the light of former Chinese govern-ments, of the civil war in the 20th century and of the subsequent great exper-iments, which have resulted in countless deaths . . ."

170 Amnesty International cited Singapore: From the individual country pages in the *Amnesty International Report 2005*.

173 what two Stanford professors did: James D. Fearon and David D. Laitin, "Eth-nicity, Insurgency, and Civil War," *American Political Science Review* (Feb. 2003).

173 Ethnic and religious splintering: This point was later disputed by Kevin Quinn et al., "Ethnicity, Insurgency, and Civil War Revisited," working paper, May 4, 2004; the new analysis did not affect the economic result cited here.

174 That leaves middle-income countries: Information on active conflicts was compiled in early 2006 from www.globalsecurity.org.

174 By February 2006, Lula's popularity: Jonathan Wheatley, "Lula Defies Doubters with Popular Revival as Polling Time Nears," *Financial Times*, Feb. 9, 2006; and further material about forecasts.

CHAPTER 10: CAN THE UNITED STATES SET THE GLOBAL ECONOMY'S RULES?

181 Left-wing politicians in Germany: Matthew Schofield, "German Truce Appears Unlikely; New Vote Possible as Politicians Fight," *Detroit Free Press*, Sept. 20, 2005.

183 That last part wasn't too popular: Daniel Altman, "I.M.F. Official Alters Plan for Debt Crises," *New York Times*, April 2, 2002.

183 In the first eleven years of the WTO's existence: The World Trade Organiza-tion's Web site offers an easy-to-use database of the cases at www.wto.org.

184 the WTO's arbitrator concluded: Carter Dougherty, "Firms in U.S. Face $4 Bil-lion in Tariffs; WTO Sets Penalty over Tax Breaks," *Washington Times*, Aug. 31, 2002.

184 from cheese to fishing rods: Jill Barshay, "EU Threat of Punitive Tariffs Forces Congress to Act on Taxes," *Congressional Quarterly Weekly*, Sept. 13, 2002.

185 the EU began to use a small one: United Press International, "EU Assesses Punitive Tariffs on US Goods," March 1, 2004.

185 the EU celebrated by promising to drop its tariffs: Paul Blustein, "EU Set to Lift Sanctions for Now; U.S. Tax Plan Prompts Move," *Washington Post*, Oct. 25, 2004.

185 The EU judged that the tax breaks: Edward Alden and Raphael Minder, "EU Set to Postpone Lifting of Trade Sanctions on US," *Financial Times*, Dec. 16, 2004.

185 It also decided to lift its tariffs: Elizabeth Becker, "Europe Is Lifting Trade Sanctions on U.S.," *New York Times*, Jan. 22, 2005.

185 The United States promised, yet again, to appeal: AFX News, "US to Appeal WTO Tax Ruling," Oct. 3, 2005.

188 China's growth has brought hundreds of millions: The United Nations measures poverty by the fraction of a country's population that lives on daily the equivalent of what $1 could buy in the United States in 1993. According to data supplied to the United Nations statistics division by the World Bank, 33 percent of China's population—about 369 million people—fit that description in 1990; by 2001, the figure was down to 17 percent, or 216 million people. China's growth has continued unabated since then, so "hundreds of millions" seems like a fair assumption.

189 known for wearing an animal-tooth necklace: Tracy Ringolsby, "Wendell Picks Geography over Money," *Rocky Mountain News*, Feb. 20, 2004; and further material.

189 apparently obsessed with the number nine: T. J. Quinn, "Mets Pact Has Turk on Cloud 9," *Daily News*, Dec. 2, 2000.

191 a database of rankings compiled from those surveys: Veenhoven's databases are online at www1.eur.nl/fsw/happiness.

191 how many happy years of life people can expect: Veenhoven scales the happiness scores to range from 0 to 1, and then multiplies them by life expectancy.

192 no one seems to know exactly how many: The Central Intelligence Agency's *World Factbook* for 2005 states that estimates range from 810,000 to 2.2 million.

192 but shortly after taking the throne in 1972: Jigmi Y. Thinley, "What Does Gross National Happiness (GNH) Mean?" speech delivered at the Second International Conference on Gross National Happiness in Halifax, Canada, June 21, 2005.

NOTES

CHAPTER 11: IS IMMIGRATION A LUXURY OR A NECESSITY?

196 Here's what he wrote: The author was contacted by e-mail in the summer of 2005 by a person using a pseudonym. The address used matched that of a contributor to Chinese Web sites dealing with the shoe industry. The e-mailer later gave his full name and telephone number. Only obvious typos have been edited out of the text, which is culled from several e-mails received over the course of five months.

199 84 percent of Haiti's college-educated citizens: Caglar Ozden and Maurice Schiff, eds., *International Migration, Remittances, and the Brain Drain* (2005).

199 153rd out of 177: United Nations Development Programme, *Human Development Report 2005* (2005).

199 figure may be inflated: Celia Dugger, "Study Finds Small Developing Lands Hit Hardest by 'Brain Drain,'" *New York Times*, Oct. 25, 2005.

199 In Nicaragua, these remittances: The figure for overall remittances, $810 million in 2004, comes from the Inter-American Development Bank; the figure for gross national income, $4.5 billion, comes from the World Bank; the choice of Nicaragua is thanks to Joachim Bamrud in the *Latin Business Chronicle*, Oct. 2005.

200 Research in various countries: A useful review of the literature is provided by Rosalía Cortés, "Social Impact of Remittances on the Fulfillment of Children's Rights," paper prepared for the global policy section of the Division of Policy and Planning, UNICEF, Nov. 2005.

208 Canada probably has about a million expatriates: John Bryant and David Law, "New Zealand's Diaspora and Overseas-Born Population," New Zealand Treasury Working Paper Series (Sept. 2004).

CHAPTER 12: DOES IT HELP THE ECONOMY WHEN IDEAS HAVE OWNERS?

211 In November of that year: The author obtained a photocopy of the letter.

211 it wasn't until March 6, 2003: According to the Web site of Pace Airlines, a charter operator that supplies the equipment for Hooters Air's flights, service began on March 6, 2003.

214 Coca-Cola only arrives there: The author has personally observed the absence of Coca-Cola and the presence of its doppelgänger in Syrian stores; however, *The Economist* reported the smuggling ("Syria's Leaders Sit Tight While the Turmoil Around Them Continues") on April 23, 2005.

214 up to 90 percent of all software: Maria Trombly and Bill Marcus, "Cost for Windows Falls—to 50 Cents—in China," *CIO Insight* online edition, Oct. 1, 2005.

214 And even Microsoft has estimated: Elizabeth Montalbano, "Microsoft Introduces Compulsory Windows Piracy Checks," IDG News Service, July 26, 2005.

214 A prime example is Tim Green: The author encountered Green in the lounge as described.

216 doing so became illegal: Randeep Ramesh, "Cheap Aids Drugs Under Threat," *Guardian*, March 23, 2005.

216 the United States became the first of the WTO's members: Agence France-Presse, "US Approves WTO Generic Drug Measure for Poor Countries," Dec. 17, 2005.

216 Taiwan began to develop a copy: BBC News, "Taiwan to Ignore Flu Drug Patent," Oct. 22, 2005.

216 Other countries, including Thailand: "In a Flap: Avian Flu," *Economist*, Oct. 22, 2005.

216 The company stopped selling: Associated Press, "Roche Halts Tamiflu Sales in China," Nov. 8, 2005.

216 Roche had no chance: Arijit Ghosh and Naila Firdausi, "Roche Says Indonesia Can Make Tamiflu for Own Market," Bloomberg News, Nov. 25, 2005.

217 In one study, Fiona Murray: Fiona Murray and Scott Stern, *Do Formal Intellectual Property Rights Hinder the Free Flow of Scientific Knowledge? An Empirical Test of the Anti-commons Hypothesis*, National Bureau of Economic Research Working Paper Series, no. 11465 (July 2005).

218 patents on a kind of wireless e-mail network: According to a list in Timothy M. O'Brien, "Patents in NTP, Inc. v. Research in Motion, Ltd.," O'Reilly Policy Devcenter (www.oreillynet.com) weblog (Dec. 17, 2005).

218 which was cofounded by a patent attorney: Ian Austen, "U.S. Patent Office Likely to Back BlackBerry Maker," *New York Times*, Dec. 20, 2005.

218 Research in Motion paid NTP over $600 million: Research in Motion, "Research in Motion and NTP Sign Definitive Settlement Agreement to End Litigation," press release, March 3, 2006.

218 According to some worried observers: See, for example, James Surowiecki, "Blackberry Picking," *New Yorker*, Dec. 26, 2005.

219 patents generally involve technical processes: U.S. Patent and Trademark Office, "General Information Concerning Patents," www.uspto.gov (Jan. 2005).

221 India joined with other developing countries: Eric Bellman, "India to WTO: Help Us Protect Herbs, Tea, Yoga," *Wall Street Journal*, Dec. 19, 2005.

CHAPTER 13: CAN A POOR COUNTRY GET RICH TOO QUICKLY?

226 Nigeria reaped hundreds of billions: World Bank, "Sustainable Management of Mineral Resources," project information document, Oct. 29, 2004.

226 oil revenue accounts for: World Bank, "Economic Reform and Governance Project," project appraisal document, Nov. 15, 2004.

227 Exports of oil, which began in 1999: Human Rights Watch, *Sudan, Oil, and Human Rights* (2003).

227 São Tomé's government agreed to give Nigeria a share: IRIN, "Waiting for the Oil Boom," Dec. 13, 2005; and further material.

227 it would allow the United States to build a military base: BBC News, "US Naval Base to Protect Sao Tome Oil," Aug. 22, 2002.

227 The discontent rose sufficiently: U.S. Department of State, Bureau of African Affairs, "Background Note: Sao Tome and Principe" (Jan. 2006).

228 the country had pledged to use 80 percent: Abraham McLaughlin, "Africa's New Model for Spreading Oil Wealth," *Christian Science Monitor*, July 28, 2004; and further material.

228 the citizens' committee complained: BBC News, "Chad's Oil Watchdog 'Powerless,'" May 25, 2004.

228 Further questions arose: Ian Gary and Nikki Reisch, "Chad's Oil: Miracle or Mirage?" Bank Information Center and Catholic Relief Services joint report, Feb. 17, 2005.

228 in December 2005, the government moved: BBC News, "Chad Angry at World Bank over Oil," Dec. 30, 2005.

228 the bank followed through on its threat: World Bank, "World Bank Suspends Disbursements to Chad," press release, Jan. 6, 2006.

228 the government, saying it needed money: BBC News, "Agreement Ends Chad Oil Dispute," April 27, 2006.

228 Major deposits of oil were discovered: Jan Hagland, "The Norwegian Oil and Gas Adventure," Ministry of Foreign Affairs, Norway, 2000; and further material.

229 only 4 percent of the annual revenue: Svein Gjedrem, "Norway and the UK," speech, Norges Bank, 2005; and further material.

231 "Why are we rushing?": Beth Jinks, "East Timor Not Ready to Handle Oil, Gas Revenue, Gusmao Says," Bloomberg News, June 15, 2005.

232 unusually fast growth for the American economy: W. Michael Cox, "Some Unpleasant Growth Arithmetic?" Federal Reserve Bank of Dallas presentation, Oct. 8, 1998; also Bureau of Economic Analysis data compiled by the author.

232 this pattern has been repeated: Daniel Altman, "With Interest: Giving Is Asia's New Class Act," *International Herald Tribune*, Oct. 22, 2005.

235 In May 2006, Timor-Leste announced: Platts, "Eni Bags Five Blocks, Reliance One in East Timor's Maiden Offer," May 22, 2006.

236 groups of disillusioned veterans: Ian McPhedran, "Diggers Fly into Dili Anarchy," *Herald Sun*, May 26, 2006.

CHAPTER 14: DO DISRUPTIVE SHOCKS HELP THE ECONOMY IN THE LONG TERM?

237 fourteenth busiest hub: Figures are from the Airports Council International's Web site, www.airports.org.

238 The Thai economy had already: For a more detailed version of this background, refer to Chalongphob Sussangkarn, "Thailand's Debt Crisis and Economic Outlook," ISEAS Regional Outlook Forum, Jan. 16, 1998.

239 its services weren't always up to the standard: The author, who travels regularly in the region, has experienced much better service and amenities on other airlines, with no clear correlation to price.

240 always managed to make a small profit: THAI's financial statements are available at www.thaiairways.com; through 2004, the company had made a profit, at least notionally, in thirty-seven consecutive fiscal years.

240 the price of jet fuel rose: Energy Information Administration, U.S. Department of Energy, *Monthly Energy Review*, Nov. 2005.

242 Thailand's prime minister, Thaksin Shinawatra: Nick Cumming-Bruce, "Thai Airways Chief Is Suspended; Accounting Problems and Big Loss Are Cited," *International Herald Tribune*, Aug. 12, 2005.

242 the board pushed him aside: Agence France-Presse, "Thai Airways Posts Third Quarter 117 Million Dollar Loss," Aug. 16, 2005.

242 the losses amounted to $114 million: Amy Kazmin, "Soaring Fuel Costs Hit Thai Airways," *Financial Times*, Aug. 16, 2005.

242 The fuel surcharges increased again: AFX News, "Thai Airways Raises Fuel Surcharges on All Flights for 2nd Time This Month," Aug. 19, 2005.

243 Kanok had said just after his suspension: Lan Anh Nguyen, "Thai Airways Hits Air Pocket," *ThaiDay*, Aug. 12, 2005.

243 the airline had decided to hedge: Anuchit Nguyen, "Thai Air May Post First Profit Gain in 3 Quarters on Levy, Baht," Bloomberg News, Nov. 22, 2005.

245 Thousands of pages have been written: Favorites among these include Dan Lovallo and Daniel Kahneman, "Delusions of Success: How Optimism Undermines Executives' Decisions," *Harvard Business Review* (July 2003); and John M. Abowd and David S. Kaplan, "Executive Compensation: Six Questions That Need Answering," *Journal of Economic Perspectives* (Fall 1999).

245 the purchases by Kohlberg Kravis Roberts: Dirk Zorn et al., "Cui Bono: Institutional Investors, Securities Analysts, Agents, and the Shareholder Value Myth," presentation at a Copenhagen Business School conference, May 2005.

246 experts suggested that some of the layoffs: Daniel Altman, "Auto-Industry Obituary for West? Not So Fast," *International Herald Tribune*, Feb. 3, 2006.

247 some analysts blamed the United States and the International Monetary Fund: An interesting entry here is by an adviser to the IMF's executive director: Jiri Jonas, "Argentina: The Anatomy of a Crisis," Center for European Integration Studies Working Papers (2002).

248 the company announced that it would start a new airline: Suchat Sritama, "THAI to Start Local Airline," *Nation* (Thailand), Feb. 8, 2006.

248 All four candidates were internal: Suchat Sritama, "Somchainuk 'Likely to Stay at THAI Helm if Candidates Flunk,' " *Nation* (Thailand), Feb. 2, 2006; and further material.

ACKNOWLEDGMENTS

I thanked many people in my first book. To them I say, consider yourselves thanked again.

Special mention this time must go to my editor, Eric Chinski, who was strangely confident that a journalist steeped in economics could also bring people and places to life. The rest of the staff at Farrar, Straus and Giroux were a delight to work with, too.

I am particularly indebted to Robert Preskill, my agent, whose patience and grit have paid off again. I am grateful also to Walter Wells, the former executive editor of the *International Herald Tribune*, for allowing me the latitude (and longitude) needed to write this book while continuing my journalism. And I must save a few lines for my niece, Sasha, who somehow made it through my first book at the advanced age of two. She has been an excellent reminder of the important things in life.

As in my first book, I would like to express my appreciation to agencies and organizations that have made useful data available to the public. On the international stage, these include the World Bank, the United Nations, the International Labor Organization, the World Trade Organization, and various foreign governments.

I also owe much to the people who made my research easier in the many cities I visited before writing this book. Many already appear in the text. Others include Jana Mancova, Charlotta Rickeby, Kristina Hägg-Blecher, Ryo Uchiyama, Josie Taylor,

ACKNOWLEDGMENTS

Agnes Kwan, Ana-Paula Laissy, Amelia Torres, R. W. Johnson, Ghimar Deeb, Bassel Kaghadou, Patricia Mota Guedes, Brookly McLaughlin, Lisa Homer, Rui Flores, and Lan Anh Nguyen. To those unintentionally left out, I offer my apologies.

Most of all, however, I want to thank all the people who made this book more than a dry scientific text. To the people in far-flung cities who met with a writer they'd never heard of, to the people who took a few minutes—or much longer—out of their days to put a few anecdotes into an e-mail, to the people who simply answered the phone to offer some expert advice: thank you for sharing your knowledge and experiences with me, and with the world.

Wangchuck, King Kigme Singye, 192
Watts, Michael, 210–12, 219, 220, 222
Wealth of Nations, An Inquiry into the Nature and Causes of the (Smith), 22
Webb, David, 32
Wei, Shang-Jin, 119
Wei Duan, 61–62, 63, 65, 84
Wellcome, 31
Wendell, Turk, 189
Whirlpool, 80
Wolfensohn, James, 42
Wolfowitz, Paul, 182
Wöllner, Miroslav, Jr., 11, 12, 13
Workers' Party, Brazil, 164, 165–66, 175
World Bank, 69, 121, 199, 226, 234; appointment of president of, 182; Chad's oil resources and, 228; preconditions for loans, 231; pro-growth

strategies, 190; U.S. power at, 182
World Cup, 175–76
World Trade Organization (WTO), 24–25, 30–31, 70, 221–22; dispute settlement system, 31, 183–85; patented drug issue before, 216; U.S. influence at, 183–85

Yahoo!, 6
Yellow Roadway Corporation (now YRC Worldwide), 81–82
Yeltsin, Boris, 231

Zhang Rongde, 196–98, 206–207
Zollars, Bill, 81–82
Zuma, Jacob, 112, 113–14, 125